Theology Proper

Knowing God the Father

The Bible Teacher's Guide

Gregory Brown

Publishing

Endorsements

"*The Bible Teacher's Guide* ... will help any teacher study and get a better background for his/her Bible lessons. In addition, it will give direction and scope to teaching of the Word of God. Praise God for this contemporary introduction to the Word of God."

—Dr. Elmer Towns
Co-founder of Liberty University
Former Dean, Liberty Baptist Theological Seminary

"Expositional, theological, and candidly practical! I highly recommend The Bible Teacher's Guide for anyone seeking to better understand or teach God's Word."

—Dr. Young–Gil Kim
Founding President, Handong Global University

"Helpful to both the layman and the serious student, The Bible Teacher's Guide, by Dr. Greg Brown, is outstanding!"

—Dr. Neal Weaver
President, Louisiana Baptist University

"Whether you are preparing a Bible study, a sermon, or simply wanting to dive deeper into a personal study of God's Word, these will be very helpful tools."

—Eddie Byun

Missions and Teaching Pastor, Venture Christian Church, Los Gatos, California
Author of Justice Awakening

"I am happy that Greg is making his insights into God's truth available to a wider audience through these books. They bear the hallmarks of good Bible teaching: the result of rigorous Bible study and thoroughgoing application to the lives of people."

—Ajith Fernando
Teaching Director, Youth for Christ
Author of A Call to Joy and Pain

"The content of the series is rich. My prayer is that God will use it to help the body of Christ grow strong."

—Dr. Min Chung
Senior Pastor, Covenant Fellowship Church, Urbana, Illinois
Adjunct Professor, Urbana Theological Seminary

"Knowing the right questions to ask and how to go about answering them is fundamental to learning in any subject matter. Greg demonstrates this convincingly."

—Dr. William Moulder
Professor of Biblical Studies, Trinity International University

"Pastor Greg is passionate about the Word of God, rigorous and thorough in his approach to the study of it... I am pleased to recommend The Bible Teacher's Guide to anyone who hungers for the living Word."

—Dr. JunMo Cho
Professor of Linguistics, Handong Global University
Contemporary Christian Music Recording Artist

"I can't imagine any student of Scripture not benefiting by this work."

—Steven J. Cole
Pastor, Flagstaff Christian Fellowship, Flagstaff, Arizona
Author of the Riches from the Word series

"Greg deals with the principles, doctrines, and applications of the text in a practical way which is useful for both individual growth or for help in preparation for teaching."

—Bob Deffinbaugh
Ministry Coordinator, Bible.org
Pastor, Community Bible Chapel, Richardson, Texas

Contents

Preface

And entrust what you heard me say in the presence of many others as witnesses to faithful people
2 Timothy 2:2 (NET)

Paul's words to Timothy still apply to us today. There is a need to raise up teachers who will correctly handle and fearlessly teach the Word of God. It is with this hope in mind that the Bible Teacher's Guide (BTG) series has been created. The BTG series includes both expositional studies and topical studies. This guide will be useful for personal devotions, small groups, and for teachers preparing to share God's Word.

Theology Proper: Knowing God the Father can be used specifically as a nine-week small-group curriculum. Every week, the members of the group will read the chapter, answer the questions, and be prepared to share in the gathering. Because each member will prepare for the small group, this will enrich the discussion and the learning. In the appendices, there are tips on how to run a study group, as well as reflection questions to help each member further prepare and even share responsibility in teaching (see Appendix 1 and 2).

I pray that the Lord may richly bless your study and use it to build his kingdom.

Introduction

Greetings! Today, we will start a study of God the Father, often called Theology Proper. However before beginning, we should consider the limitations of our study. No study of God can be considered comprehensive for three reasons.

1. A limitation of the human mind. A finite mind cannot fully grasp an infinite being.

Psalm 139:6 says, "Your knowledge is beyond my comprehension; it is so far beyond me, I am unable to fathom it."

David said he found the knowledge of God beyond him—too complex for him to fathom. Specifically, he was acknowledging that God knew his thoughts from afar (v. 2), and that God knew exactly what he was going to say before he said it (v. 4). How could anyone fully understand such things?

Life holds many limitations for all of us, apart from attempting to fully understand God. Some of us cannot do math. Some of us cannot work with our hands or build things. Some of us lack administrative abilities. How much more shall we struggle in understanding God? One of our limitations is that of the human mind.

2. A moral problem. We each have been affected by the presence of sin. Consider how Scripture talks about the unregenerate—those who are not saved:

First Corinthians 2:14 says,

The unbeliever does not receive the things of the Spirit of God, for they are foolishness to him. And he cannot understand them, because they are spiritually discerned.

Paul said that an unbeliever "cannot understand" the things of the Spirit. It is impossible. Sin has affected people in such a way that they cannot understand the things of God. Paul speaks about this more in Romans 8. He says, "the sinful

13

mind is hostile to God. It does not submit to God's law, nor can it do so" (Romans 8:7 NIV 1984).

Paul says the sinful mind is hostile toward the things of God, and even when the sinful mind does understand, it lacks the power to submit. Sin has drastically affected the ability of the unconverted person.

However, this is not only true of the unconverted. Even believers are still affected by sin, and this keeps us from fully understanding the revelation of God. Consider what Jesus said:

> "My teaching is not from me, but from the one who sent me. If anyone wants to do God's will, he will know about my teaching, whether it is from God or whether I speak from my own authority
> John 7:16–17

Jesus said if anyone wanted to know if his teaching came from God, they would have to want to do God's will. If they didn't want to do God's will, they would not be able to properly evaluate it. This is still true today. Sin affects our ability to properly evaluate God and his Word. James said this: "So put away all filth and evil excess and humbly welcome the message implanted within you, which is able to save your souls" (James 1:21).

In speaking to Christians James said, in order for us to accept God's Word, we must get rid of sin. The presence of unconfessed sin and even sin we are not aware of, always affects our ability to truly accept revelation from God. What makes this problem even greater is the fact that we will never be completely free of sin until we have glorified bodies in heaven. We each have a sin problem.

3. A resource problem. The final reason a study of God cannot be comprehensive is because we have a resource problem. God simply has not told us everything about himself. What he has told us we can know, but he has chosen in his sovereignty to not reveal everything. Look at Deuteronomy 29:29:

> Secret things belong to the Lord our God, but those that are revealed belong to us and our descendants forever, so that we might obey all the words of this law.

I urge you to keep these limitations in mind as we navigate through this study. My prayer is that God will reveal himself to you in new and profound ways.

Knowing God as the Highest Good

In Latin, there is a term *summum bonum,* which means "the highest good out of which all other good flows." In this section, we will see how Scripture teaches that knowing God is the highest good above all other good things. The highest good is not helping people; it is not attaining great wealth; it is not attaining tremendous knowledge. The highest good is to know God and as a result every other virtue flows from this knowledge.

Intimate Knowledge

Look at what Jeremiah said about this:

This is what the LORD says: "Let not the wise man boast of his wisdom or the strong man boast of his strength or the rich man boast of his riches, but *let him who boasts boast about this: that he understands and knows me.*
Jeremiah 9:23–24 (NIV 1984)

Here the Lord says through Jeremiah that the knowledge of him is our greatest pursuit. God names three of the more common pursuits of men and women in life. He names the pursuit of wisdom, as education is a major priority in most societies. He names the pursuit of strength, as many give themselves to the endeavor of developing their bodies and beauty. He names the pursuit of wealth. Wealth many times is the fuel behind building the mind and the body. God says the greatest boast, and therefore, the greatest pursuit is understanding and knowing God.

J. I. Packer eloquently said the same thing in his book *Knowing God.* He said:

What makes life worthwhile is having a big enough objective, something which catches our imagination and lays hold of our allegiance, and this the Christian has in a way that no other person has. For what higher, more exalted, and more compelling goal can there be than to know God?[1]

There is no higher or more exalted goal than knowing God and that will be the goal of this study. It is not just a desire to have "knowledge about God." The word "know" as it is used in the Scripture typically implies intimacy. In Genesis 4:1 (KJV), the word "know" is used to describe sexual relations. It was said of Adam that he "knew" his wife and they had a child.

God is not saying that academic knowledge of him is great, though that is part of it. It is an "intimate and experiential" knowledge of God that we are to pursue. God used the word "know" to describe our relationship with him, a word that was used of the "closest union" one can have with a person on the earth—a sexual relationship. Let this study not just be an academic venture. This should be a pursuit of intimately knowing God.

Example of Paul

Similarly, Paul said this: "But these assets I have come to regard as liabilities because of Christ. More than that, I now regard all things as liabilities compared to the far greater value of knowing Christ Jesus my Lord, for whom I have suffered the loss of all things—indeed, I regard them as dung!—that I may gain Christ" (Phil 3:7–8).

Paul was a top Pharisee of his day. However, he lost his career, his family, his friends, and his comfort, all for the sake of knowing Christ. He saw this as the highest goal of life and one worth giving up all things for. In fact, he said he counted everything as dung, or rubbish, in order to know Christ and have an intimate relationship with him.

Have you found knowing Christ such a worthy pursuit that you are willing to give up everything to know him?

This often occurs when people get married. They find a man or a woman and the trajectory of their lives changes. In a similar way, God is the highest good and worth leaving all other pursuits for (cf. Matt 13:45-46).

Transformational Knowledge

Finally, it should be noted that we will not be considering God primarily from an academic perspective or simply for intimacy. We will be considering him also to be transformed. Listen to what Paul said about beholding God:

> And we all, with unveiled face, beholding the glory of the Lord, are being *transformed into the same image from one degree of glory to another*. For this comes from the Lord who is the Spirit.
> 2 Corinthians 3:8 (ESV)

Paul uses a picture of Moses going up on the mountain in Exodus and viewing God. He came down from the mountain and his face was shining. In the same way, studying God is like going up on the mountain to see God. As we study his personality and his characteristics, it should make us look more like him and change us from glory to glory. As God was a shining light so also Moses came down from the mountain with his face shining.

Our hope is that by spending time with God, we will start to be transformed into his very image (cf. Rom 12:2, Col 3:10). He is not an object to look at and speculate about in the museum. He is God, and therefore, worthy to be adored, feared, and modeled, and that is our hope. If we studied for any other purpose alone, it would be misguided.

Jesus described people who heard his words and did not live by them as fools who built their house on the wrong foundation and it was destroyed in the storm (Matt 7:24–27). Studying God and modeling him is the foundation on which to build our lives and that is the purpose of this study.

Benefits of Knowing God

What makes knowing God the highest good? As we said the *summum bonum* is the highest good out of which all good flows. What do we receive from knowing God? What are the benefits?

If we are going to fully give ourselves to the endeavor of studying and knowing God, we must be fully convinced of the benefits of this endeavor. What does the Bible teach as benefits of knowing God?

Eternal Life/Quality of Life

The first benefit is eternal life. Look at what Jesus said:

> When Jesus had finished saying these things, he looked upward to heaven and said, "Father, the time has come. Glorify your Son, so that your Son may glorify you—just as you have given him authority over all humanity, so that he may give eternal life to everyone you have given him. *Now this is eternal life—that they know you, the only true God, and Jesus Christ, whom you sent.*
> John 17:1–3

Jesus said this is eternal life, knowing God. Eternal life is not primarily about length of life, for everybody will live eternally in one of two places. It is also

17

about quality of life. This means the more we know God and the more we understand and build a relationship with him, the more our quality of life increases. We start to live life the way it was meant to be lived.

This is one of the reasons we should pursue a knowledge of God. Life can never be what it was meant to be apart from the knowledge of God. In the beginning, God walked with Adam and Eve in the Garden of Eden, but when sin came into the world, their relationship with God eroded. They died spiritually, and therefore, intimacy with God was no longer their primary pursuit. Pursuing God through Christ restores us to what was lost in the Garden.

This is the reason Christ came to earth and died on the cross for our sins, in order to grant eternal life to those who accept him as Lord and Savior. We study God to have life and to fulfill the purpose God created us for. Most people are living only for temporary things when in reality our purpose is eternal. Jesus said, "I am come that they *might have life and that they might have it more abundantly"* (John 10:10, KJV).

Though eternal life does not just refer to length of time, for we all will live forever, it should be said that it does include eternity in the kingdom of heaven with God. Listen to what Jesus said in Matthew 7:21–23:

> "Not everyone who says to me, 'Lord, Lord,' will enter into the kingdom of heaven—only the one who does the will of my Father in heaven. On that day, many will say to me, 'Lord, Lord, didn't we prophesy in your name, and in your name cast out demons and do many powerful deeds?' *Then I will declare to them, 'I never knew you. Go away from me, you lawbreakers!'*

Christ said the reason these people would not enter the kingdom of heaven was because they never knew him. They didn't have an intimate relationship with him through faith (cf. Heb 10:38). Salvation is not for those who say a prayer; it is for followers of Jesus, meaning those who have a vital relationship with him. Certainly, that will start at a confession of Christ, but nevertheless, it is a relationship.

We study God to have a relationship with him that enriches our quality of life and will continue throughout eternity as we know God. We study God to know what life is, and therefore, what life is not.

Proper Evaluation of Humanity

Something else happens when we encounter God. We begin to rightly evaluate ourselves and others. Studying God is like looking at a mirror. We see our faults, our problems, and maybe even our virtues. This happens in order that we may be changed.

Knowing God Reveals Our Sin

Isn't this what happened when Peter first came in contact with Jesus? Peter's response was, "Go away from me, Lord, for I am a sinful man!" (Luke 5:8).

When Peter realized that Jesus was God, he cried out for Jesus to leave because he was a sinner. When we start to realize who God is, it helps us have a proper perspective of ourselves.

We see the same thing happen with Isaiah when he saw God in Isaiah 6:5. He said, "I said, 'Too bad for me! I am destroyed, for my lips are contaminated by sin, and I live among people whose lips are contaminated by sin. My eyes have seen the king, the Lord who commands armies.'"

Many people have a tendency to wrongly evaluate themselves because they judge themselves by looking at other people. I am really smart in comparison with him. I am really beautiful in comparison with her. I am really holy in comparison with those people. Pride exists because people are looking at the wrong person. They are looking at themselves or one another instead of God. Pride would be eliminated if people had a proper relationship with God.

Knowing God not only helps us evaluate ourselves but also others. Isaiah, after seeing God said, "I live among a people whose lips are contaminated." He saw the people and the world around him differently because he was looking at the glory of God. Hear this: you will evaluate the music you listen to, the TV programs that you watch, your friends, and society differently when you are living in the presence of God.

This explains why a woman continually dates the wrong guy; she doesn't know God, and therefore, cannot properly evaluate herself or others. This explains why we take in ungodly music and unedifying TV because most of us cannot properly evaluate. This is why the world exalts drug dealers, murderers, alcoholics, cheaters, thieves, etc., who talk about their crimes in the music they write or the movies they produce. This is because without knowing God, man cannot properly evaluate others. Listen to what Isaiah says:

> Those who call evil good and good evil are as good as dead, who turn darkness into light and light into darkness, who turn bitter into sweet and sweet into bitter.
> Isaiah 5:20

As our society turns farther away from God, the more it will be common for man to praise evil and hate good.

19

Knowing God Helps Us Give Value to Humanity

It should also be noted that knowing God will help us give value to humanity. We see this in Genesis 9:6. It says, "Whoever sheds human blood, by other humans must his blood be shed; for in God's image God has made humankind."

When we look at our society and see the killing of innocent babies, sex trafficking, the growing murder rates and suicide rates around the world, we should realize this is happening because people don't know God and can't properly value human life. Man is made in the image of God, and therefore, has value. I have value because in some way or another, even though I sin, I bear the image of God. Having God as my maker and having been created in his likeness, gives me innate value. Humanity has value.

Depression often arises because of a lack of knowing God. One says, I am unattractive; I can't do anything right; nobody loves me. These types of thoughts happen because we do not truly know our value as people made in the glory and image of God. Listen to how David thought about himself because of his knowledge of God:

> I praise you because I am fearfully and wonderfully made; your works are wonderful, I know that full well.
> Psalm 139:14 (NIV 1984)

David knew God's works were good. Can you imagine a society that saw the true beauty and value in each human because they knew God? Can you imagine how that would decrease murder, suicide, human trafficking, and even plastic surgery? "God, we are fearfully and wonderfully made. We know this full well."

It is this understanding of human value that has led Christians around the world to often be the ones to start hospitals, orphanages, crisis pregnancy centers, and universities. Why? It's because they have a proper view of God that affects their view of man. If man is made in the image of God, then there is a great dignity in serving them, building them up, and caring for them. These people are made in the image of God and have dignity and glory. This dignity and glory even extends to the poor, the sick, the aged, and the mentally challenged. Given that all men are made in the image of God, it should also exclude racism. Therefore, to show partiality is to sin against God and one another (cf. James 2:1-9).

We will have a greater evaluation of humanity because of our study of God, and it will give us a more accurate worldview.

Proper Evaluation of Morality

The next benefit of knowing God is a proper evaluation of morality. We have hinted at this already in looking at humanity, but a proper understanding of God also affects how we evaluate morality—what is right and wrong. We see varying lifestyles in society based on our understanding of God.

We see this in Romans 1:21–32, though we will not study this passage here in its entirety, it shows how the world is affected by not acknowledging God. Look at what the text says:

> For although they knew God, they neither glorified him as God nor gave thanks to him, but *their thinking became futile and their foolish hearts were darkened.* Although they claimed to be wise, they became fools. Romans 1:21–22 (NIV 1984)

In speaking about the Gentile world, Paul says that they knew God but did not glorify him as God. What were the consequences of denying God?

Paul said a consequence of denying God was *futile thinking* (v. 21). Futile means useless, pointless, or without purpose. The thinking of society became useless and without purpose. A lack of acknowledging God negatively affected the thinking of mankind.

Another consequence of denying God was a *darkened heart* (v.21). Darkness is the absence of light. We cannot see properly without light. God is the light and without him we cannot properly evaluate anything else. Professing to be wise, they became fools (v. 22). They evaluated all of life improperly because they had refused the light (cf. John 8:12). This darkened heart also may suggest much more including the inability to love God or others. Romans 1:31 later describes these people as "without natural affection" (KJV). Those who had ceased to acknowledge God had lost the ability to love even in the most fundamental relationships: God, family, friends, etc. In fact, the word "heart" is a comprehensive term referring to the mind, will, and emotions. When we deny God we will not be able to properly understand things, make decisions, or even love—everything is affected. Man's heart becomes dark without God.

When society starts to deny God, they will become an unwise, incompetent, and loveless society. Without proper thinking, proper decision making, and proper love, the whole value system of society will be fractured. Let's consider more consequences of not glorifying and knowing God.

What are further consequences?
Romans 1:24–26 says:

21

Therefore God gave them over in the desires of their hearts *to impurity, to dishonor their bodies among themselves.* They exchanged the truth of God for a lie and *worshiped and served the creation rather than the Creator,* who is blessed forever! Amen. For this reason God gave them over to dishonorable passions. For *their women exchanged the natural sexual relations for unnatural* ones,

Paul says a consequence of a society denying God is *sexual impurity* (v. 24). Surely, we see this in our society. Pornography, prostitution, sexual abuse, trafficking, and rampant adultery are all repercussions of a society that has denied God.

Paul also says that *false worship* is a result of denying God (v. 25). When man denies God, he starts to worship and serve created things instead of the Creator. We see this in the gamut of religions and cults around the world. We also see it in how man worships entertainers, athletes, authors, etc. Man was made to worship God, and if he doesn't worship God, he will worship something else. We also see this false worship in selfishness. Most people live their lives as though life is about their pleasure and their happiness instead of God's. In society, we essentially see the idolatry of the self. Everything is about self-actualization, self-awareness, self-esteem, self-help, self-achievement, etc. Man worships himself. Without God, society becomes a haven of idols.

The next consequence of denying God that Paul mentions is *homosexuality* (v. 26). The society that has turned away from God will be increasingly prone to the acceptance and practice of homosexuality. No one can deny the increasing acceptance of homosexuality in the world today. It has been accepted in many Christian denominations as an alternative lifestyle; some have even accepted homosexual pastors. Homosexual marriage is an acceptable practice in many nations, and those who do not accept it are increasingly scorned and harassed. We live in a world that has denied God and is reaping the consequences of that denial.

What are the other consequences of denying God? Look at what else Paul says in Romans 1:28–31:

And just as they did not see fit to acknowledge God, God gave them over to a depraved mind, to do what should not be done. They are filled with every kind of unrighteousness, wickedness, covetousness, malice. They are rife with envy, murder, strife, deceit, hostility. They are gossips, slanderers, haters of God, insolent, arrogant, boastful, contrivers of all sorts of evil, disobedient to parents, senseless, covenant-breakers, heartless, ruthless. Although they fully know God's righteous decree that

22

those who practice such things deserve to die, they not only do them but also approve of those who practice them.

Paul simply says that society will continually practice "what should not be done" (v. 28). He describes a myriad of vices that will show up in society including envy, murder, strife, deceit, hostility, slander, the hatred of God, disobedience, senselessness, heartlessness, etc. Senseless murders will constantly be talked about on the daily news. The slander of God, the Bible, and any type of moral values will be common. Society will become loveless and senseless. People will be left scratching their heads at the corruption in the government, business, education, and the home. This will all be an effect of not knowing God. If every good thing comes from knowing God, then it just makes sense that every bad thing will come from denying him and his rule over society (cf. James 1:17).

What is the final result Paul gives of not knowing God?

Not Knowing God Leads to Approval of Sin

Paul says that not only will denying God lead to all types of sin, but it also will lead to "approval" of sin. Look at what Romans 1:32 says:

Although they fully know God's righteous decree that those who practice such things deserve to die, they not only do them but also approve of those who practice them.

When you look at society and see the movies, the media, and the people that are elevated or put on pedestals, it is a picture of the result of not knowing God. In the US, some of the biggest stars are what would be called "gangsta rappers." Their song lyrics glamorize the abuse of drugs, stealing, killing, gang violence, sex, and disrespect of women. People flock to buy their records and they are given lucrative movie and book deals.

The young people listen to their music, sing their songs, and dress like them. When we start to not only practice sin but approve of sin, it is a picture of a society that has turned fully away from God. What's wrong and right has been inverted.

Society says sex before marriage is right, homosexuality is right, pornography is right, the murder of the innocent is right, drug and alcohol abuse is right, and the worship of the biblical God and the practice of biblical values is wrong, and often met with persecution.

The knowledge of God is necessary to help us properly evaluate morality—what is right and wrong. We must study God to properly calibrate our hearts and minds.

Peace and Security

What else does knowing God bring? Listen to what Solomon says: "The name of the Lord is like a strong tower; the righteous person runs to it and is set safely on high" (Proverbs 18:10).

In this verse, Solomon says the name of the Lord is a strong tower. We need to understand two things about this passage to fully grasp it. The first thing is that "name" in the Hebrew culture meant more than something you called somebody; it had to do with their character. That is why at times in the Bible we see God intervene in someone's life and change their name. Jacob, who was a thief and swindler, was named Israel meaning "one who has wrestled with God and prevailed." He received a new name because he had a change of character.

We could translate the proverb this way: "The characteristics of the Lord are a strong tower." Towers in those days were used for safety. If there was a war, people would run into a stone tower for safety. A strong tower would protect the community from an approaching enemy or a great storm.

Therefore, the proverb means that those who "know God and his characteristics" will find safety, security, and peace. When others are afraid and fearful at events in life, God keeps those who know him at peace and protects them. Listen to what Isaiah says: "Thou wilt keep him in perfect peace, whose mind is stayed on thee: because he trusteth in thee" (Isaiah 26:3 KJV).

Isaiah says the person whose mind is always thinking about God stays at peace in the storms of life because he knows and trusts him. They know that even if they die, they will spend eternity in heaven. They know that even when they fail, it is all part of God's sovereign plan that he is working out for their good (Romans 8:28). Where others panic, get depressed, or run to protect themselves, the one who knows God's name has peace and security. J. I. Packer said this: "There is no peace like the peace of those whose minds are possessed with full assurance that they have known God, and God has known them, and that this relationship guarantees God's favor to them in life, through death and on forever."[2] We seek to know God to increase our peace and security.

Increased Wisdom

Knowing God also increases our wisdom. Listen again to Solomon: "The fear of the LORD is the beginning of wisdom, and knowledge of the Holy One is understanding" (Prov 9:10 NIV 1984).

The fear of the Lord is the beginning of wisdom. Next, when Solomon says, the knowledge of the Holy One is understanding, he probably is just using

Hebrew parallelism to say the same thing. To fear the Lord means to know the Holy One, and to receive wisdom is the same as understanding. Solomon is using a parallel statement for emphasis. If you begin to seek the knowledge of God, you will gain wisdom for life. This fits the theme of Proverbs: seek after wisdom and it will bless your life. God is the source of all wisdom.

Many people in the world have head knowledge because you can get that from books and degrees. But few people have wisdom—who know how to apply knowledge. Wisdom answers the question, "How can I apply this knowledge to my life?" or "What should I do in this situation?" Wisdom comes from fearing God and knowing him.

A lack of wisdom is part of the reason the counseling industry has become so large. It's part of the reason people seek psychics and read their horoscopes. If you look at Hollywood, everybody has a shrink and a psychic. This is true because people lack the wisdom to make decisions. And, people can't make wise decisions because wisdom starts with God and a knowledge of him.

Proverbs 3:6 says this: "Acknowledge him in all your ways, and he will make your paths straight." The New Living Translation says, "He will show you which paths to take." The person who is acknowledging God and seeking his face will receive wisdom from God to direct his paths. God will guide his career, marriage, finances, etc. However, the person who denies God will lack wisdom for all these decisions, and he will reap the consequences of this denial as seen in a life marked by foolish decisions.

Wisdom begins with knowing God and fearing him. We study God in order to make us wise.

Multiplication of Blessings

Peter names several blessings that come from the knowledge of God. Look at what he says:

> May grace and peace be multiplied to you in the knowledge of God and of Jesus our Lord. His divine power has granted to us all things that pertain to life and godliness, through the knowledge of him who called us to his own glory and excellence
> 2 Peter 1:2-3 ESV

Peter says the knowledge of God leads to "multiplied" blessings. It is through the knowledge of God that grace, peace, and power are multiplied to believers.

Multiplied Grace

The first multiplied blessing he names is "grace," which means unmerited favor (2 Peter 1:2). It is interesting that when you consider the life of Joseph (Genesis 37–45), we see a man who went through many trials but received God's favor in each one of them. He was sold into slavery and taken to Egypt, but while he was serving as a slave, he prospered. Potiphar, his master, prospered because of him, and therefore, placed him over his whole household. Soon after, he was put in prison. But even there, he prospered and was eventually placed in charge of all the prisoners. Finally, he was put in charge over the kingdom of Egypt under Pharaoh. There was unmerited favor over his entire life, even in the midst of trials, because he knew the Lord.

We also see this displayed in Jacob's life. While he was a shepherd for his uncle Laban, Laban became very wealthy because of him (Gen. 30:27–29). In fact, Laban says that he knew God was blessing him because of Jacob (v. 27). Grace is multiplied to those who know the Lord. This does not mean the eradication of trials; however, it does mean one will have God's favor while in the trials. The knowledge of God, an intimate relationship with him, brings grace—unmerited favor.

Multiplied Peace

Although discussed previously, "peace" is mentioned here again by Peter (2 Peter 1:2). "May grace and peace be multiplied to you in the knowledge of God and of Jesus our Lord." The Bible mentions two kinds of peace. There is peace *with God* that we receive by accepting Christ as Lord and Savior (Rom 5:1). Before we were born again, the Bible says that because of our sins, we were at enmity with God and his wrath abided on us (John 3:36). But because of our faith in Christ, we now are at peace with God.

The second peace is the *peace of God*. Philippians 4:7 calls it "the peace of God that surpasses all understanding."

> Do not be anxious about anything. Instead, in every situation, through prayer and petition with thanksgiving, tell your requests to God. And the peace of God that surpasses all understanding will guard your hearts and minds in Christ Jesus.
> Philippians 4:6–7

Think about that. A person receives peace by always praying and thanking God for everything. Peace is multiplied to this person. The more you know God, the more you will receive peace.

Multiplied Power

Finally, we also receive power. Being in God's presence and knowing him brings a certain amount of power in the life of the seeker. Peter says the person who knows God receives power to be godly. "His divine power has granted to us all things that pertain to life and godliness, through the knowledge of him who called us to his own glory and excellence" (2 Peter 1:2-3 ESV).

The more we know God, the more we will experience God's power in our life, power to do the things God has called us to do. It should be noted that people who have a weak knowledge of God will find themselves very prone to fall into sin because they lack power. However, the more we know God, the more we will find spiritual power in our life to be godly and to glorify God through great works.

Did we not see great power in the life of Abraham, Moses, David, Elijah, Mary, and the apostles? Power is in the life of the person who is intimate with God (cf. John 15:5), and therefore, God uses them in a special way for his glory. Second Chronicles 16:9 in the KJV says, "For the eyes of the LORD run to and fro throughout the whole earth, *to shew himself strong in the behalf of them whose heart is perfect toward him.*"

A Worthy and Pleasing Life

The next benefit of knowing God is a worthy and pleasing life. Colossians 1:9–10 says this:

> For this reason we also, from the day we heard about you, have not ceased praying for you and asking God to *fill you with the knowledge of his will* in all spiritual wisdom and understanding, so that you may live *worthily of the Lord and please him in all respects*—bearing fruit in every good deed, growing in the knowledge of God

Paul prays for this church to be "filled" with the knowledge of God's will "so that" (v. 9) the congregation would live a life "worthy" of the Lord and "pleasing" to him in every way (v. 10).

The word "worthy" comes from the root word "worth." If you go to a gym and purchase a membership, the only reason you pay for it is because you believe that it is worth the asking price. When people look at how Christians live, they can tell how much God really means to them—his value. They can tell by how much time they invest in their relationship with him through church, service, and devotion. They can tell by the cost. Similarly, Paul is praying that this congregation would know God more so that their life would properly reflect how much God is worth—in essence his value.

What should be the value of God to the believer? Simply said, God is worth everything plus. Listen to what Romans 12:1 in the KJV says: "I beseech you therefore, brethren, by the mercies of God, that ye present your bodies a living sacrifice, holy, acceptable unto God, *which is your reasonable service.*"

Paul says in view of everything God has done, a believer should offer his entire life as a sacrifice. In fact, he says it is the only "reasonable" offering one who knows God can give.

Christians who offer God "everything plus" are people who are "pleasing" to God. He enjoys them and rejoices over them with songs (cf. Zephaniah 3:17). That is what happens when a person really knows God; they start to demonstrate God's worth in varying ways. This is why a person who claims to know God and fails to experience any real change in their life is deceived. Listen to what John said: "If we say we have fellowship with him and yet keep on walking in the darkness, we are lying and not practicing the truth" (1 John 1:6).

We cannot live a lifestyle like the world and truly have a relationship with God. John says this is impossible. A true relationship with God—a true knowledge of him—will always change us; we will no longer be able to walk in darkness. It will enable us to start walking worthy of him and pleasing him in every way.

Fruitfulness

The next benefit of knowing God is a fruitful life. Look again at what Paul says in Colossians 1:9–10:

> For this reason we also, from the day we heard about you, have not ceased praying for you and asking God to *fill you with the knowledge of his will* in all spiritual wisdom and understanding, so that you may live worthily of the Lord and please him in all respects—*bearing fruit in every good deed,* growing in the knowledge of God

Paul says the knowledge of God will make us bear fruit in every good deed. A person who knows God will bear fruit. Jesus said something similar in John 15:4–5:

> Remain in me, and I will remain in you. Just as the branch cannot bear fruit by itself, unless it remains in the vine, so neither can you unless you remain in me. "I am the vine; you are the branches. The one who remains

in me—and I in him—bears much fruit, because apart from me you can accomplish nothing.

A person who is remaining in Christ—spending intimate time with him—will produce much fruit.

Fruit always has two characteristics. First, it always represents the tree. An apple comes from an apple tree. An orange comes from an orange tree. When you bear fruit from the knowledge of God and spending time with him, it will be fruits or characteristics that represent God and his will. Galatians 5:22-23 says, "But the fruit of the Spirit is love, joy, peace, patience, kindness, goodness, faithfulness, gentleness, and self-control..."

Secondly, a tree always bears fruit so others can eat from it (cf. Psalm 1:2-3). This will happen in your life through your words and actions. People will be blessed by you; people will be led to Christ by you; people will be encouraged by you. You will give people wisdom, encouragement, strength, and you will help them be fruitful.

These are the benefits of knowing God. Listen to what God said to Abraham: "I will make you into a great nation and I will bless you; I will make your name great and you will be a blessing" (Gen 12:2).

Those who are growing in the knowledge of God will increasingly be a blessing to others as well.

Patience, Endurance, Joy, and Thanksgiving

There are still more benefits to being filled with God's will. Again, Colossians 1:9-12 says,

> For this reason we also, from the day we heard about you, have not ceased praying for you and asking God to fill you with the knowledge of his will in all spiritual wisdom and understanding, so that you may live worthily of the Lord and please him in all respects—bearing fruit in every good deed, growing in the knowledge of God, *being strengthened with all power according to his glorious might for the display of all patience and steadfastness, joyfully giving thanks* to the Father who has qualified you to share in the saints' inheritance in the light.

Paul says the knowledge of God's will brings power to endure, to be patient, to be joyful, and to be thankful.

Patience

Next, Paul mentions patience. In this context, patience seems to deal primarily with people (since steadfastness focuses on trials). God gives us power to endure difficult people without retaliation.

No doubt, it was David's relationship with God that allowed him to endure the constant assaults and attacks of King Saul without retaliation. Even when David had opportunities where he could have killed Saul, he always said, "I will not touch God's anointed." It was David's relationship with God that enabled him to be patient with Saul and also to be patient in waiting for God to fulfill his promise of making him king.

Endurance

"Steadfastness" can be translated "endurance" (NIV 1984). It means "to bear up under a heavy weight" (cf. Col 1:9, 11). Through knowing God, we receive power to endure a hard life situation. God gives us grace to persevere through trials.

It has often been said that you are either in a trial or about to enter one. Christianity does not make a person exempt from the trials of life; in fact, it may actually cause more trials. However, knowing God gives us the precious fruit of endurance for these trials.

Joy

Joy is an inward attitude that has nothing to do with circumstances, but is based on one's relationship with God. A person who is growing in the knowledge of God can go through difficult situations with joy (cf. Col 1:9, 11). Look at what Paul said to the Philippians: "*Rejoice in the Lord* always. Again I say, rejoice! Let everyone see your gentleness. *The Lord is near!*" (Phil 4:4-5).

Why could Paul rejoice in the Lord always and also be gentle in serving others? It was because he was "in" a relationship with the Lord and also because the Lord was "near." This doesn't seem to be focusing on the fact that Christ is coming soon, but the fact that God was near in proximity. God promises that he will never leave us nor forsake us (Heb 13:5); he abides in the hearts of those who love him (John 14:23). This should give the believer joy no matter what circumstances they are going through. We can have joy because we are growing in relationship with our Lord and because he is always near us.

Thanksgiving

Finally, we see that thanksgiving is also a result of knowing God (cf. Col 1:9, 11). Thanksgiving is the outward expression of this internal joy in all circumstances. We saw this perfectly modeled by Job as he thanked God even in the midst of his trials. This was a man filled with the knowledge of God's will (Col 1:9). Listen to what he said: "He said, 'Naked I came from my mother's womb, and naked I will return there. The Lord gives, and the Lord takes away. May the name of the Lord be blessed!'" (Job 1:21).

For many Christians, we not only don't give God thanks or praise when things are bad, but we often forget to give thanks when things are good or when God has answered our prayers.

We saw this lack of thanksgiving in the story of the ten lepers who approached Christ for healing. He told them to go to the temple and show themselves to the priest. On the way there, all of them were healed. One of them was so happy and grateful, he ran back to tell Christ, "Thank you." Look at how Christ responded: "Were not ten cleansed? Where are the other nine? Was no one found to turn back and give praise to God except this foreigner?" (Luke 17:17–18).

Everybody went their own way, and only one returned to give God thanks. Giving thanks to God in trial and in blessing is a result of knowing God and his will. The world is full of complainers (cf. Rom 1:21), and sadly many of them are Christians. As we grow in knowing God more, we will find the fruit of praise and thanksgiving on our lips (cf. Heb 13:15).

Conclusion

The benefits of knowing God are vast. Knowing him is the summum bonum, the highest good out of which all good flows. One might ask, "How can we turn this study about God and the accumulated knowledge about him into intimacy with him?" J. I. Packer asks and answers this question in his book *Knowing God*. He said,

> How can we turn our knowledge about God into knowledge of God? The rule for doing this is simple but demanding. *It is that we turn each Truth that we learn about God into matter for meditation before God, leading to prayer and praise to God.*[3]

Let this be our prayer and our practice so that we may truly come to know him through this study. Amen.

Review Questions

1. What are some reasons why a study of God is always incomprehensive?

2. What are some negative effects on a person or society for not seeking God? In what ways do you see these negative effects happening in the world?

3. What are some positive benefits of seeking and knowing God? How have you experienced these in your own life or seen them in the lives of those around you? How is God calling you to seek to know him more and help others do the same?

Prayer Prompts

- Pray that God would anoint your study and that you would truly come to know him more through its duration. Pray that knowing God will become your life's goal and that as you know him more, you might truly embrace his worth and adore him even more.

- Pray that our churches, communities, and nations would come to know God more through the preaching of his Word and that they would be transformed by this knowledge.

- Pray that this knowledge of God would lead to the reverence of humanity as made in the image of God especially for the unborn, the poor, different races, and cultures, and that there would be an increase of love and unity that can only come through Christ.

General Revelation

After studying the benefits of knowing God and seeing how knowing him is the attainment of the highest good, we now will answer the questions: "How can we get to know God more?" and also "How can we know that God exists? What is the evidence?"

Let's start by looking at how Scripture handles the existence of God.

The Bible Assumes the Existence of God

When we open our Bibles, some might expect to find a large apologetic treatise on the existence of God. It would be expected that the writers of the Bible would begin by proving and defending his existence. "These are the reasons and proofs that there is a God..." However, the Bible does not begin this way, because the Bible assumes that all mankind believes in God. Genesis begins with this: "In the beginning God created the heavens and the earth" (Gen 1:1).

Similarly, Paul speaks of the entire world having knowledge of God, and therefore, being without excuse for not believing in him. Romans 1:20 says this:

> For since the creation of the world his invisible attributes—his eternal power and divine nature—have been clearly seen, because they are understood through what has been made. So people are without excuse.

Why does the Bible teach that every person knows that there is a God? How is God revealed? What are the evidences of his existence?

The reason Scripture does not argue the existence of God is because God has made himself known to all of mankind. Theologians call God making himself known "revelation." God has revealed himself to man, and therefore, man is without excuse for not believing in him (Romans 1:20).

Implied in the word "revelation" is the fact that God must make himself known to us. On our own, we cannot know God. Revelation must come from his initiative. Consider what Wayne Grudem says about revelation: "If we are to know God at all, it is necessary that he reveal himself to us. Even when discussing the revelation of God that comes through nature, Paul says that what can be known about God is plain to people 'because God has shown it to them'" (Rom. 1:19).[4]

33

In what ways has God revealed himself? There are *two primary forms of revelation.* The first is called *general revelation,* which is revelation that everybody has received. Charles Ryrie explains general revelation this way:

> General revelation is exactly that—general. It is general in its scope; that is, it reaches to all people (Matt. 5:45; Acts 14:17). It is general in geography; that is, it encompasses the entire globe (Ps. 19:2). It is general in its methodology; that is, it employs universal means like the heat of the sun (vv. 4–6) and human conscience (Rom. 2:14–15). Simply because it is a revelation that affects all people wherever they are and whenever they have lived it can bring light and truth to all, or, if rejected, it brings condemnation.[5]

The second is *specific revelation,* which only some people have. Erickson defines special revelation this way: "God's manifestation of himself to particular persons at definite times and places, enabling those persons to enter into a redemptive relationship with him."[6] We will look at both of these revelations, but we will be considering general revelation first.

General Revelation Shows That God Exists

As mentioned previously, some of the greatest evidence that we have of a creator is his creation. David says in Psalm 19:1–4:

> The heavens declare the glory of God; the sky displays his handiwork. Day after day it speaks out; night after night it reveals his greatness. There is no actual speech or word, nor is its voice literally heard. Yet its voice echoes throughout the earth; its words carry to the distant horizon. In the sky he has pitched a tent for the sun.

David says the "heavens declare the glory of God." He says they speak about him day after day and night after night. Creation declares that there is a God.

Here is an apologetic for the evidence of God. Let's say a tribal person was walking outside and found a watch on the ground. He had previously never seen a watch or heard of anything like it before. He would pick up the watch and notice seconds moving, the hours moving. If he managed to open the watch, he would see screws, chips, and advanced technology.

The tribal person would not say, "Wow, this must have all just come together somehow." No, he would say to himself, "I don't know what this is, but I'm sure it had a creator." In fact, by looking at the dynamics of the watch, he would probably say, "This creator must be very intelligent because I have never seen anything like this." The watch's features would scream, "Designed by some great intelligence!" It certainly wouldn't suggest that it came together accidentally and without purpose. It had to have intention behind it. It had to have purpose. Accidents like this don't happen. A tribal person would naturally believe there was a creator, and you could not tell him otherwise.

If that is the normal conclusion when seeing a watch, how much more should we come to that same conclusion when seeing the human body. If the body is at 98.6 degrees Fahrenheit, the body is stable, but if it gets a little bit hotter, a person will overheat and have a fever. If the body was a little bit colder, it would freeze. It's the same when looking at the earth: if we were a little farther away from the sun, we would freeze to death. If we were a little closer, we would burn. The science in the body and throughout creation says, "Creator." In fact, because the intelligent design behind the creation is so magnificent, it says, "This creator must be great!" A person can come to no other conclusion. That's why Scripture says man is "without excuse" (Rom 1:20).

One of the greatest evidences for the Creator is his creation. How do I know that the Mona Lisa had a creator? It's simply because I have seen the creation. I don't have to meet Leonardo Da Vinci to know he existed because I have seen what he created. Again, it would be ludicrous to come to any other conclusion. This is why Scripture says, "Fools say to themselves, 'There is no God'" (Psalm 14:1). It would be foolish to come to any other conclusion when looking at creation.

Another aspect of general revelation which reveals God to man is the *conscience.* Look at what Paul says in Romans 1:19 (NASB): "Because *that which is known about God is evident within them*; for God made it evident to them."

Paul says the knowledge of God is "evident within them" when referring to mankind. It seems Paul is referring to the conscience as a mechanism that reveals God to man. The conscience is an internal witness within man that affirms or accuses him of right and wrong. The ultimate basis of right and wrong is God. This is how the knowledge of God is "evident within them." In fact, this knowledge is so strong in the conscience that every person will be judged on their response to their conscience. Listen to Romans 2:14–16:

> For whenever the Gentiles, who do not have the law, do by nature the things required by the law, these who do not have the law are a law to themselves. *They show that the work of the law is written in their hearts, as their conscience bears witness* and their conflicting thoughts accuse or else defend them, on the day when God will judge the *secrets of human hearts,* according to my gospel through Christ Jesus.

Paul says the "work of the law is written in their hearts." The summation of God's law is to love God and to love our neighbor (Matt 22:34–40). The knowledge of God is evident within man by the internal witness God has given in the conscience.

Evidence for the conscience can be seen by looking at the majority of religions in the world. Even in tribal areas, they typically believe in a God and his judgment. They believe they will be judged by God for their sins. This is common among the religions of the world because of the conscience. God has made the knowledge of himself "evident within them," and therefore, they are without excuse. Another evidence of the conscience is seen in mankind's similar moral laws. It doesn't matter what culture a person is from; we typically have the same laws, "Do not lie, do not steal, do not kill, etc." These all reflect the conscience of man.

This is general revelation. God has revealed himself to man through his creation and also through the conscience. We have a God that wants to be known, and therefore, he reveals himself to us. Creation declares his existence and glory, and our hearts declare it as well.

General Revelation Shows Certain Attributes of God

Not only do we see that God exists when looking at creation, but we can also discern some of his characteristics. Many characteristics of a person can be discovered by looking at his creation or something he has done.

For example, when I was single, I was very disorganized. If you went into my room, you would have seen clothes all over my desk, my bed unmade, and hundreds of books on my floor. Because of my room (my creation) you would be able to tell a lot about me without ever meeting me. You would probably surmise that this person must be a pretty disorganized guy. You would probably also surmise that this person likes to study because of all the books. You could tell some things about me by what I had created. It's the same with God.

What are some characteristics we can learn about God through general revelation?

God Is Glorious

We can tell from creation that God is glorious—he is great. Psalms 19:1–3 says this:

The heavens declare the glory of God; the sky displays his handiwork. Day after day it speaks out; night after night it reveals his greatness. There is no actual speech or word, nor is its voice literally heard.

David says the heavens "declare the glory of God." The Hebrew word for *glory* has the connotation of weight, how heavy something is. When we look at something as wonderful as the stars, you have to say, "This God must be great. He must be big. Look at what he has created." When you look at the sun and its size and power, you can come to no other conclusion. This God is glorious. We can see his glory in creation.

God Is Powerful

Another characteristic that can be discerned from creation is the power of God. It takes great power to create the heavens and the earth. Consider again what Romans 1:19–20 says:

> *because what can be known about God is plain to them,* because God has made it plain to them. For since the creation of the world his *invisible attributes—his eternal power* and divine nature—have been clearly seen, because they are understood through what has been made. So people are without excuse.

Paul says God's eternal power has been made clear. When you look at all of creation, you cannot but discern that this creator is very powerful.

God Is Transcendent or Immortal

Romans 1:20 also says that God has made other "invisible attributes" plain, such as his "divine nature." What does Paul mean by the revelation of God's divine nature?

The word *divine* means "of, relating to, or proceeding directly from God or a god."[7] Essentially, divine means that the Creator is unlike anything in all of creation. There is nothing like him!

In fact, this is one of the ways that Paul stated that mankind sinned in refusing to acknowledge the Creator's immortality or what some would call his *transcendence*. Transcendence means that God is "beyond comprehension."[8] Instead of recognizing that God is immortal, they created idols in the form of creation. They made idols of men and animals. Romans 1:22–23 says,

37

Although they claimed to be wise, they became fools and exchanged the glory of *the immortal God* for an image resembling mortal human beings or birds or four-footed animals or reptiles.

When you look at the glory of God's creation, it is natural to assume that the Creator must be greater than his creation. He must be different; he must be immortal.

But instead of acknowledging the immortal God, people professing to be wise became foolish and started to worship the creation itself. They worshiped cows, snakes, and humans. Most people worship themselves by the way they live their life. They essentially declare *that I am the chief end of my existence.* That's why people say, "All that matters is that you are happy. Do what makes you happy." That means they are the chief end of their existence. They worship their own image; they are their own God.

In fact, one of the major temptations throughout history has been to worship other individuals or become deities ourselves. Wasn't that the temptation of Eve when the serpent said, "Eat of this tree and you will be like God?" Similarly, many kings have fallen into this temptation, claiming divinity, and desiring to be worshiped (cf. Daniel 3). This also has happened with many of the cults and religions of the world. A person or persons are viewed as divine and are worshiped as such. Because men refuse to acknowledge God, they instead worship the creation.

Paul says this is foolishness. God is divine; he is immortal and transcendent. There is nothing like him.

What else can we learn about the nature of God from creation?

God Is Kind and Loving

Another characteristic we can learn about God through creation is the fact that he is kind. This is often referred to as the goodness of God. God has made it clear that he loves and cares for people even those who do not love him. Listen to what Paul says in Acts 14:17 (NIV 1984):

Yet he has not left *himself without testimony: He has shown kindness* by giving you rain from heaven and crops in their seasons; he provides you with plenty of food and fills your hearts with joy.

Paul teaches that the natural provisions of creation show that God is kind. He cares for animals and people (cf. Jonah 4:11). He has given us many things such as rain, food, and, even joy. All these actions testify to the fact that he cares.

38

Certainly, we also see bad things in creation. We see such things as famine, flood, and disease. However, it wasn't God's original design for things to be this way; he made everything originally good (cf. Genesis 1:31).

In fact, Jesus uses an argument from general revelation when teaching the disciples not to worry. In Matthew 6:25–34, he says, "Look at how God provides for the birds of the air and the lilies of the field. Aren't you more valuable than the birds of the air and lilies of the field?" He essentially says nature should teach us about the kindness and care of God. If we observed nature more intentionally, it would encourage us not to worry about our life, but to entrust our life and future with God.

We also see Christ giving a lesson on the kindness of God through nature when he teaches that we should love and pray for our enemies. Listen to his instruction:

> But I say to you, love your enemy and pray for those who persecute you, so that you may be like your Father in heaven, since *he causes the sun to rise on the evil and the good, and sends rain on the righteous and the unrighteous.*
> Matthew 5:44–45

Certainly, there are times when God displays his anger, but even his anger is a picture of his kindness (Hebrews 12:6). God is constantly showing his mercy and kindness through daily acts such as rain and sunshine.

Knowing that God is kind should affect us. It should keep us from worry, and it should challenge us to be kind to others, even our enemies. Nature teaches us about the kindness of God.

God Is a Living Being

Another clear characteristic we can discern about God from creation is the fact that he is a living being. God is alive and not dead. We learn this from his creation of humanity as living beings. Look at what Paul says to the Athenians in the book of Acts who were worshiping images of gold and silver:

> For in him we live and move about and exist, as even some of your own poets have said, 'For we too are his offspring.' *So since we are God's offspring, we should not think the deity is like gold or silver or stone, an image made by human skill and imagination.*
> Acts 17:28–29

Paul is saying that if we consider the fact that God created mankind to be his children, it should become abundantly clear that he is a living person. He is alive, not an idol that is without breath. We shouldn't think that God is something made by man like an image of gold or silver.

Paul essentially says, "Don't you think it's ludicrous to bow down to an image that you made?" However, like the people in Athens, many religions throughout the world worship idols. They behave as though God is living inside a statue or religious object. Paul says, "Look at us! We're alive, and therefore, so is God." It's foolish to think that the one who created us is something without life.

God Is a Moral Being

The next characteristic we can discern about God from creation is that he is a moral being. How has it been made clear to us that God is moral? This seems to be discerned by how God created man. God created man with a conscience as mentioned previously. Because man is made in God's image, there is a natural law residing in the heart of man. It is something that has been affected by sin, but it nevertheless is still present. It both affirms and accuses man of righteousness and sin.

Throughout history, mankind has typically had the same laws. It is wrong for a man to steal, lie, kill, rob, and people who do such things should be punished. These are not laws based on culture but conscience. It is a moral code that resides inside of man, regardless of whether they live in Africa, Asia, Australia, Europe, or the Americas. We all have the same moral laws and God will judge us on the basis of them as seen in Romans 2:14–16:

> For whenever the Gentiles, who do not have the law, do by nature the things required by the law, these who do not have the law are a law to themselves. They show that *the work of the law is written in their hearts, as their conscience bears witness* and their conflicting thoughts accuse or else defend them, on the day when God will judge the secrets of human hearts, according to my gospel through Christ Jesus.

This is how we discern that God is a moral being. Though man has been marred by sin, a natural law still resides within his heart. This shows us that the Creator must be moral.

Then Why Do Some People Not Believe in God?

Well, the natural question then must be, why do some people not believe in God if the facts are so evident? What about atheists? The reason people deny God is because of sin. Listen again to what Paul says in Romans 1:18–19:

> For the wrath of God is revealed from heaven against all ungodliness and unrighteousness of people who *suppress the truth by their unrighteousness,* because what can be known about God is plain to them, because God has made it plain to them.

Paul says mankind suppresses the truth because of their unrighteousness. The practice of sin makes man suppress the knowledge of God. No one wants to think about a God that is both holy and just when they are living in sin.

Sin hardens man's conscience which has an innate awareness of God. The conscience can be so hardened that it no longer works properly. Listen to 1 Timothy 4:1–2 (NIV 1984):

> The Spirit clearly says that in later times some will abandon the faith and follow deceiving spirits and things taught by demons. *Such teachings come through hypocritical liars, whose consciences have been seared as with a hot iron.*

In this passage, Paul is talking about the overflow of false teaching that will continue to spread in these last days. The conduits of this teaching will be people whose consciences have been seared as with a hot iron. This means their consciences are hard and have lost sensitivity to sin.

This has happened to all of us at some point. Some may have experienced this with cursing. When they were young, they felt really bad about cursing, but eventually, by practicing it, their consciences no longer were pricked by their sin. This happens with pornography, cheating, lying, stealing, etc. It is possible to harden the conscience in such a way that it no longer functions properly. In the same way, a person can deny God so much through their sin that their conscience loses sensitivity to the Divine.

Paul is essentially saying that these teachers, because of their continual practice of sin and the subsequent searing of their conscience, exposed themselves to all kinds of deception from demons. The world has suppressed the truth by sin for so long that they will believe all kinds of lies as well, so much so that many will deny the very existence of God.

In summary:

1. The Bible assumes we believe in God's existence because of revelation.

2. General revelation shows God's existence.
3. General revelation shows many of God's attributes.

What else does general revelation do?

General Revelation Leaves Man without Excuse

Romans 1:20 says, "For since the creation of the world his invisible attributes—his eternal power and divine nature—have been clearly seen, because they are understood through what has been made. *So people are without excuse.*"

General revelation, though it cannot save anyone, will condemn people. Man is without excuse for not believing in God because of the witness of creation. All of creation will rise up to witness against mankind. The sun, the moon, the stars, the trees will all stand as witnesses declaring that man did know about God and his divine nature (cf. Psalm 19:1, Rom 1:20). But mankind will also be condemned because of the witness in their heart, which they have denied. Jesus will judge men in the last days based on the secrets of their heart as their conscience affirms and accuses them (cf. Rom 2:16, 1 Cor 4:5).

Again, general revelation is not enough to save a person, but it is enough to condemn a person for not believing in God and living up to the revelation given.

What else should general revelation do? How else does it witness for God?

General Revelation Leads People to Seek God

Listen to what Paul says to the people living in Athens in Acts 17:24–27:

> *The God who made the world and everything in it*, who is Lord of heaven and earth, does not live in temples made by human hands, nor is he served by human hands, as if he needed anything, because he himself gives life and breath and everything to everyone. From one man he made every nation of the human race to inhabit the entire earth, *determining their set times and the fixed limits of the places where they would live, so that they would search for God and perhaps grope around for him and find him, though he is not far from each one of us.*

Paul says that this God, who created the whole earth, gives every person life, breath, and everything else (v. 25). He created all the nations from one man (v. 26). He determined the times when the nations would live, where they would live, and the whole purpose of these things was for mankind *to seek him* (v. 26–27).

The heavens, the earth, and all of the blessings God has given to man were given for the purpose of man seeking God. The date a person was born, the time, the family, and the country, were all part of God's infinitely wise plan of helping mankind pursue a relationship with him. Certainly, it may be easier for some than others based on their circumstances; however, the truth is the same for everybody. God wants mankind to seek him, and he has left his witnesses for us.

Listen again to Psalm 19:1–4:

The heavens declare the glory of God; the sky displays his handiwork. Day after day *it speaks out*; night after night it reveals his greatness. There is no actual speech or word, nor is its voice literally heard. Yet *its voice echoes throughout the earth*; its words carry to the distant horizon. In the sky he has pitched a tent for the sun.

Why do they speak out and why throughout the earth? They are telling people about God so that they will seek after him and know his presence. God has left witnesses. Listen to what Paul says in Acts 14:17: "*yet he did not leave himself without a witness by doing good*, by giving you rain from heaven and fruitful seasons, satisfying you with food and your hearts with joy."

God has left testimony—revelation—to draw people to himself. His kindness is seen in the seasons of the earth. He provides rain for crops and food so that man can eat. His characteristics are clearly displayed daily so that people will seek and find him (cf. Jeremiah 29:13).

The Result of Responding

This naturally leads to the question, "What if man responds to general revelation? What will God do then?"

If a person believes that God exists, that he is moral and seeks to live according to the moral laws in his conscience, God will give him more revelation. Listen to a general principle that Christ teaches in Luke 8:18: "So listen carefully, for *whoever has will be given more, but whoever does not have, even what he thinks he has will be taken from him.*"

The Bible teaches that if we respond to the revelation God gives, then he will give us more, and if we don't respond, he takes away. Each one of us is always living under this principle. If we respond to revelation, whether that of nature or of Scripture, then God will give us more revelation. But if we do not respond, he will take away what we have.

I have seen this principle at work in many ways. I know many Christians, pastor kids, and missionary kids who have been exposed to the teaching of the Word of God since they were young, but because they have not heeded or acted upon it, it has had the opposite effect. It has hardened their hearts instead of softening it. Eventually, many of them turn away from God all together.

As we consider this, we should ask, "How is this principle affecting my life? Am I receiving more because I have been faithful or am I losing for lack of faithfulness?"

Taking Away Revelation

How do we see this "taking away" happening throughout the world as people choose not to respond to general revelation both around them and inside of them? We learn something about this "taking away" as we look at Israel and also the pagan world in Scripture. Look at Isaiah 6:8–12:

> I heard the voice of the sovereign master say, "Whom will I send? Who will go on our behalf?" I answered, "Here I am, send me!" He said, "*Go and tell these people: 'Listen continually, but don't understand! Look continually, but don't perceive!' Make the hearts of these people calloused; make their ears deaf and their eyes blind*! Otherwise they might see with their eyes and hear with their ears, their hearts might understand and they might repent and be healed." I replied, "*How long, sovereign master?" He said, "Until cities are in ruins and unpopulated*, and houses are uninhabited, and the land is ruined and devastated, and the Lord has sent the people off to a distant place, and the very heart of the land is completely abandoned.

In this text, God is looking for a missionary to send, and therefore, Isaiah responds, "Here am I. Send me!" However, God then calls him to go and make the hearts of the Israelite people calloused, their ears deaf, and their eyes blind until God had destroyed their cities. *How was Isaiah supposed to harden them?* He was going to do this by giving them revelation, specifically the revelation of the Word of God. As he preached, it would harden them as they chose not to obey it. Eventually, because of continued disobedience, God would destroy their cities and exile them from their land.

Israel was continually exposed to the revelation of God. They were the nation to receive the Ten Commandments. God lived among them. He sent them prophets to speak his Word, however, they still did not respond. Therefore, the revelation Isaiah gave was going to have the opposite effect on them. The preaching of Isaiah was going to harden their hearts. God was going to take his revelation away from them. If we are faithful to God's revelation, he gives more, but if not, he takes away.

In fact, when we look at Israel today, the majority of the nation is either atheist or agnostic (cf. Rom 11:8, 25). Very few Jews believe in God or practice religion as their faith; it is now just part of their culture. This was the result of hearing God's revelation but not responding.

Jesus spoke more about this in Matthew 13:10–16. He explained why he spoke in parables to the Jews instead of clear teaching. He said it was because they had not responded to revelation in the past, and therefore, their hearts had become hardened (v.15). Listen to what was said:

> Then the disciples came to him and said, "Why do you speak to them in parables?" He replied, "You have been given the opportunity to know the secrets of the kingdom of heaven, but they have not. For whoever has will be given more, and will have an abundance. But whoever does not have, even what he has will be taken from him.
> Matthew 13:10–12

Why were the secrets given to the disciples and not to Israel? Why was Jesus giving stories and riddles instead of clear doctrine? It was because Israel had not responded and there was a "taking away." I often say this about the church in our day. I fear there is a "taking away" happening in the church. We too often get stories from the pulpit instead of the Word of God. I fear this is a form of judgment happening in the church throughout the world. The Word of God has been taken, and now we simply get stories like Israel did.

Some people consider this a form of grace. If Israel continued to hear the Word of God, they would have had a greater accountability and, therefore, judgment. They would be more responsible for what they heard. For this reason, many see God's removal of clear teaching as a grace so that they wouldn't be judged as harshly.

Let's look at the example of the pagan nations. Up to this point with Israel, we have talked about not responding to the revelation of Scripture, but let's see the effects of not responding to general revelation. We saw this previously in Romans 1. Let's look at it a little closer.

Romans 1:18 says this: "*For the wrath of God is revealed from heaven against all ungodliness and unrighteousness of people who suppress the truth by their unrighteousness.*" God's wrath is revealed against those who suppress the truth. This means they are not responding to his revelation, and therefore, they invoke his anger. How does he respond, and what does God's wrath look like?

Paul describes this wrath throughout the rest of the chapter. It is the "taking away" of revelation.

Romans 1:22–24 says:

Although they claimed to be wise, they became fools and exchanged the glory of the immortal God for an image resembling mortal human beings or birds or four-footed animals or reptiles. *Therefore God gave them over in the desires of their hearts to impurity,* to dishonor their bodies among themselves.

The nations rejected the knowledge of God and began to worship the created thing. Paul then says that this denial of God led to God giving them over to sexual immorality. The wrath of God is essentially seen in the removal of this revelation in the conscience. The conviction of certain actions being sin was no longer there because the conscience had stopped functioning properly. Man then began to indulge in all types of sexual immorality without the restraint of the conscience. What else do we see?

They exchanged the truth of God for a lie and worshiped and served the creation rather than the Creator, who is blessed forever! Amen. For this reason *God gave them over to dishonorable passions. For their women exchanged the natural sexual relations for unnatural ones,* Romans 1:25–26

The wrath of God is seen in the practice of homosexuality. The revelation in the conscience of this being wrong is essentially suppressed. Because the conscience no longer works in this area, homosexuality in this culture becomes accepted and promoted. What else did God do?

Romans 1:28–31 says:

And just as they did not see fit to acknowledge God, God gave them over to a depraved mind, to do what should not be done. They are filled with every kind of unrighteousness, wickedness, covetousness, malice. They are rife with envy, murder, strife, deceit, hostility. They are gossips, slanderers, haters of God, insolent, arrogant, boastful, contrivers of all sorts of evil, disobedient to parents, senseless, covenant-breakers, heartless, ruthless.

As a judgment for not responding to God's revelation, the pagan world was given a depraved mind that led them into all kinds of immorality. What does the word "depraved" mean? It means corrupt, wicked, or perverted.

46

They refused the revelation of God and their minds were given over to all kinds of sin. As a judgment by God, the unbelieving world could not even distinguish between right and wrong anymore. Listen to Romans 1:32: "Although they fully know God's righteous decree that those who practice such things deserve to die, they not only do them but *also approve of those who practice them.*"

Because the Gentiles rejected God's natural revelation, God took away the natural revelation in the conscience. The natural law in man became skewed, and they approved of the very things that they once knew were wrong. They promoted sexuality, homosexuality, murder, and all kinds of evil became acceptable in society. They experienced a "taking away" because they rejected God's revelation. When we don't respond, God takes away the gift of his revelation.

Many times, we think of God's wrath like a spanking: he judges with a flood, he destroys by angels as with Sodom and Gomorrah, he brings poverty and war as with Israel. But sometimes, his wrath comes by saying, "Have your own way," and he takes away his revelation. He says, *"Okay, do whatever you want."*

I was an assistant coach for a college basketball team in Chicago for five years. I coached two years with guys and three years with girls. I remember coaching with the guys and sometimes certain players felt like the coach had it out for them. It seemed from their perspective that he was harder on them in practice than on other players. I would often tell them, "When coach stops talking to you, then you have a problem. That means you won't be playing and he's given up on you."

In some ways that's similar to revelation. God speaks to us because he wants us to know him, but if we choose to suppress his revelation through sin, he says, "OK. Have it your own way. I'm going to stop speaking but not only that, I'm going to withdraw what I have given," and he allows us to reap the consequences of our sin. I believe many of the tragedies we have experienced both individually and corporately come from the consequences of this principle, a "taking away" of revelation—a hardening of the conscience.

The Giving of More Revelation

What if a person heeds the call of general revelation?

Scripture indicates that God would give them more revelation and potentially even knowledge leading to salvation. We see people in the Scripture who God miraculously saves though they had limited revelation of him. However, they had been faithful with the little they had. We see this in the story of Cornelius in Acts 10:1–5:

47

Now there was a man in Caesarea named Cornelius, a centurion of what was known as the Italian Cohort. He *was a devout, God-fearing man, as was all his household; he did many acts of charity for the people and prayed to God regularly.* About three o'clock one afternoon he saw clearly in a *vision an angel of God who came in* and said to him, "Cornelius." Staring at him and becoming greatly afraid, Cornelius replied, "What is it, Lord?" The angel said to him, "*Your prayers and your acts of charity have gone up as a memorial before God. Now send men to Joppa and summon a man named Simon, who is called Peter.*

In the story, there is a man named Cornelius. He is a man who worships God, but with inadequate saving revelation. He is clearly moral and worships the God of the Jews. As the story progresses, God sends an angel to Cornelius telling him to send for Peter. Peter goes to the man's house and there he preaches to his household. In response, the whole house was filled with the Spirit and then baptized (v. 44-48). I share this because this man responded to his limited revelation of God and God gave him more revelation.

As we respond to general revelation, God will provide more revelation for us to respond to. We see another example in the story of Philip and the Ethiopian in Acts 8:26–31:

Then an angel of the Lord said to Philip, "Get up and go south on the road that goes down from Jerusalem to Gaza." (This is a desert road.) So he got up and went. There he met an Ethiopian eunuch, a court official of Candace, queen of the Ethiopians, who was in charge of all her treasury. He had come to Jerusalem to worship, and was returning home, sitting in his chariot, reading the prophet Isaiah. Then the Spirit said to Philip, "Go over and join this chariot." So Philip ran up to it and heard the man reading Isaiah the prophet. He asked him, "Do you understand what you're reading?" The man replied, "How in the world can I, unless someone guides me?" So he invited Philip to come up and sit with him.

Similar to the Roman Cornelius, we see here an Ethiopian. He also worshiped God, but with limited revelation. He probably was a convert to Judaism. Here we see God meet with him in a supernatural way in order to give him more revelation.

As the story goes on, the Ethiopian is reading a passage in Isaiah that he does not understand and miraculously Philip is brought to the Ethiopian and explains the gospel to him. The Ethiopian was saved and then baptized. Then, the narrator says the Spirit of the Lord suddenly took Philip away; Philip just vanished (v. 48). If people respond to the revelation that God gives, then he will give more.

But if revelation is rejected, God is just in not offering more. Listen to Luke, "So listen carefully, for whoever has will be given more, but whoever does not have, even what he thinks he has will be taken from him" (Luke 8:18).

No one can accuse God of injustice for it is by mercy that anybody is saved at all. We do not deserve eternal life. It was forfeited because of man's sin. Therefore, God is merciful in choosing to reveal himself at all, and he is justified in removing revelation when we choose not to respond to it.

Some people may say this is not fair. How can God give the gospel to some and not to others if only the gospel can save? What about the tribal person in the forest who has never heard? God is just because he has given us witnesses, and if we respond, he will give more; if not, he takes away even the revelation we have. It is only by his mercy that any of us are saved because as sinners, we only deserve his wrath.

We must understand that general revelation is given in order to lead man to seek God more (cf. Acts 17:27). We must ask ourselves, how are we responding to what God has taught us? Based on our response to his revelation, God is always giving us more or he is taking away.

What else does general revelation teach us?

General Revelation Places the Burden on Christians to Share the Gospel

As shared previously, general revelation cannot save anyone. It should draw people to seek God, and if they are faithful to the revelation given, Scripture says he will give more. But it should be noted that because general revelation does not save, it puts a great burden on Christians to share the gospel with others.

The gospel of Jesus Christ dying on the cross for our sins is a part of "specific revelation," which we will study next. Christ himself has given each Christian a call to share the gospel to the ends of the earth. Listen to what Jesus says in Matthew 28:19–20:

> *Therefore go and make disciples of all nations,* baptizing them in the name of the Father and the Son and the Holy Spirit, teaching them to obey everything I have commanded you. And remember, I am with you always, to the end of the age."

We must go to the nations and share the gospel, for general revelation is not enough to save anyone. General revelation helps prepare the hearts, but it places the burden on us to sow the seed (Matt 13:3-8, 18-23). Creation does its part, but we must do our part as well. Listen to what Romans 10:14–15 says:

49

How are they to call on one they have not believed in? *And how are they to believe in one they have not heard of? And how are they to hear without someone preaching to them? And how are they to preach unless they are sent?* As it is written, "How timely is the arrival of those who proclaim the good news."

How can people believe in Christ and be saved unless we share the message? God has sent each one of us to preach his good news so that all will hear the Gospel of Jesus Christ. Just as each one of us were saved through someone sharing the gospel, our faithful witness will be used by God to save others as well.

Conclusion

How do we know there is a God? The Bible does not argue for it or give an apologetic treatise because God has revealed himself to man through revelation.

He reveals himself through creation. It declares that there is a God and gives us his characteristics: he is powerful, he is transcendent, he is moral, and he is kind, among other things.

He reveals himself through our conscience as man innately knows there is a God and the law of God is written on the heart of man (Romans 2:15).

General revelation leaves man without excuse for not believing in God. However, it is a form of grace meant to make man seek after God. If man responds to the revelation he has been given, God will give more, but if not, he takes away. Finally, general revelation reminds us of our need to share the gospel since general revelation by itself cannot save.

We will look at the other ways that God reveals himself, which is called special revelation. It is special because only some people receive this revelation.

Review Questions

1. What is general revelation, and what are the primary ways God reveals himself?

2. What happens when people respond to general revelation? What happens when people reject it?

3. How would you respond to a person who questions God's justice because of people who have never heard the gospel? Can God still be just if every person does not get the opportunity to hear the gospel?

4. Explain the concept of natural law. What evidences are there of this concept, especially when considering it teaches that everybody has an innate knowledge of God?

Prayer Prompts

- Pray for forgiveness for the sins of the world and that God would be gracious and remove his wrath.

- Pray that Christians would proclaim the gospel in every nation so that God may be made known and that people may be saved.

- Pray that we as Christians would faithfully respond to God's revelation so that he may reveal more of himself to us.

Special Revelation

We have been talking about how we know that God exists. Is there evidence? What are the ways that God has revealed himself?

The first thing we looked at was general revelation. God has given revelation to all people showing that he exists. There are two primary aspects of general revelation, and the first is creation. We see his witness very clearly in his creation. Creation boasts of the existence of God. David said, "The heavens declare the glory of God; the sky displays his handiwork" (Psalm 19:1). When we look at creation and how beautiful, complex, and dynamic it is, it boasts of a greater being and intelligent design. To think that it all happened by accident is foolish. The Psalmist says, "Fools say to themselves, 'There is no God.'" (Psalm 14:1). It is foolish to think that there is no God.

The second form of general revelation is natural law or the conscience of man. Because God has made man in his image, there remains a conscience, a moral code among all men. In every nation, despite different cultures and experiences, we naturally have the same laws: do not steal, do not kill, etc. This comes from God and it witnesses explicitly of him. Romans 1:29 says, "Because that which is known about God is *evident within* them" (NASB). The knowledge of God is within man, being revealed through the conscience.

What other evidences attest to the existence of God?

In this lesson, we will look at special revelation. "Whereas general revelation is available to all people generally, specific (or special) revelation is only available to specific people and at specific times and places."[9] We will be looking at six primary ways which God has chosen to reveal himself specifically to people throughout history.

Angels

The first aspect of special revelation comes in the form of angels. Throughout the Old and New Testament, we see many accounts where God revealed himself through angels. *What are angels?*

Ministers to the Saints

"Are they not all ministering spirits, sent out to serve those who will inherit salvation?" (Hebrews 1:14).

Angels are spirits sent from God to minister to those who are saved. Since they are spirits, they typically cannot be seen unless God chooses to reveal them. First Corinthians 11:10 tells us that they are involved in church services in some manner. "For this reason a woman should have a symbol of authority on her head, because of the angels" (1 Cor 11:10).

He calls women to wear a sign of authority over their heads so that they will not lose the ministry of angels. It seems the wives were disrespecting their husbands by taking off their covering, which would keep them from receiving angelic ministry. God has always used angels to serve the saints, though most times it is done invisibly.

Angelic Protection

We saw this form of revelation in the story of Lot in Genesis 19. In response to the prayers of Abraham, God sent two angels to warn Lot and lead him out of Sodom and Gomorrah as God was about to judge the city. This revelation of God through angels was given specifically to Lot and earlier to his uncle Abraham (Gen 18). They watched God move and intervene to save his elect.

We also saw a special revelation of angels with Elisha in 2 Kings 6. In that narrative, King Aram's armies were surrounding the house of Elisha while he and his servant were waiting inside. The servant was fearful so Elisha prayed for God to open the eyes of his servant. As his eyes were awakened to special revelation, he saw angels surrounding the camp with horses and chariots of fire to protect them. The angels then struck the soldiers with blindness, and Elisha and his servant were protected (v.17).

This may seem unique, but the Bible teaches that angels are always protecting us as well. Listen to what Psalm 91:11 says: "For he will order his angels to protect you in all you do." Christ, in fact, said this about angelic protection: "See that you do not disdain one of these little ones. For I tell you that *their angels* in heaven always see the face of my Father in heaven" (Matt 18:10). Throughout history because of this some have even believed in "guardian angels." We know the early church did. Look at what the church said when Peter showed up at their door after being released from prison.

When she recognized Peter's voice, she was so overjoyed she did not open the gate, but ran back in and told them that Peter was standing at

the gate. But they said to her, "You've lost your mind!" But she kept insisting that it was Peter, and they kept saying, "*It is his angel!*"
Acts 12:14-15

We are always being protected by them, though we do not see it. This is a unique revelation of God.

Angelic Messengers

In addition, the Bible shows angels being messengers of his words. Scripture says that even the Law of Moses was given through angels. Acts 7:53 says this: "You received the law by decrees *given by angels*, but you did not obey it."

Another time we see God using angels to give his revelation was with the births of John the Baptist and Jesus. In Luke 1, an angel revealed himself to Zechariah, the father of John the Baptist, to share that he would have a son whose name would be John. Around the same time frame, the angel Gabriel was sent to share with Mary that she also would soon give birth to a baby who would be the Son of God. After the birth of Jesus, another angel announced the birth of Christ to shepherds in a field in Luke 2. God sent angels to prepare people for the birth of his Son and also for John the Baptist who would prepare the way for his Son.

In the book of Daniel, we also see an angel delivering a message. In Daniel 10, Daniel had been praying for two weeks that God would deliver his people from the rule of Babylon and send them back to their land, and at the end of two weeks, an angel appeared giving him a prophecy about the future of Israel.

We can be sure that when God is speaking to us through the Bible, sermons, or through other people, his angels are often involved, even though we don't see them. But sometimes, God allows his angels to be visible and for his people to receive revelation directly through them.

Angels are a form of special revelation which he only gives at times to specific people.

Proof of Angels

Do we have any proof that angels exist? Yes, we do.

Interestingly, the Bible is not the only resource that teaches about angels. Before the Bible was even written, belief in angels existed. Ancient ruins show us that virtually all ancient societies believed in angels. Ancient Egypt, ancient Phoenicia, and ancient Babylon all have figures of winged people, animals, and combinations of them throughout their ruins.[10]

One specific ancient ruin we should consider is that of ancient Babylon, which lies right in the place where most believe the Garden of Eden was located. According to Genesis 3, when Adam and Eve sinned, God removed them from the Garden of Eden so that they would not eat of the Tree of Life and live forever in their sin. But interestingly, God placed a cherub in front of the garden to guard the way to the tree (Gen 3:24). In Babylon, ancient ruins have been found of winged creatures with the face of bulls and lions, which are two of the faces of a cherub. Cherubs actually have four heads according to Scripture as seen in Ezekiel 1:10.

> Their faces had this appearance: Each of the four had the face of a man, with the face of a lion on the right, the face of an ox on the left and also the face of an eagle.

All this supports the belief in angels and that God has, throughout history, chosen to give special revelation through them to some people.

Prophets and Apostles

What other forms of special revelation do we have? We have the prophets and apostles who spoke authoritatively for God throughout the history of Scripture. They were the primary writers of Scripture. The prophets wrote the Old Testament, and the New Testament was written primarily through the apostles.

Prophets

In the Old Testament, God would speak through people called prophets such as Moses, Isaiah, and Jeremiah who gave the people God's Word for them to follow. A common phrase of the prophet was, "This is what the Sovereign Lord says" (Ezekiel 13:3, 21:16, 34:11), as they often gave the instructions of God verbatim. The prophets would correct the nations of their sin and call them back to following God's commands.

Do prophets exist today?

In the New Testament, prophets ministered in the early church (Acts 13:1), and Scripture indicates that people still receive prophetic gifts today (1 Cor 12:10). However, these would not be the same as the Old Testament prophet. The Old Testament prophet was to be without error in his ministry, and if he did commit an error, he was to be killed because that would prove he was not a prophet of God (Deut 18:20–22). Hebrews seems to indicate that the prophets stopped speaking when Christ came. Hebrews 1:1–2 says:

After God spoke long ago in various portions and in various ways to our ancestors through the prophets, in these last days he has spoken to us in a son, whom he appointed heir of all things, and through whom he created the world.

And Jesus seemed to imply that the last prophet was John the Baptist (Matt 11:13). He said: "For all the prophets and the law prophesied until John appeared" (Matt 11:13). After the prophets, Christ came to speak and his ministry was continued through his apostles. Prophets today are not equivalent to the Old Testament prophet. Their primary ministry is to strengthen, encourage, and comfort the church. First Corinthians 14:3 says, "But the one who prophesies speaks to people for their strengthening, encouragement, and consolation."

Apostles

The apostles are the New Testament counterpart to the prophets in the Old Testament. They were witnesses of the resurrection (1 Cor 9:1) and established the foundations of the church both by their teaching and mission work (Eph 2:20). They also were the primary writers of the New Testament and spoke with the authority of the Lord. The apostles were the twelve, Paul, James, and maybe a few others.[11]

Where the prophets often spoke verbatim, exactly what God said, God spoke through the apostles in Scripture by using their personality, experiences, and education, and, yet, their writing remained without error. This is clearly demonstrated through the books in the New Testaments. They show different styles of expression and different writing abilities. God spoke through them without circumventing their personalities.

Are there still apostles today?

The word apostle in the Greek just means "sent one." There are apostles today in the sense of those who are sent as missionaries to plant churches and to serve in various ministries. However, Scripture seems to indicate that Paul was the last apostle in the sense of establishing the foundation of the church (Eph. 2:20). Look at what Paul says in 1 Corinthians 15:4–9:

> and that he was buried, and that he was raised on the third day according to the scriptures, and that he appeared to Cephas, then to the twelve. *Then he appeared to more than five hundred of the brothers and sisters at one time, most of whom are still alive, though some have fallen asleep. Then he appeared to James, then to all the apostles. Last of all, as though to one born at the wrong time, he appeared to me also. For I am the least*

of the apostles, unworthy to be called an apostle, because I persecuted the church of God.

In talking about Christ's resurrection, Paul shares that Christ revealed himself to "all the apostles" and "last" to him, as one "born at the wrong time" (v.7). Paul seems to be saying that he was the "last" and that his calling to apostleship was not normal. All the other apostles had been with Christ from the beginning of his ministry (cf. Acts 1:21) but Paul became a follower after his resurrection through a vision in Damascus (Acts 9). It seems from Paul's teaching that he was the last official member of the apostles who served a special role in establishing the church. The prophet and the apostle were a form of special revelation given by God to reveal himself.

Various Methods: Visions, Dreams, Research, Study, Etc.

How else has God revealed himself throughout history?
God has revealed himself throughout history in various ways. He would speak through dreams as with Joseph (Gen 37:5). Sometimes, he would speak through visions as with Daniel (Daniel 8:1). Sometimes, he would speak verbally as with Abraham (Gen 12:1–3). Sometimes, God would speak to people in regular methods like doing historical research as we see with the writers of the gospels. Listen to what Luke said about his writing in Luke 1:1–3:

> Now many have undertaken to compile an account of the things that have been fulfilled among us, like the accounts *passed on to us by those who were eyewitnesses and servants of the word from the beginning.* So it seemed good to me as well, because I have *followed all things carefully from the beginning,* to write an orderly account for you, most excellent Theophilus,

Luke was not sitting in his room and God gave him a miraculous vision. He studied and looked at primary and secondary historical resources like a researcher and yet was guided by God in the writing of his Word.
For others, their writing or revelation seems to have been developed in the same way a sermon was. They studied the Old Testament, looked at historical events, found applications, and wrote a letter demonstrating these insights.
For example, the book of Hebrews is essentially a topical book comparing the old covenant to the new covenant. It argues that the new covenant and Christ are better than the law and the shadows of the old covenant. The author quotes the Old Testament more than any other New Testament author. The writer

obviously thoroughly studied the law yet, at the same time, clearly received special revelation from God while studying and writing. He expands on previously taught concepts such as Christ's new role as high priest who prays daily in heaven for believers (cf. Psalm 110:4, Hebrews 7). God used both irregular and regular methods to give revelation to the writers.

Wayne Grudem sums up the process of revelation nicely in this quote:

> In between these two extremes of dictation pure and simple on the one hand, and ordinary historical research on the other hand, we have many indications of various ways by which God communicated with the human authors of Scripture. In some cases Scripture gives us hints of these various processes: it speaks of dreams, of visions, of hearing the Lord's voice or standing in the council of the Lord; it also speaks of men who were with Jesus and observed his life and listened to his teaching, men whose memory of these words and deeds was made completely accurate by the working of the Holy Spirit as he brought things to their remembrance (John 14:26). Yet in many other cases the manner used by God to bring about the result that the words of Scripture were his words is simply not disclosed to us. Apparently many different methods were used, but it is not important that we discover precisely what these were in each case.
>
> In cases where the ordinary human personality and writing style of the author were prominently involved, as seems the case with the major part of Scripture, all that we are able to say is that God's providential oversight and direction of the life of each author was such that their personalities, their backgrounds and training, their abilities to evaluate events in the world around them, their access to historical data, their judgment with regard to the accuracy of information, and their individual circumstances when they wrote, were all exactly what God wanted them to be, so that when they actually came to the point of putting pen to paper, the words were fully their own words but also fully the words that God wanted them to write, words that God would also claim as his own.[12]

Considering all this, one might ask, "Does God still speak through dreams and visions?" Certainly, God is done speaking in the sense of adding to the revelation of Scripture (cf. Rev 22:18–19, Jude 1:3), but does God still speak in charismatic ways?

There is no clear Scripture that declares God will never speak in these ways. However, his primary method of speaking will always be through his completed Word. Scripture presents many of these various methods as unusual such as Jesus giving a vision to Paul and him being miraculously converted (Acts 9:3-6). With that said, we are hearing stories of Muslims being converted through visions all the time. Often, these stories are very similar to Paul's. These people are typically very antagonistic towards Christianity, and yet God shows mercy and saves them. Look at what Paul says about himself: "even though I was formerly a blasphemer and a persecutor, and an arrogant man. But I was treated with mercy because I acted ignorantly in unbelief" (1 Tim 1:13).

No doubt, when God saves this way, it is an act of mercy as well. Even though this may not be the normal method or our daily bread, we should not exclude this as a way that God may choose to speak to his saints. God still chooses to speak to his people miraculously; however, these forms of revelation can be counterfeited, and therefore, must be tested and approved by God's written Word (1 John 4:1).

Applications

Are there any applications we can take from God often choosing to use various methods throughout history to speak to people?

One of the encouraging applications I think we can take from the various methods of special revelation is that God speaks and sometimes ministers to people differently. Some people may have very charismatic experiences where God speaks to them through dreams, visions or an audible voice. But to others, God speaks primarily through less dramatic ways such as his sovereignty over circumstances, strong impressions (cf. 2 Cor 2:12-13), and studying or researching his Word.

However, often, people come to God and expect him to speak very miraculously. They expect him to clearly answer questions such as: "Who should I marry?" "What school should I go to?" "What job should I take?" "What car should I buy?" Sometimes, people have these expectations because they have met people whom God ministers to more charismatically. It is good to remember that God sometimes chooses to minister to his children in different ways. This should help keep us from becoming discouraged when we don't receive something unique or prideful when we do.

Example of Peter and John

Don't be discouraged about how God relates to others or how they experience him. Trust God's faithfulness to you. We see an illustration of this when Christ restored Peter at the end of the Gospel of John. In John 21:19–22, Christ told Peter the manner in which he was going to die. He was going to die a martyr's death. Afterwards Peter responded, "What about him?" in referring to John the Apostle. Let's look at the passage:

(Now Jesus said this to indicate clearly by what kind of death Peter was going to glorify God.) After he said this, Jesus told Peter, "Follow me." Peter turned around and saw the disciple whom Jesus loved following them. (This was the disciple who had leaned back against Jesus' chest at the meal and asked, "Lord, who is the one who is going to betray you?") *So when Peter saw him, he asked Jesus, "Lord, what about him?"* Jesus replied, *"If I want him to live until I come back, what concern is that of yours? You follow me!"*

Christ said, "What is that to you? You must follow me." This is important because God works and sometimes speaks differently to his children. If we spend our time focusing on others, we may find ourselves discouraged, wanting their experiences. Or you may find yourself prideful because of how God ministers to you.

Sometimes, we see this inclination with certain gifts like tongues or prophecy. People find themselves desperate to have tongues when that may not be a gift that God chooses to give them. Others find themselves prideful over their gift, and they are always seeking a place to display or bring honor to themselves. We must be careful about desiring other people's experiences or relationship with God. We are unique and God deals with each of us uniquely.

Jesus told Peter, "What is it to you how I choose to work in this man's life? You must follow me." For one false prophet named Balaam in the OT, God chose to speak to him through a donkey in order to get his attention (Numbers 22). It wasn't because this man was special, but because this man wasn't listening. His extra revelation wasn't an honor; it came because he wouldn't listen any other way. As with Paul's conversion, sometimes, a dramatic revelation is the only way to get a person to respond.

Ask anyone who has multiple children, and they will tell you that good parenting necessitates ministering to each child in different ways simply because they are unique. God is the same way with us. I think that's a lesson we can gain from looking at the unique and various ways God has revealed himself throughout the history of the Bible.

Theophanies

Are there other special revelations? Yes, there are theophanies.

Theophanies are manifestations of God in ways that are tangible to the human senses. In its strictest sense, it applies to visible or auditory appearances of God often, but not always, in human form.[13] What identifies a theophany is

61

typically a sudden and temporary appearance of God in order to deepen his relationship with his people. At times, in the Old Testament, we would see God appear as an angel, a man, or in some other form to reveal himself to his people.

God Appeared as Men

We see this with Jacob wrestling with a man who is called God (Genesis 32:24–32). The new name given to Jacob was Israel, which means "God commands" or "prevails with God." Jacob wrestled with God in human form.

We also see this with Abraham right before God destroyed Sodom and Gomorrah. Look at what Genesis 18:1–2 says:

> *The Lord appeared to Abraham by the oaks of Mamre* while he was sitting at the entrance to his tent during the hottest time of the day. Abraham looked up and saw three men standing across from him. When he saw them he ran from the entrance of the tent to meet them and bowed low to the ground.

This text says that God appeared to Abraham, and he did it through three men. As the story goes on, it becomes clear that two of these men were angels and one was God. In Genesis 19:1, we see that the two angels went down to Lot's house while God stayed and talked to Abraham. Again, God showed up as a man in this text.

We see another one in the book of Daniel with Shadrach, Meshach, and Abednego in Daniel 3. They were thrown into the fiery furnace by Nebuchadnezzar, King of Babylon. But while in the furnace, they were not burned, and Nebuchadnezzar saw another person in the fire. Look at how he responded:

> He answered and said, Lo, I see four men loose, walking in the midst of the fire, and they have no hurt; and the form of the fourth is like the Son of God.
> Daniel 3:25 (KJV)

He responded, we put three in there, but we see four and the other looks like the Son of God. It would seem again that God shows up in the form of a man to protect his faithful servants.

Angel of the Lord

We also see God choosing to reveal himself as an angel at times in the Old Testament, specifically the Angel of the Lord. This happened with Gideon as he was called to lead Israel in rebellion against the Midianites. Let's look at Judges 6:11–16 (NIV 1984):

> *The angel of the LORD came and sat down under the oak in Ophrah* that belonged to Joash the Abiezrite, where his son Gideon was threshing wheat in a winepress to keep it from the Midianites. When the angel of the LORD appeared to Gideon, he said, "The LORD is with you, mighty warrior." "But sir," Gideon replied, "if the LORD is with us, why has all this happened to us? Where are all his wonders that our fathers told us about when they said, 'Did not the LORD bring us up out of Egypt?' But now the LORD has abandoned us and put us into the hand of Midian." *The LORD turned to him and said, "Go in the strength you have and save Israel out of Midian's hand. Am I not sending you?"* "But Lord," Gideon asked, "how can I save Israel? My clan is the weakest in Manasseh, and I am the least in my family." The LORD answered, "I will be with you, and you will strike down all the Midianites together."

It is clear that Gideon did not initially recognize that this man was an angel. At some point in the conversation, Gideon recognized that he was in fact the Angel of the Lord and began to cry out with fear to God (v. 22-23). However, what's interesting about this discourse is the fact that the narrator begins to address the Angel of the Lord as God. In verse 14 the narrator says, "The LORD turned to him and said" with capital letters, which means it was God's covenant name YAHWEH. The Angel of the Lord was God.

We also see an appearance of the Angel of the Lord in a fiery bush speaking to Moses in the book of Exodus. Look at Exodus 3:1–4:

> Now Moses was shepherding the flock of his father-in-law Jethro, the priest of Midian, and he led the flock to the far side of the desert and came to the mountain of God, to Horeb. *The angel of the Lord appeared to him in a flame of fire from within a bush.* He looked—and the bush was ablaze with fire, but it was not being consumed! So Moses thought, "I will turn aside to see this amazing sight. Why does the bush not burn up?" When the Lord saw that he had turned aside to look, *God called to him from within the bush and said,* "Moses, Moses!" And Moses said, "Here I am."

Here we see that Moses saw the Angel of the Lord in the bush and after that the narrator said, "God called to him from within the bush" (v.4). The Angel of the Lord and God were the same person.

63

It would seem that these appearances of God in human or angelic form were always for the purpose of some special calling or for grace to be bestowed upon a servant. They were not normal at all.

Many would suggest that when God showed up in the form of the Angel of the Lord, who seemed to always appear as a man, those appearances were actually early sightings of the Son of God. Why do they believe that? It is simply biblical reasoning. After Christ came to the earth, we still have appearances of angels but no appearances of the Angel of the Lord. Also, it would seem logical that since Christ has always eternally existed, he was active and would have manifested himself in the world at various times. Many believe Christ commonly did this as the Angel of the Lord.

Various Expressions

However, God did not only appear in human or angelic form, he appeared in various forms. For example, with Abraham, God appeared as a smoking fire pot to confirm the covenant of making his descendants a great nation (Genesis 15:17). When God was leading Israel through the wilderness, he appeared as a cloud by day and a fire by night (Exodus 13:21).

Tabernacle and Temple

Another form of a theophany is God's appearance to Israel in the glory cloud in the tabernacle and then later in the temple. Look at Exodus 33:9: "And whenever Moses *entered the tent, the pillar of cloud would descend* and stand at the entrance of the tent, and the Lord would speak with Moses."

This verse speaks of the tabernacle by calling it a tent. God's presence would descend in a cloud to meet with Moses in the tent. This was God's temporary dwelling for traveling with Israel. As Israel moved, God went with them; wherever they went, he went as well. God wanted to be with his people in peace, in battle, in rain, and sunshine. God dwelt in the midst of Israel.

When they took over the land of Canaan, it was then that his permanent dwelling, the temple, was built. In 2 Chronicles 7:1–3, we see the glory of God fill the temple:

> When Solomon finished praying, fire came down from heaven and consumed the burnt offering and the sacrifices, *and the Lord's splendor filled the temple. The priests were unable to enter the Lord's temple because the Lord's splendor filled the Lord's temple.* When all the Israelites saw the fire come down and the Lord's splendor over the

temple, they got on their knees with their faces downward toward the pavement. They worshiped and gave thanks to the Lord, saying, "Certainly he is good; certainly his loyal love endures!"

Though the tabernacle and the temple are not theophanies themselves, they were the place that God would appear in a theophany and make his presence known to Israel. These dwellings demonstrated God's desire for intimacy with man. Many people see the tabernacle and temple as very similar to the Garden of Eden. It was in the garden that God walked among the people and had intimacy with them.

However, this desire for intimacy is taken to an even higher level in the new covenant as the body of individual believers becomes his temple. We see this in 1 Corinthians 6:19: "Or do you not know that your body is the temple of the Holy Spirit who is in you, whom you have from God, and you are not your own?"

Though we may not classify this as a theophany, because it is a permanent manifestation, it is still a revelation of God. He has chosen to make his home in the body of his saints.

Throughout history, God has made himself known through theophanies, temporary appearances of his glory. He appeared as a human, an angel, a fiery bush, a glory cloud, etc. He appeared to Israel on a regular basis at the tabernacle and the temple. However, in one sense, we experience him in an even greater way than a theophany because he has chosen to permanently dwell within us.

Jesus Christ

God's ultimate special revelation was seen in his Son coming to the earth. The Jews knew that no one could ever look upon God and live because of his glory, beauty, and holiness. They always sought to see the Father but knew that it was impossible. God told Moses nobody could see his face and live (Exodus 33:20). In fact, people lived in fear of seeing the presence of God. But in Christ, the impossible became possible, the God of heaven and earth could be clearly seen and known.

John says this about Jesus: "No one has ever seen God. The only one, himself God, who is in closest fellowship with the Father, has made God known" (John 1:18).

How did Jesus make the Father known? How did he reveal more about God? Jesus brought the revelation of God in many ways, but we will look at *three primary ways.*

Jesus Revealed God's Teachings

The first way that Jesus made God known was by his teaching. Listen to what he said to Philip in John 14:10:

> Do you not believe that I am in the Father, and the Father is in me? *The words that I say to you, I do not speak on my own initiative, but the Father residing in me performs his miraculous deeds.*

When Jesus said God was doing his work, he was referring to his own teachings as coming directly from God. God was speaking through Jesus on the earth. Christ taught this truth at various times. He declared:

> Then Jesus said, "When you lift up the Son of Man, then you will know that I am he, and I do nothing on my own initiative, *but I speak just what the Father taught me.*
> John 8:28

In fact, this is best illustrated by the name John called Christ. Listen to John 1:1: "In the beginning was the Word, and the Word was with God, and the Word was fully God."

When John called Jesus the "Word," the name is an expression of one of the functions or purposes of Jesus. "Word" essentially means that *Christ was the communication of God.* One of the reasons that Christ came was to communicate God's words to us—he was the "Word" of God incarnate.

When we look at the teachings of Jesus, we see the very words of the Father. When Jesus taught to love your enemy and pray for them, when he taught that hatred was equivalent to murder, that lust was equivalent to adultery, we hear the words of God. In Christ's words, we find a standard that is much higher than our own because it is divine. In Christ's words, we see the revelation of the Father.

If we want to know God's word on how to live, how to choose a career, how to be saved, how to make decisions in life, it all comes through God's Word, and Christ came to reveal his word in a greater way.

Jesus Revealed God's Person

The second way that Christ revealed God was simply through his person. The Bible says he is the physical representation of God. Listen to Colossians and Hebrews:

> He is the image of the invisible God, the firstborn over all creation.

Colossians 1:15

The Son is *the radiance of his glory and the representation of his essence,* and he sustains all things by his powerful word, and so when he had accomplished cleansing for sins, *he sat down at the right hand of the Majesty on high.*
Hebrews 1:3

Philip said, "Show us the Father and it will be enough for us. We just want to see God and that will be enough, that will satisfy us." Jesus told Philip, "If you have seen me, you have seen the Father" (John 14:9 paraphrase). People could not look upon God face to face in the OT, but we have beheld him in the image of Christ.

Only one time in the gospels did Christ fully reveal his God-head and power. On the Mount of Transfiguration, Christ took three disciples up the mountain and there he was transfigured. Consider the account in Luke 9:28–36 (NIV 1984):

About eight days after Jesus said this, he took Peter, John and James with him and went up onto a mountain to pray. *As he was praying, the appearance of his face changed, and his clothes became as bright as a flash of lightning.* Two men, Moses and Elijah, appeared in glorious splendor, talking with Jesus. They spoke about his departure, which he was about to bring to fulfillment at Jerusalem. Peter and his companions were very sleepy, but when they became fully awake, *they saw his glory and the two men standing with him.* As the men were leaving Jesus, Peter said to him, "Master, it is good for us to be here. Let us put up three shelters—one for you, one for Moses and one for Elijah." (He did not know what he was saying.) While he was speaking, *a cloud appeared and enveloped them, and they were afraid as they entered the cloud. A voice came from the cloud, saying, "This is my Son, whom I have chosen; listen to him."* When the voice had spoken, they found that Jesus was alone. The disciples kept this to themselves, and told no one at that time what they had seen.

The Scripture says that he shined as bright as lightning (Luke 9:29). This lightning probably symbolized his deity. We see that God similarly revealed himself through lightning at Mt. Sinai (Ex 20:18). On the "Mount of Transfiguration," God was making himself known through Christ. The disciples saw God's glory in Christ, and there the Father said, "This is my one dear Son; in him I take great delight."

67

What Christ shielded in his human body was all at once revealed; he was the full representation of God in human flesh.

Since Christ is the exact image of God, we not only saw God's glory, but also his power in Christ. Jesus calmed storms; he demonstrated power over nature. He cast out demons, showing his power over the spirit realm. He healed physical diseases and even showed the ability to suspend his own laws in multiplying bread and making water from wine. When we saw Christ, we saw God.

Philip said that seeing God the Father would be enough; it would be the greatest experience of life. Jesus said, "If you have seen me, you have seen him." If we want to know God and see him, we must see him in Christ. He is the person of God.

We know that Christ revealed God, but what did Christ reveal about God that wasn't fully revealed previously?

God Is a Servant

He revealed many things not known fully about God. Paul said this about Jesus in Philippians 2:6–7:

> who though he existed in the form of God did not regard equality with God as something to be grasped, but emptied himself *by taking on the form of a slave*, by looking like other men, and by sharing in human nature.

The word "form" in this text means an "outward expression of an inward nature."[14] Christ did not become a servant at his incarnation. He just demonstrated what he always was as God. Jesus was the prototype of a servant, not only did he serve God in doing his will (John 6:38), but he served man. Look at what Mark 10:45 says: "For even the Son of Man did not come to be served *but to serve, and to give his life as a ransom for many.*"

Jesus revealed that God is a servant and that we serve a servant-God. It's a phenomenal concept that we could never understand without Christ. Jesus bent down and washed the feet of his disciples, something only the slaves would do (John 13:1–17). Peter was so shocked, he said, "You will never wash my feet." He found this hard to understand about God.

Jesus served us by dying for us. Look at what Paul says: "and by sharing in human nature. He humbled himself, by becoming obedient to the point of death —even death on a cross!!" (Phil 2:7–8).

Jesus humbled himself by becoming a man and then dying. But Jesus didn't simply become humble in the incarnation. He revealed what he has always been as God. We worship a humble Creator.

How does Jesus and thus God still serve us?

Ephesians 5:25–27 says that he *washes the church with the Word of God* to make us a pure and holy bride.

> Husbands, love your wives just as Christ loved the church and gave himself for her *to sanctify her by cleansing her with the washing of the water by the word*, so that he may present the church to himself as glorious—not having a stain or wrinkle, or any such blemish, but holy and blameless.

When we spend time in our devotions, when we hear sermons at church, Christ is present. He leans over, as he did with Peter, and washes us. He washes sin off of us; he removes discouragement and anger. If you have received his Word, then you have been washed by our servant-God.

But that's not all. He also serves us through *prayer*. Listen to the writer of Hebrews: "So he is able to save completely those who come to God through him, because he *always lives to intercede for them*" (Hebrews 7:25).

If it weren't for Christ, we would not have a concept of a God who prays for his people. To the pagans, that wouldn't make any sense. Prayer is only offered to the deity; the deity doesn't pray for man. However, we have a servant God who serves others and calls us to be servants as well (cf. John 13:14-15, Rom 12:13).

It's a phenomenal concept. Christ didn't become something he wasn't already as far as his nature. He just demonstrated what he already was as God in human form, so we could better understand God. It's phenomenal.

Are there any other ways God serves us? Yes, *God will serve us in his coming kingdom.* Look at Luke 12:35–37:

> "Get dressed for service and keep your lamps burning; be like people waiting for their master to come back from the wedding celebration, so that when he comes and knocks they can immediately open the door for him. *Blessed are those slaves whom their master finds alert when he returns! I tell you the truth, he will dress himself to serve, have them take their place at the table, and will come and wait on them*!

Look at what Christ said about God. He gives us a paradox. He shares the story of a servant who has faithfully served his master while he was gone. When the master returns, you might expect a thank you or, simply, for the master to go about his business. But not this master. The master dresses himself to serve, the servants sit at the table, and the master waits on them—he serves them (v. 37).

This refers specifically to the second coming of Christ. He will come and serve his people. He will reward them with crowns, authority, and property on the earth. As a master, he will refresh them through his service. We serve a servant God. These are phenomenal concepts that were not fully revealed until Christ displayed the exact representation of God.

How should we respond to this? Paul says in Philippians 2:5, "*You should have the same attitude toward one another that Christ Jesus had.*" We should serve others as well. Are we putting others first? In what ways are we seeking to serve those around us?

Jesus Revealed the Way to God

What else did Jesus reveal about God? He revealed the way to have a relationship with the Father. He revealed the way to true salvation. Jesus said, "I am the way and the truth and the life. No one comes to the Father except through me" (John 14:6).

Listen to John 17:1–3:

When Jesus had finished saying these things, he looked upward to heaven and said, "Father, the time has come. Glorify your Son, so that your Son may glorify you—*just as you have given him authority over all humanity, so that he may give eternal life to everyone you have given him. Now this is eternal life—that they know you, the only true God, and Jesus Christ, whom you sent.*

God gave Christ authority to grant salvation and eternal life to those who would come to God through him. He is the door to salvation; he is the door to spending eternity in heaven. Christ is also the door to continually knowing God for the rest of our lives. "This is eternal life: to know God." All this was revealed through Christ.

Christ demonstrated God's love for man when he died on the cross for the sins of the world. He also teaches us the way to receive this love, by faith, as we believe in his death, burial, and resurrection, and take him as Lord of our lives. Christ taught this especially through his apostles. Romans 10:13 says, "For everyone who calls on the name of the Lord will be saved."

He is the only person we can call on to have eternal life and to have a relationship with God. This power does not exist in false gods. Acts 4:12 says,

"And there is salvation in no one else, for there is no other name under heaven given among people by which we must be saved."

Have you come through the door of Jesus Christ? There is no other way to the Father; there is no other way to eternal life.

God so desired to have a relationship with mankind that he sent his Son to the earth. In fact, not only did he send him, he sacrificed him for our sins so we could have a relationship with a Holy God.

Even as followers, saved and redeemed by the Son, we still come to God daily through Christ. First Peter 2:5 says this: "you yourselves, as living stones, are built up as a spiritual house to be a holy priesthood and to *offer spiritual sacrifices that are acceptable to God through Jesus Christ.*"

Christ is not just the door but the atmosphere in which the believer worships and has a relationship with God. We offer spiritual sacrifices acceptable to God "through Jesus Christ." We approach the throne room of God based on the competence of our high priest. Hebrews 4:15–16 says this:

> For we do not have a high priest incapable of sympathizing with our weaknesses, but one who has been tempted in every way just as we are, yet without sin. Therefore let us confidently approach the throne of grace to receive mercy and find grace whenever we need help.

In fact, Christ taught that our prayers must be offered in his name (John 16:24), meaning that Christ is our daily sufficiency to come to God, and we must pray in alignment with his will. Christ is the doorway to God.

Christ revealed the "teachings of God," he revealed the "person of God," and he revealed "the way to know God and have salvation." Christ is a form of special revelation, one of the primary ways God has revealed himself to us.

Application

How should we apply this?

1. If we are to know God in salvation, we must realize it is only through Christ.

He is not a way among other ways. He is the way to the Father. His is the only name given among men by which we must be saved.

2. Second, we must daily relate to God on the basis of Christ's work.

This should create humility in us as we seek to worship and glorify God. We are incapable of coming to God, even in sanctification, on our own accord. It must be through the Son. We pray through Christ; we approach the throne through Christ; we offer spiritual sacrifices through Christ. He is the atmosphere in which we worship the Father (cf. 1 Cor 1:30).

3.   Third, if we are to know God, we must study Christ.

We must study his teachings. We must study how he lived because it is there that we know God. He only said the words of his Father; therefore, he is worth listening to and building our lives upon.

The guards were commissioned by the Pharisees to grab Jesus and take him, but they could not. Why? In John 7:46 they replied, "No one ever spoke like this man!" This is because he spoke the very words of God. We should study his words for in them we come to know God.

4.   Fourth, we must imitate Christ.

What does it look like for a man to live like God? We see it in Christ. He gave up everything, heaven, and the full display of his authority and power, to serve others. In Christ, we see a godly life and the secret to being exalted (Phil 2:6–11). It is the opposite of the world, who seeks exaltation by seeking to be first and the greatest. Christ became last and is now first.

Are you a servant like your God? If not, you are falling short of God's image in your life (Rom 3:23). We see these characteristics in Christ, and they must be modeled. "You should have the same attitude toward one another that Christ Jesus had" (Phil 2:5).

5.   Finally, we must come to Christ for help.

As a servant, he desires to help us, and therefore, we should call on him. He understands us and knows exactly how to minister to our situation. We do not have a God that cannot sympathize, but one who hungered and thirsted just like us. Listen again to the writer of Hebrews 4:15–16:

For we do not have a high priest incapable of sympathizing with our weaknesses, but one who has been tempted in every way just as we are, yet without sin. *Therefore let us confidently approach the throne of grace to receive mercy and find grace whenever we need help.*

Some have said, "How can Christ help me if he never sinned? How can he relate to me?" Here is a good illustration. Say you were seeking help to train in power lifting, and while at the gym, you saw two people pick up 200 lbs. and try to put it over their head for ten seconds. One picked it up but dropped it in two seconds, but the other held it the whole time. Who held more weight, the one who picked it up but dropped it, or the one who held it the entire time? The one who held it to the end is the one who held more weight. Christ bore the full weight of temptation without succumbing to it. He was tempted in the wilderness like Adam but did not fail. How much more can he help us defeat sin? He held the weight to the end and, therefore, can help us most in our time of need.

Conclusion

How do we know there is a God? We know because of revelation. God has chosen to reveal himself. He has revealed himself "generally" through creation but "specifically" throughout history in the means of angels, prophets and apostles, visions, dreams, theophanies, and in his son Jesus Christ.

The greatest thing about these revelations is the fact that we have a God that wants to be known. He wants us to know him. He is not hiding, but is seeking to reveal himself in various ways every day. However, it is typically those who are seeking him that truly find him. Look at what Jeremiah 29:13 says: "When you seek me in prayer and worship, you will find me available to you. If you seek me with all your heart and soul." He says this through James: "Draw near to God and he will draw near to you" (James 4:8).

Our current knowledge and intimacy with God is proportional to our effort in seeking to know him. He is always trying to reveal himself to us, but we must respond by seeking after him. When we respond, he draws us even closer and reveals more of himself to us. Are you pursuing a relationship with the God who wants to be known?

He wants to be known so much that he broke into time by coming down as a man to reveal himself so that some may be saved. We must respond to God, and we must make him known to others.

In the next chapter, we will look at the last form of special revelation: God's written Word.

Review Questions

1. What is special revelation? What are some of the various forms of special revelation?

2. Does God still reveal himself through dreams, visions, and prophecy? If so, how do we test such forms of revelation (1 John 4:1)? In what ways have you seen these forms of revelation abused?

3. Who were the prophets and apostles? Are there still prophets and apostles today? Why or why not?

4. One of the primary ways God has revealed himself is through Jesus Christ. In what ways did Christ reveal God?

Prayer Prompts

- Pray that God would continue to reveal himself and make himself known to all men. Pray that people would have a spirit of wisdom and revelation to know God better (Eph 1:17).

- Pray for the church to have discernment and protection from false forms of revelation (1 John 4:1).

- Pray for the church to be faithful in proclaiming his Word and making Christ known (Matt 28:118, 19).

Special Revelation: The Bible

What is the final form of special revelation?

God's Word, the Bible, is the final form of special revelation. It must be remembered that it is through general revelation that one is without excuse for not believing in God, but it is only through specific revelation that man can be saved. It is only through hearing the message of the gospel, shared from the Word of God, that one can come to saving faith. Romans 10:17 says, "Consequently faith comes from what is heard, and what is heard comes through the preached word of Christ."

The Bible is God's primary and final way of revealing himself to his people.

How We Received the Bible

How did we receive the Bible? The Bible has two authors: the first is God and the second is man.

In fact, God began writing the Bible himself. God wrote the Ten Commandments with his own hand. We see this in Exodus 31: "He gave Moses two tablets of testimony when he had finished speaking with him on Mount Sinai, tablets of stone *written by the finger of God*" (Exodus 31:18).

But not only did he write the Ten Commandments, the Bible teaches that every word of Scripture is "inspired by God"—the actual breath of God, even though it was written by human authors as well. Second Timothy 3:16 says: "Every scripture is inspired by God and useful for teaching, for reproof, for correction, and for training in righteousness."

Both the Old Testament and the New Testament are God's words. Wayne Grudem said this:

> All the words in the Bible are God's words. Therefore, to disbelieve or disobey them is to disbelieve or disobey God himself. Oftentimes, passages in the Old Testament are introduced with the phrase, "Thus says the LORD" (see Ex. 4:22; Josh. 24:2; 1 Sam. 10:18; Isa. 10:24; also Deut. 18:18 – 20; Jer. 1:9). This phrase, understood to be like the command of a king, indicated that what followed was to be

75

obeyed without challenge or question. Even the words in the Old Testament not attributed as direct quotes from God are considered to be God's words... The New Testament also affirms that its words are the very words of God. In 2 Peter 3:16, Peter refers to all of Paul's letters as one part of the "Scriptures." This means that Peter, and the early church, considered Paul's writings to be in the same category as the Old Testament writings. Therefore, they considered Paul's writings to be the very words of God. In addition, Paul, in 1 Timothy 5:18, writes that "the Scripture says" two things: "You shall not muzzle an ox when it treads out the grain" and "The laborer deserves his wages." The first quote regarding an ox comes from the Old Testament; it is found in Deuteronomy 25:4. The second comes from the New Testament; it is found in Luke 10:7. Paul, without any hesitation, quotes from both the Old and New Testaments, calling them both "Scripture." Therefore, again, the words of the New Testament are considered to be the very words of God. That is why Paul could write, "the things I am writing to you are a command of the Lord" (1 Cor. 14:37).[15]

How can it be possible that the Scripture has two authors—both God and man? What was the process? Peter gives us a hint in 2 Peter 1:20–21. Listen to what he says: "Above all, you do well if you recognize this: No prophecy of scripture ever comes about by the prophet's own imagination, for no prophecy was ever borne of human impulse; rather, men *carried along by the Holy Spirit spoke from God.*"

Peter says the prophecies of Scripture did not come about by a prophet's interpretation or volition, but men were carried along by the Holy Spirit.

What does it mean to be carried along by the Holy Spirit?

In Acts 27, the writer, Luke, uses the same phrase to describe a ship being carried by a storm. Look at what he says: "When the ship was caught in it and could not head into the wind, we gave way to it and were *driven along*" (Acts 27:15).

In the same way the ship was "driven" by the storm, so the authors of the Bible were "carried" by the Holy Spirit in the writing of Scripture. The Holy Spirit drove them along in the writing of the content and also kept them from error. The writers were there; they were thinking and writing, but they were being moved by the Spirit.

Let's look at specific instances where we see the Bible being written by men.

When Moses finished writing on a scroll the words of this law in their entirety, he commanded the Levites who carried the ark of the Lord's

covenant, "Take this scroll of the law and place it beside the ark of the covenant of the Lord your God. It will remain there as a witness against you, for I know about your rebellion and stubbornness. Indeed, even while I have been living among you to this very day, you have rebelled against the Lord; you will be even more rebellious after my death!
Deuteronomy 31:24–27

God commanded *Moses* to write everything down, and it was written to be a witness against the people because of their propensity to sin. Then, it was kept in the Ark of the Covenant. After Moses wrote in the Book of the Law, we see *Joshua* continue the writing. "Joshua wrote these words in the Law Scroll of God. He then took a large stone and set it up there under the oak tree near the Lord's shrine" (Joshua 24:26).

We see Joshua, previously Moses's assistant, writing down the events that happened in the book of Joshua. Similarly, we see the same call to write given to the *prophet Jeremiah.* "The Lord God of Israel says, 'Write everything that I am about to tell you in a scroll" (Jeremiah 30:2). Again, God did this with the rest of his prophets throughout the Old Testament.

In the New Testament, we see the same process, except the work of the Holy Spirit is more emphasized. Jesus told the disciples that when he left, he was going to give them the Holy Spirit. "But the Advocate, the Holy Spirit, whom the Father will send in my name, will teach you everything, and will cause you to remember everything I said to you" (John 14:26).

We see Christ repeat this in John 16. It says:

"I have many more things to say to you, but you cannot bear them now. But when he, the Spirit of truth, comes, he will guide you into all truth. For he will not speak on his own authority, but will speak whatever he hears, and will tell you what is to come.
John 16:12–13

God sent the Holy Spirit to inspire and bring to remembrance all the words that Jesus said. The Holy Spirit would not only bring things to remembrance, but he would teach the writers of Scripture future revelation. This is how the New Testament and the Old Testament were written: the Holy Spirit moved upon men to write the actual words of God because God desired to reveal himself to people.

Scripture Is Powerful

We don't only see the revelation of God in the writing of Scripture, but also in the power of Scripture. Second Timothy 3:16 says that "Every scripture is inspired by God." It can also be translated "All Scripture is *God breathed*" (NIV 1984), which not only speaks of God's authorship of Scripture but also its power. When you think about God's breath or words in Scripture, it's always a demonstration of his power. Let's look at a few texts:

> The Lord God formed the man from the soil of the ground and *breathed into his nostrils the breath of life, and the man became a living being.*
> Genesis 2:7

> *God said,* "Let there be lights in the expanse of the sky to separate the day from the night, and let them be signs to indicate seasons and days and years.
> Genesis 1:14

> The Son is the radiance of his glory and the representation of his essence, and he *sustains all things by his powerful word,* and so when he had accomplished cleansing for sins, he sat down at the right hand of the Majesty on high.
> Hebrews 1:3

Wherever God's breath is, life is created and sustained. God's breath or spoken word has the ability to create life, just as it created the heavens and the earth, and it has the ability to sustain all of creation. In the same way, God has given us his "breath"—his Word— in the writings of the Holy Bible, and it has great power.

Power like a Fire, a Hammer, and a Sword

In what ways do we see this power? Listen to what God said to Jeremiah about his Word: "My message is like a fire that purges dross! It is like a hammer that breaks a rock in pieces! I, the Lord, so affirm it!" (Jeremiah 23:29).

God described the power of his Word like a fire that heats and like a hammer that breaks a rock into pieces. Sometimes, man's heart is so cold, it needs to be warmed by Scripture. Sometimes, man's heart is so hard, it needs to be broken in order to respond to God. The Word of God has this power.

The writer of Hebrews says something similar, comparing the Word of God to a sword. Listen to what he says: "For the word of God is living and active and sharper than any double-edged sword, piercing even to the point of dividing soul from spirit, and joints from marrow; it is able to judge the desires and thoughts of the heart" (Hebrews 4:12).

God's Word is alive and active. It's like a sword that does surgery on the hearts of men. It reveals sin and secret attitudes of the heart. Many times, we are blind to our sin until the Word of God discerns and reveals it through a sermon or Scripture reading.

The Word of God is active; it cuts and reveals our heart condition. It's like going to the hospital for a checkup. Sometimes the diagnosis can be hard to hear, but it is healthy for us. Listen to Luke's description of the Israelites after Peter's sermon at Pentecost: "When the people heard this, they were *cut to the heart* and said to Peter and the other apostles, 'Brothers, what shall we do?'" (Acts 2:37 NIV 1984).

Has the Word of God been convicting and cutting you? What else is Scripture compared to?

Power like a Seed

Scripture would also compare itself to a seed. It has the power to give life. Look at what Peter says about the Word of God: "You have been born anew, not from perishable but from imperishable seed, through the living and enduring word of God" (1 Peter 1:23).

A person's eternal destiny is affected by how he or she responds to the seed of the Word of God. James says something similar: "So put away all filth and evil excess and humbly welcome the message implanted within you, which is able to save your souls" (James 1:21).

Second Timothy 3:14–15 says:

You, however, must continue in the things you have learned and are confident about. You know who taught you and how from infancy you have *known the holy writings, which are able to give you wisdom for salvation through faith in Christ Jesus.*

We can only be saved through the revelation of the Word of God. This is one of the things that makes the Word our chief revelation—salvation comes through it. The Word of God is powerful like a seed that brings life.

Power to Bear Fruit

In continuing the metaphor of the Word of God being a seed, it not only brings life through saving, but it also bears fruit in one's sanctification. It has the power to change us continually. We get a good picture of this in the Parable of the Sower. Look at what Matthew 13:23 says:

> But as for the seed sown on good soil, this is the person who hears the word and understands. *He bears fruit, yielding a hundred, sixty, or thirty times what was sown.*

The person who has truly received the seed of the Word will naturally produce fruit. This fruit represents many things. It represents leading others to Christ (1 Cor 16:15, KJV), it represents praise and thanksgiving to God (Hebrews 13:5), it represents giving (Rom 15:28), but primarily it represents an inward character change. Look at what Paul says in Galatians 5:22-23: "But the fruit of the Spirit is love, joy, peace, patience, kindness, goodness, faithfulness, gentleness, and self-control. Against such things there is no law."

The Word of God is a seed that bears fruit in the lives of those who accept it. It is the seed that is continually sown in the soil of our hearts in order to produce a harvest of righteousness.

Power That We Should Be Unashamed Of

Finally, Scripture would say that the Word of God is so powerful that the minister should never be ashamed to speak it. Listen to what Paul said about the Word of God: "For I am not ashamed of the gospel, for it is God's power for salvation to everyone who believes, to the Jew first and also to the Greek" (Romans 1:16).

He was not ashamed of the Bible, or specifically the gospel, because it is the power of God. It works. It convicts and confronts on its own. It doesn't need an apologetic because it has power. It has changed the lives of many. It has overthrown corruption in governments and changed nations. It is powerful. God said through Isaiah that the Word of God would never return to him void (Isaiah 55:11).

We should not be ashamed of it as well. We should not leave it on our bookshelves at home collecting dust. We shouldn't be quiet about it when we are around our friends. It has the ability to change lives, and it will change ours if we let it. It's worth talking about.

Many churches have abandoned the clear exposition of Scripture and specifically the gospel. They say, "How can we reach the world with this? The world cannot understand the Word and they don't care about it." Therefore, they have given their church services over to entertainment. They have focused primarily on playing games to win the youth, and therefore, the kingdom of God has suffered greatly because of it. They may grow in numbers, but while they do that, their spiritual health decreases; there is no true lasting fruit.

This happens because people start to believe and/or treat the Word of God as if it's anemic. It is not powerful enough to change the lives of people. It is not all that is needed. People essentially start to become ashamed of it. Paul said, "I am not ashamed of the gospel," for it has power. The power of teaching the Word does not come through homiletics or oratory (cf. 1 Cor 2:3-4); it comes simply because it is the "breath of God." Scripture reveals God because it shows us his power.

Scripture Is Sufficient

Another way that Scripture reveals God is in its sufficiency. One of the characteristics of God is his independence. He does not need anything because he is sufficient in himself (cf. Acts 17:25). We see something of this in the "sufficiency" of Scripture. Wayne Grudem defines "sufficiency" this way:

> The sufficiency of Scripture means that Scripture contained all the words of God he intended his people to have at each stage of redemptive history, and that it now contains everything we need God to tell us for salvation, for trusting him perfectly, and for obeying him perfectly.[16]

The Word of God is sufficient to teach a person about what is right and wrong and also to equip him or her to live righteously. It doesn't need any support. We see this clearly in 2 Timothy 3:16–17:

> Every scripture is inspired by God and useful for teaching, for reproof, for correction, and for training in righteousness, that the person dedicated to God may be capable and equipped for every good work.

What type of good works? What exactly is Paul talking about? God wants you to be a good husband, good wife, good child, good leader, good servant, good student, etc. Anything that is a good work, the Bible will thoroughly equip us for. Do you want to get rid of a habitual sin? You must come to the Bible. Do you want to be a good leader? Come to the Bible. The Bible is sufficient to equip us for every good work.

Listen to what 2 Peter 1:3–4 says:

I can pray this because his divine power has *bestowed on us everything necessary for life and godliness through the rich knowledge of the one* who called us by his own glory and excellence. Through these things he has bestowed on us *his precious and most magnificent promises, so that by means of what was promised you may become partakers of the divine nature, after escaping the worldly corruption* that is produced by evil desire.

Peter says God has given us everything we need for life and godliness through our knowledge of him. Where do we get this knowledge? We get it in his Word. He also says that we can participate in the divine nature and escape the corruption of the world through his "magnificent and precious promises." We have promises in the Bible that will enable us to look more like God and also enable us to remain untainted from the corruption of sin and the world.

According to one person's count, the Bible contains 3573 promises.[17] Each of these will help us look more like God and also escape the corruption of this world. What are some examples? There are promises for those who struggle with worry and depression. God has given us promises like Philippians 4:6-7:

Do not be anxious about anything. Instead, in every situation, through prayer and petition with thanksgiving, tell your requests to God. And the peace of God that surpasses all understanding will guard your hearts and minds in Christ Jesus.

How do we get free of worry? (1) We must choose not to worry, as it is not God's will for our lives. (2) We must learn to pray about everything. (3) We must learn how to give thanks in everything. The result of practicing this type of lifestyle is that God will protect our hearts (emotions) and minds (thoughts) with his peace. Many people are destroyed and crippled by fears, but God says, learn to reject anxiety, learn how to live in an atmosphere of prayer, give thanks in all things, and I will protect your heart and mind with my peace.

The Bible includes tremendous promises that will help us be more like God, but we have to know them. We have to study them. We have to practice them in order to live the righteous life God has called us to.

We see another promise in Philippians 4:19. It says, "And my God will supply your every need according to his glorious riches in Christ Jesus."

We look at many Christians who have great needs. They lack physically, emotionally, mentally, financially, socially, and in various other ways. However, Scripture promises that God will meet all our needs. How do we tap into this promise? This promise is given to the Philippian church for their faithful support of Paul's missionary work (cf. Phil 4:18). This is a promise for every believer who is a faithful giver. Paul essentially gives the same promise in 2 Corinthians. Look at what he says:

> Each one of you should give just as he has decided in his heart, not reluctantly or under compulsion, because God loves a cheerful giver. *And God is able to make all grace overflow to you so that because you have enough of everything in every way at all times, you will overflow in every good work.*
> 2 Corinthians 9:7–8

God promises that if you are a cheerful giver, "all grace" will abound in your life, you will always have what you need, and you will abound in every good work. When you give to God's work, he will graciously meet all your needs and also supply grace to abound in everything righteous that you put your hands to. However, we must realize that this is the very reason so many are in lack. They do not faithfully support the work of building God's kingdom, and therefore, they lack grace in having their needs met and also in producing good works.

The prophet Malachi actually calls for the Israelites to test God in the area of giving to see if God would not in response abundantly supply all their needs. Look at what he says in Malachi 3:10:

> "Bring the entire tithe into the storehouse so that there may be food in my temple. Test me in this matter," says the Lord who rules over all, "to see if I will not open for you the windows of heaven and pour out for you a blessing until there is no room for it al.

God's Word is sufficient. It is sufficient to equip the man of God for all righteousness. God has revealed his character in his Word, and we see something of this character in the sufficiency of Scripture. In the Word of God, he has given us everything we need in order to be righteous. The Bible is God's training manual to make a sinful depraved people righteous.

Sufficient Compared to Other Revelation

Finally, because Scripture is sufficient, it is greater than other forms of revelation. We have talked about prophecies, visions, and even miracles being a revelation of God. Some sadly begin to seek these over God's Word. Let me emphasize again, Scripture is the primary means of God's revelation given to us today, and it will equip us for all righteousness. It is greater than any other revelation.

We see this truth clearly in the story of the rich man and the beggar named Lazarus, which Jesus told in Luke 16:19–31. As the story goes, a rich man and a beggar both died. In hell, the rich man was in torment while Lazarus was safe across a gulf of water in paradise—Abraham's Bosom. The rich man eventually asks for Abraham to send Lazarus back to warn his family so that they would not come to the same place of torment. Look at their conversation and specifically Abraham's replies in Luke 16:27–31:

> So the rich man said, 'Then I beg you, father—send Lazarus to my father's house (for I have five brothers) to warn them so that they don't come into this place of torment.' But Abraham said, '*They have Moses and the prophets; they must respond to them.*' Then the rich man said, 'No, father Abraham, but if someone from the dead goes to them, they will repent.' He replied to him, '*If they do not respond to Moses and the prophets, they will not be convinced even if someone rises from the dead.*'"

Abraham said, "*They have Moses and the prophets…If they do not respond to Moses and the prophets, they will not be convinced even if someone rises from the dead.*" Moses and the prophets were dead, but their writings were captured in Scripture. Abraham was saying the Word of God has more power than miracles, such as a resurrection. Essentially, he says, "If they won't accept what the Bible says, they won't even accept a miracle." Certainly, we saw this reality with Christ's resurrection. The Pharisees, who had him killed, still did not repent. They had already rejected the Scripture, and therefore, the resurrection was unprofitable.

This speaks a great deal to the many churches that have forsaken the sufficiency of the Word of God in pursuit of revelation through healings and miracles. Many claim that the gospel cannot go forth without such revelations. There is nothing wrong with miracles, but the greatest and most powerful miracle is the "written breath of God." It is sufficient on its own.

Our great commission is to make disciples by teaching them to obey "everything" that Christ has commanded through the Scripture (Matt 28:19). The Scripture is our greatest revelation as it testifies about Christ (the living Word), and it is the way we test all other revelations such as visions, dreams, prophecies, etc. (cf. 1 John 4:1).

This truth of the Word's sufficiency in comparison to other forms of revelation is also tremendously challenging to us. Many times we condemn Israel for not responding to all the miracles that God did for them in the wilderness or that Christ did during his first coming. However, the reality is if we do not respond to the truth of the Word of God today then we also would not have responded to all the great miracles that God did for the nation of Israel in the past. To make our accountability greater, they only had Moses and the prophets, but we have Matthew, Mark, Luke, John, Peter, Paul, and others. We have a greater revelation than Israel and also the early church. How much more accountable will we be if we neglect the revelation that God has given us in his completed Word?

Scripture Is Reliable

Another way Scripture reveals God is in its accuracy and reliability. The Bible is reliable because it is without error or in other words "inerrant." "Inerrancy" has many definitions.

Wayne Grudem said, "The inerrancy of Scripture means that Scripture in the original manuscripts does not affirm anything that is contrary to fact."[18] The Lausanne Covenant declared the Bible to be "inerrant in all that it affirms."[19] The International Council on Biblical Inerrancy said in its Chicago statement that "Scripture is without error or fault in all its teaching."[20] Millard Erickson said it this way: "Inerrancy is the doctrine that the Bible is fully truthful in all of its teachings."[21]

Inerrancy simply means that the Bible is true and without error in the original manuscripts, and for that reason, we can trust its copies.

How do we know that? Why should we believe in its inerrancy? *What are some evidences for the inerrancy of Scripture?*

1. Evidence for the inerrancy of Scripture is the character of God.

God cannot lie. Look at Titus 1:2: "to further the faith of God's chosen ones and the knowledge of the truth that is in keeping with godliness, in hope of eternal life, *which God, who does not lie, promised before time began.*"

Paul encourages Titus with the fact that God cannot tell a lie. That's why we can trust the Scripture and everything said in it. Scripture is God's Word, and God cannot tell a lie. Numbers 23:19 says this: "God is not a man, that he should lie, nor a human being, that he should change his mind. Has he said, and will he not do it? Or has he spoken, and will he not make it happen?"

In fact, Christ called himself "the way, and the truth, and the life" (John 14:6). Jesus is the truth because there is nothing false in him. Everything he says and does is true because he is God and that is his character.

Another proof of the truthfulness of God, and therefore, the truthfulness of Scripture, is seen in how God instructs Israel to test prophets. Look at what he says in Deuteronomy 18:21–22:

Now if you say to yourselves, 'How can we tell that a message is not from the Lord?'—whenever a prophet speaks in my name and the prediction is not fulfilled, then I have not spoken it; the prophet has presumed to speak it, so you need not fear him.

The way God tells Israel to test prophets also teaches the truthfulness of God. If a prophet made an error in his prophecy, he wasn't speaking for God because God cannot make errors. He knows all things and cannot lie or be tempted (cf. James 1:13). Since the Bible is God's Word, it cannot have errors.

2. Evidence for the inerrancy of Scripture is what the Bible teaches about itself—that every word is true, not just the ideas of Scripture.

This is important because some liberal theologians teach against this. They would say that the ideas of the Bible are true but not necessarily every event, such as Jonah being swallowed by a big fish, the virgin birth of Jesus, etc.
However, this teaching contradicts what the Bible says about itself. Look at what Christ taught in Matthew 4:4: "It is written, 'Man does not live by bread alone, but by every word that comes from the mouth of God.'"
Jesus said that man lives on "every word" that comes from the mouth of God, not SOME words or SOME events. Similarly, the Psalmist said this about Scripture:

The law of the Lord is perfect and preserves one's life.
Psalm 19:7b

Your instructions are totally reliable; all your just regulations endure.
Psalm 119:160

The Lord's words are absolutely reliable. They are as untainted as silver purified in a furnace on the ground, where it is thoroughly refined.
Psalm 12:6

Scripture teaches that every part of it is true, not just some parts or the main ideas of Scripture.

3. Evidence of inerrancy is the perseverance of Scripture.

Jesus said this, "I tell you the truth, until heaven and earth pass away not the smallest letter or stroke of a letter will pass from the law until everything takes place" (Matthew 5:18).

This is important because some liberal theologians say that the Scriptures we have today are not the same as the original writings. Essentially, they are saying that God did not preserve his Word. However, Jesus declared that even the smallest letter, the least stroke of a pen will not disappear from the Law until all is accomplished. We can believe that the Word of God is inerrant because God has preserved it.

4. Evidence of inerrancy is that Scripture uses Scripture in such a way that supports its inerrancy.

In the Bible, at times an entire argument rests on a single word (e.g., John 10:34–35 and "God" in Psalm 82:6), the tense of a verb (e.g., the present tense in Matt 22:32), and the difference between a singular and a plural noun (e.g., "seed" in Gal 3:16). Let's look at an example.

In Matthew 22:30–32, the entire argument rests on a single word. The Sadducees were the liberal believers in Christ's day; they did not believe in miracles, the resurrection, or even an afterlife. So one day, they tested Christ on his belief in the resurrection. They concocted a scenario where a woman's husband dies and then she marries his brother. The brother dies and she marries another brother. He dies and she marries another and so on until the seventh died. Then she eventually died. "Basically, they argued that the idea of resurrection posed insuperable difficulties, hence it was not reasonable, therefore it was not true."[22] Then the Sadducees asked Christ, "At the resurrection whose wife will she be?" Look at how Christ responded in Matthew 22:30–32:

> For in the resurrection they neither marry nor are given in marriage, but are like angels in heaven. Now as for the resurrection of the dead, *have you not read* what was spoken to you by God, '*I am the God of Abraham, the God of Isaac, and the God of Jacob*'? *He is not the God of the dead but of the living!*

Here, Christ's argument rests on the tense of the word "am." Essentially, Christ says, "Didn't you notice that 'I am the God of Abraham, the God of Isaac, and the God of Jacob' was written in the present tense?" Christ was saying that Abraham, Isaac, and Jacob are all still alive, and therefore, would one-day be resurrected. This confronted their lack of belief in the afterlife and the resurrection. Every word has been chosen by God even down to the tense.

We also see this in how Paul handled the words of Scripture. Look at what Paul says:

The promises were spoken to Abraham and to his seed. The Scripture does not say "and to seeds," meaning many people, but "and to your seed," meaning one person, who is Christ."
Galatians 3:16 (NIV 1984)

When looking at the promise of Abraham, Paul argues that the promise was not just to Israel specifically, but that it was to Christ and therefore, everybody in Christ. He says in Genesis the promise was to Abraham's "seed," singular, and not "seeds," plural. Here the argument rests on the word "seed" being singular.

The Bible is inspired and inerrant even down to the tense and plurality of the words. Every word is inspired by God and not just the ideas. This gives credence to studying and meditating on each word of the Bible since we believe God chose them for a purpose. This is one of the reasons many Bible students study the original languages of Scripture. They do this because they are convinced of the validity of each word. Jesus said, "*Man does not live by bread alone, but by every word that comes from the mouth of God*" (Matt 4:4).

Questions About Inerrancy?

1. Some might ask, "How can the Bible be without error if mere humans wrote it? I know God made it but so did man, and man is fallible."

This is true, and, because of this reality, it must be clearly recognized as a miracle. Man is sinful and prone to error; however, God is perfect and cannot err. The Holy Spirit inspired the authors in such a way that he kept them from error in the writing of the Scripture.

2. Then someone might ask, "If, we do not have the original manuscripts, isn't the argument of inerrancy in the original manuscripts a moot argument?"

When we look at the way that the apostles and the early church handled the copies of Scripture, we see their belief in the reliability of the copies.

In the early church, the copies of the originals were passed around from church to church, and, yet, the copies were always still considered authoritative. We see this in several ways.

- When Paul spoke about the Scripture being God-inspired in 2 Timothy 3:16, he was using copies, not the originals. The early church was using copies just as we are now. The original texts were copied and passed from church to church. Yet, they still believed they were inspired and, therefore, authoritative.

- We also see how the early church believed the copies were authoritative in the Old Testament quotations used in the New Testament. The majority of the OT quotes in the NT were from the Septuagint, which was the Greek version of the Old Testament.[23] Even though the original verses were in Hebrew, the writers of the NT still considered the copies, the translated verses, authoritative and without error. We even see Jesus quote the Septuagint in his rendering of Isaiah 29:13 in Mark 7:6–7:

> He said to them, "Isaiah prophesied correctly about you hypocrites, as it is written: '*This people honors me with their lips, but their heart is far from me. They worship me in vain, teaching as doctrine the commandments of men.*'

Again, this is a quote from a copy, but it was still inspired by God. The apostles primarily used Greek copies in the quotes placed in the inspired New Testament. If Jesus and the apostles used copies, then, similarly, we can trust the copies we have.

Here is a contemporary argument. If I apply for a job, the company will most likely take a photocopy of my driver's license and keep it for their records. They know the copy is not perfect. It may have a smudge here or there, but, in general, the copy is considered accurate and acceptable.

This is how the early church handled the copies of Scripture and so do we. God has preserved his words, and it is still authoritative. In fact, when we compare the thousands of copies of Scripture, they are 95 to 99 percent the same.[24] The copies of the OT and NT manuscripts contain no great variances. The errors are typically copyist errors such as an undotted "i" or an uncrossed "t," but nothing that affects any doctrine in the Bible. God has preserved his Word.

Any errors are in our understanding of the text, the copy of the manuscript itself, or the translation. But the Bible cannot have error because God is without error. If we cannot trust the Bible on one thing, then the whole Bible comes into question.

Application

What does all this mean for us?

1. The inerrancy of Scripture means we can trust the Word of God.

We should not doubt even spectacular stories in the Scripture, such as Jonah being swallowed by a big fish, Moses parting the Red Sea, or the earth being destroyed by a flood. Listen, God cannot tell a lie, and therefore, you can trust his Word.

It also means you can trust his word for salvation. You can trust his word on how to raise your kids and how to run a business. The Scripture holds the very words of God and so not only is it powerful, but it is also trustworthy.

2. The inerrancy of Scripture should guide us on how we meditate on the Word of God.

It is good at times to meditate on single words, noting their tenses and their pluralities, because each word was chosen by God. They are God-inspired and every aspect of them has meaning for us.

With the Sadducees, Jesus said, "Have you not read?" Sure, they had read, but they really didn't study and meditate on each word as given. Many times, we miss a great deal in our study of the Bible because we forget that every word was chosen by God and that man shall live by every word (Matt 4:4). This type of study will greatly enrich our devotional time.

Scripture Is Eternal

Another way that Scripture reveals God is in its eternality. God has always existed and will continue to exist eternally (cf. Deut. 33:27). In the same way, Scripture is eternal because it comes from God. Listen to what Peter says: "You have been born anew, not from perishable but from imperishable seed, through the living and enduring word of God" (1 Peter 1:23).

Peter calls it the "enduring word of God" or it can be translated as the "everlasting word of God" (cf. International Standard Version). It is true that the Scriptures did not always exist in written form, but they have always existed in that they are a representation of the character and person of God. And, it will always exist because God will preserve it.

As mentioned before, this is one of the reasons we can trust that no manuscripts have been lost or ultimately corrupted (cf. Matthew 5:18). God has preserved his Word because it is a reflection of him and his eternality.

Scripture Brings God's Blessing

Finally, we see the revelation of God through the Word in how it brings God's blessing. Scripture teaches that it is the character of God to bless. He blessed the sea creatures and birds of the air (Gen 1:22). He blessed Adam and Eve (Gen 1:28). Hebrews 11:6 says he rewards those who seek him. God is a God of blessing.

We see the revelation of this blessing on those who love God's Word. It is a truth taught throughout the Bible. Look at what God says in Psalm 1:1–3:

> How blessed is the one who does not follow the advice of the wicked, or stand in the pathway with sinners, or sit in the assembly of scoffers! Instead he finds *pleasure in obeying the Lord's commands; he meditates on his commands day and night. He is like a tree planted by flowing streams; it yields its fruit at the proper time, and its leaves never fall off. He succeeds in everything he attempts.*

"Blessed" is a word that can be translated "happy." People who give their lives to the study of God's Word will find that they are happier than others. They will find joy even in the midst of trials because they meditate on his Word. David also teaches this in other passages. Look at what he says in Psalm 19:8: "The Lord's precepts are fair and make one joyful." Those who love God's Word and meditate on it day and night will find joy and happiness. They will find an inner peace that can only come from God.

"Blessed" is a word that also has the meaning of approval. When a man asks a father for his daughter's hand and the father gives him his blessing, it means he approves. One of the greatest things we should want in life is the approval of God. God approves those who delight in and study his Word. Paul teaches this as well in 2 Timothy 2:15 (NIV 1984): "Do your best to present yourself *to God as one approved,* a workman who does not need to be ashamed and who correctly handles the word of truth."

Who is the one that God approves on the earth? It is those who do their best, those who work tirelessly at understanding God's words. They study it and correctly handle it when they are teaching it to others. God will approve of Christians who do this. We see this reality in other texts as well. Listen to what Paul says in 1 Corinthians 4:1–2 (KJV): "Let a man so account of us, as of the ministers of Christ, and *stewards of the mysteries of God.* Moreover it is required in stewards, that a man *be found faithful.*"

Paul says believers are "stewards of the mysteries of God." In ancient times, if a master went away on business, he would leave his household under the care of a steward. The steward would manage the affairs of the house until the master came home. When the master came home, he would inspect the *faithfulness* of the steward's ministry.

Similarly, God has given us his Word. He has given it for us to study, to live, and to teach to others so that they may know God. One day, he will come to inspect our faithfulness and those who were faithful will be "approved" and rewarded (1 Corinthians 3:12–14).

Are you being faithful with God's Word?

The word "blessing" also has to do with *receiving abundant grace*. He gives abundant grace to those who delight in his Word. In fact, David describes those who delight in God's Word as a tree that bears fruit (Psalm 1:3).

Trees are not made for their own benefit, but for the benefit and enjoyment of others. The fruits can provide food and medicinal benefits; the tree itself provides shelter and protection. Trees are a blessing to others and that's how the man who meditates on God's Word is described. He will bear fruit that brings blessings, protection, and healing to others. His life will not be about himself, but it will be used for the enrichment of those around him.

David says this type of man will prosper in everything he does (Psalm 1:3). In whatever God calls him to do, he will find prosperity and success. Certainly, the success God is talking about does not mean the absence of trials. Joseph was sold into slavery, which doesn't seem like prosperity. But even as a slave, he was exalted to manager over the household. Soon, he was sent to prison, but even there he was exalted to the head of the prisoners. Ultimately, he was made second in command over all of Egypt. Even the evil Joseph's brothers committed against him was used for good (Gen 50:20). It's the same with those who delight in God's Word. He gives them rich blessings even in the midst of their trials. God's prosperity doesn't mean an exception from trials, but favor and perseverance through the trials of life. The trials that destroy others make the one who meditates on the Word of God strong.

Are you one who meditates on God's Word? He blesses those who do. This blessing is a special revelation from God. It is his favor on the lives of those who love him and revere his Word. "This is the one I esteem: he who is humble and contrite in spirit, and trembles at my word" (Isaiah 66:2b).

Conclusion

The primary way God reveals himself to people today is through his Word. His Word reveals his characteristics. The Word is powerful; the Word is truthful and reliable in all that it affirms. It is sufficient in that it trains the man of God for all righteousness. The Word of God is eternal; it cannot be corrupted or destroyed as it is a reflection of God. God's blessing is on those who delight and study it. Those who love it will know God more, but they also will see his favor over their lives.

Are you delighting in God's Word?

Review Questions

1. What does the sufficiency of Scripture mean? How can you support this biblically?

2. In what ways do we see the power of God's Word? How do we utilize this power?

3. What is inerrancy? In what ways does Scripture teach its inerrancy? Why is it important for the church to believe in and to defend the doctrine of the inerrancy of Scripture? How is this doctrine being attacked?

4. In what ways does God bless the person who delights in his Word? How do we develop and/or protect our delight? In what ways do you practice meditating on Scripture?

Prayer Prompts

- Pray that God would draw us individually and corporately to delight in his Word, that we would faithfully study it, and that we may grow up into full maturity as a body of Christ (Psalm 1, John 6:44, 1 Peter 2:2).

- Pray that the Word of God would be proclaimed throughout the world in churches, schools, businesses, and nations. Pray that it would be received and glorified among the people (2 Thess 3:1).

- Pray that God would continue to protect his Word from distortion and the lies of the evil one. Pray that the church would faithfully guard the Scripture given to us and also be faithful stewards of it (2 Tim 1:14, 1 Cor 4:1–2).

Characteristics of God

What are the characteristics of God? Millard Erickson said this about the characteristics or attributes of God, "When we speak of the attributes of God, we are referring to those qualities of God that constitute what he is, the very characteristics of his nature."[25] Ryrie instead calls God's characteristics, his "perfections" because all of the qualities or attributes of God are perfect.[26] In this portion of our study, we will be considering God's attributes—his characteristics—his perfections.

In considering God's characteristics, I think a good analogy is looking at a married couple. One of the great things about being married is the ability to get to know one person in an intimate way, potentially, for the rest of life. This growing knowledge enables us to learn how to better serve and love him or her daily.

Similarly, Scripture teaches that we are the bride of Christ, and we will be married to God for all eternity (cf. Eph 5:23, Rev 19:7). Since God is the bridegroom of the church, we must devote ourselves to knowing him intimately so that we might please him and effectively serve him in this loving union throughout this life and the next.

We can only do this properly if we give ourselves to the discipline of study. We must understand his characteristics—his person, his being, what brings him pleasure, what brings him displeasure, etc. Therefore, in this section we will focus on his characteristics with the hope of better serving our Heavenly Bridegroom for the rest of eternity.

What are some characteristics of God?

God Is Spirit

The first characteristic is that God is spirit. Look at what Christ taught the woman at the well: "God is spirit, and the people who worship him must worship in spirit and truth" (John 4:24).

What did Christ mean by "God is spirit"? He meant that the essence of God, his makeup, is immaterial. Listen to what Jesus said when he was resurrected from the dead in Luke 24:39: "Look at my hands and my feet; it's me! Touch me and see; a ghost does not have flesh and bones like you see I have."

Jesus said a "ghost," or it can be translated "spirit," does not have flesh and bones. In the same way, our God does not have a physical makeup. Yes, Jesus does. But Jesus did not eternally exist as a man. He humbled himself and took the form of man in order to save us from our sins (Phil 2:7). God is spirit.

Anthropomorphisms

Now one might ask, "If God is not material, how come so many Scriptures use illustrations of God having human body parts?" We see this particularly when God revealed his glory to Moses in the Old Testament. Listen to what God said in Exodus 33:22–23:

> When my glory passes by, I will put you in a cleft in the rock and will cover you with my hand while I pass by. Then *I will take away my hand, and you will see my back, but my face must not be seen.*

Did you see that? God talks about himself having a back, hands, and a face. How can this be? This is what we call an *anthropomorphism*. This comes from the Greek words "anthropos," which means "man," and "morphe," which means form. These are times when Scripture talks about God in the form of a man. Why does God speak about himself in these terms? He speaks like this to give us a frame of reference, so that we can better understand him.

How can one describe God in understandable words when nothing on earth is like him? You cannot, so God seeks to give us an understanding by using human points of reference like a hand or body. We see many Scriptures like this. The Psalmist said, "Save us and help us with your right hand" (Psalm 60:5 NIV 1984). Similarly, Jesus said this:

> My sheep listen to my voice, and I know them, and they follow me. I give them eternal life, and they will never perish; no one will snatch them from my hand. My Father, who has given them to me, is greater than all, and *no one can snatch them from my Father's hand.*
> John 10:27-29

Again, these are given to help us relate to and understand God, even though every illustration falls short of his true glory.

I think we get some type of understanding of anthropomorphisms when we consider the illustrations often given to represent the Trinity. I remember being confused about the doctrine of the Trinity while in Sunday school class, along with every other student. Because of this, the teacher described the Trinity by using the illustration of ice melting and becoming water, then evaporating as steam. Another time somebody used the illustration of an egg—the yoke, the white, and the shell representing the Father, the Son, and the Holy Spirit. However, each of these illustrations fails miserably in representing the Trinity. Each member of the Trinity is fully God, operates independently and, yet, are one. It's a paradox. With that said, the illustrations of the Trinity, though they fell far short of the glory of God, were mildly helpful at that young age. Similarly, even though God does not have material form, he uses illustrations we can relate to in order to help us comprehend something of his glory.

The fact that anthropomorphisms are simply points of references is also seen when God uses animal forms to describe himself. Scripture talks about him covering us with his wings like a bird (cf. Psalm 91:4). Does God really have wings? No, he is a spirit, but he wants us to understand that he cares for us like a mother hen cares for her chicks. That's an illustration we can understand even though it still falls miserably short of God's true glory. God's care for us is infinitely greater than any hen could ever possibly care for her chicks.

What else can we learn about God since he is spirit?

Invisible

Because God is spirit, this also means he is "invisible." We cannot see God. This is what John taught in his Gospel. Look at what he said in John 1:18: "No one has ever seen God. The only one, himself God, who is in closest fellowship with the Father, has made God known." The only human that has ever seen God in his full glory is Jesus, and, therefore, it is through Jesus that we can have a better understanding of God.

However, even though God is invisible, it should be noted that at times in the Scripture God chose to take physical form to reveal himself to man in sensible ways. As mentioned previously, these temporary physical manifestations are called theophanies. We saw one of these in the book of Isaiah. Isaiah saw the Lord in physical form. He said this in Isaiah 6:1 "In the year of King Uzziah's death, *I saw the sovereign master seated on a high, elevated throne. The hem of his robe filled the temple.*"

In addition, God revealed himself throughout biblical history in many different physical forms. He revealed himself in a flame with Moses (Ex 3:2), through a man with Abraham (Gen 18:1-2), through a cloud with Israel (Ex 13:21), through an angel with Gideon (Judges 6:22), etc.

Ultimately, the fullest expression of God has been given in Jesus Christ. This appearance would not be considered a theophany because this appearance was not temporary. Christ will dwell throughout eternity as the God-man (cf. 1 Tim 2:5), and it is through Christ that we can see God. The writer of Hebrews said this:

> *The Son is the radiance of his glory and the representation of his essence,* and he sustains all things by his powerful word, and so when he had accomplished cleansing for sins, he sat down at the right hand of the Majesty on high.
> Hebrews 1:3

Jesus said, "The person who has seen me has seen the Father!" (John 14:9). The ultimate expression of God is seen in Jesus Christ, his Son.

God is spirit, and therefore, he is invisible. However, at times he has chosen to reveal himself to men in theophanies and ultimately through his Son, Jesus Christ.

How can we apply the reality that God is spirit?

Application

What does this mean for us?

When Jesus says, "God is spirit, and the people who worship him must worship in spirit and in truth" (John 4:24), he essentially is saying this reality should affect how we worship him. Since God is spirit, "we must worship God in spirit and in truth" (John 4:24).

What does it mean to worship in spirit? To worship in spirit means to worship with the right heart or the inner man.

In the context, Christ was trying to teach a Samaritan woman that worship is not a matter of being in Jerusalem at the temple or being in Samaria. It is not primarily a matter of where you are or what you are doing, because worship is a matter of the heart. God is spirit, so we must worship him in spirit.

Some have primarily seen this as Christ referring to our need for the Holy Spirit in worship, but most translators do not capitalize the word "spirit" because it has no article behind it. It doesn't say "the Spirit." Worship is primarily a matter of the heart—the inner man. It is not so much about location or activity. You can sing a song and not worship, give an offering and not worship. It is a matter of the inner man; it is a matter of having the right heart.

We see this in the New Testament with the Pharisees. Jesus said, "This people honors me with their lips, but their heart is far from me, and they worship me in vain" (Matthew 15:8-9). Christ warned his disciples to not worship in the same way the Pharisees did. He said: "Be careful not to display your righteousness merely to be seen by people. Otherwise you have no reward with your Father in heaven" (Matthew 6:1). When the Pharisees worshiped, their hearts were not in the right place. They gave to be seen by men; they prayed and fasted to be seen by others, and therefore, that was their reward. They did not approach God properly in the inner man. God is spirit, and he must be worshiped with our spirit.

Certainly, it's the same for us. Consider what Paul said about giving in 2 Corinthians 9:7: "Each one of you should give just as he has decided in his heart, not reluctantly or under compulsion, because God loves a cheerful giver." Giving weekly or monthly is not the most important aspect; it is the manner of the heart. It must not be reluctant or under compulsion, but out of a joyful heart. Otherwise, it means nothing.

Consider what Paul taught in 1 Corinthians 13:1–3:

> If I speak in the tongues of men and of angels, but I do not have love, I am a *noisy gong or a clanging cymbal*. And if I have prophecy, and know all mysteries and all knowledge, and if I have all faith so that I can remove mountains, but do not have love, I am nothing. If I give away everything I own, and if I give over my body in order to boast, but do not have love, I receive no benefit.

Paul names all these things that would typically be worship to God. He names speaking in tongues, prophecy, faith, giving everything to the poor, and even being given to the flames as a martyr, but without love—without the right heart—it is nothing to God. It is like a resounding gong or a clanging cymbal.

Much of worship on Sundays is just a bunch of clanging cymbals. Clanging cymbals create a loud noise nobody wants to hear, and there is a lot of that in the church. I have no doubt that many times on Sunday, God is in pain by hearing the worship. He hears a constant clanging because it comes from hearts that are not serious, not contemplative, and not reverent. True worship is a matter of the inner man. It is a matter of the heart, will, and emotions. God is spirit and so we must worship him in spirit.

Understanding that God is spirit should drastically affect our worship. *How can we practically worship in spirit in order to honor God?*

To worship in spirit, with the right heart, means that our worship is universal.

That means everything we do can be worship. It is not localized. It is not only a Sunday thing or about being in a church building. First Corinthians 10:31 says: "So whether you eat or drink, or whatever you do, do everything for the glory of God." Paul says our eating, our drinking, and whatever else we do should glorify God.

1. To worship in spirit, with the right heart, means to give God our best.

99

We saw this throughout the Old Testament. God would never accept anything that was not the best. This is specifically seen in the instructions given for offering a burnt sacrifice. It had to be a lamb without blemish. It had to be the worshiper's best (cf. Malachi 1:6–10) or it would be rejected.

2. To worship in spirit, with the right heart, means that worship must be our priority.

Christ said this in the Beatitudes: "Blessed are the pure in heart, for they will see God" (Matthew 5:8).

The pure in heart has the meaning of being single in mind or focus. It is the single in focus that see God and have his blessing. Their focus—their priority—is knowing God and bringing pleasure to him. Too often, our hearts are divided, and it quenches our worship. David said this: "Teach me your way, O LORD, and I will walk in your truth; *give me an undivided heart, that I may fear your name*" (Psalm 86:11 NIV 1984).

3. To worship in spirit, with the right heart, means to be zealous in pursuing God.

Listen to what God said through Jeremiah: "When you seek me in prayer and worship, you will find me available to you. If you seek me with all your heart and soul" (Jeremiah 29:13). Worship must involve zeal. The zealous and they alone will find God and receive his blessing. They are like a deer who is desperate for water. It is those he rewards. The casual worshiper receives nothing from God. The Psalmist modeled acceptable worship when he prayed this: "As a deer longs for streams of water, so I long for you, O God! I thirst for God, for the living God I say, 'When will I be able to go and appear in God's presence?'" (Psalm 42:1–2). True worship must be zealous (cf. Romans 12:11).

4. To worship in spirit, with the right heart, means to worship with holiness.

David said this: "If I had harbored sin in my heart, the Lord would not have listened" (Psalm 66:18). Sin quenches not only our prayer life but also our worship. If I enjoy nurturing my anger towards someone who hurt me, or if I cherish an impure relationship, the Lord will not hear me. If I cherish music so much that I will illegally download it, the Lord will not hear me. Worship must be in holiness.

5. To worship in spirit, with the right heart, means to live peaceably, without division.

100

Listen to what Christ said in Matthew 5:23–24:

So then, if you *bring your gift to the altar and there remember that your brother has something against you,* leave your gift there in front of the altar. First go and be reconciled to your brother and then come and present your gift.

Jesus said one should not offer a gift in worship if he is walking in discord with another brother. As much as it depends on us, we must live in peace with our brothers and sisters (Romans 12:18).

The fact that God is spirit should challenge us in our worship. He is looking at the spirit of man, the heart of man, when we approach him for worship (1 Sam 16:7).

God Is a Person

As we think about God as spirit, we might be tempted to think that God is not a person. God is a person. Wayne Grudem said this about God's personhood:

In the teaching of the Bible, God is both *infinite* and *personal:* he is infinite in that he is not subject to any of the limitations of humanity, or of creation in general. He is far greater than everything he has made, far greater than anything else that exists. But he is also personal: he interacts with us as a person, and we can relate to him as persons.[27]

In fact, his personhood may be most clearly seen in the fact that God made man in his image. Listen to Genesis 1:27: "God created humankind in his own image, in the image of God he created them, male and female he created them."

Because God made man in his image, we can probably learn a lot about God's person by studying humanity and vice versa. In what ways do we see God's personhood? We see it in the fact that God demonstrates characteristics of personality such as anger, joy, and consciousness. Scripture teaches he is angry at sin all the time (Psalm 7:11). Also, when we are walking in holiness and living the life he has called us to, he rejoices over us and even sings. Zephaniah 3:17 (NIV 1984) says this:

The LORD your God is with you, he is mighty to save. He will *take great delight in you, he will quiet you with his love, he will rejoice over you with singing.*

Scripture also teaches that he demonstrates the emotion of jealousy. God declares that he is a jealous God who will share his glory with no one. Deuteronomy 6:15 says this: "for the Lord your God, who is present among you, is a jealous God and his anger will erupt against you and remove you from the land."

We also see that God demonstrates consciousness. We see this in the fact that he makes decisions. He plans and foreordains things. This is clearly demonstrated in the doctrine of election. God chose people for salvation before time. Ephesians 1:4–5 says this:

For he chose us in Christ before the foundation of the world that we may be holy and unblemished in his sight in love. He did this by predestining us to adoption as his sons through Jesus Christ, according to the pleasure of his will—

As we study the rest of his characteristics, they all in some way demonstrate his personhood. It is because God is a person that we can have an intimate relationship with him.

Applications

How can we apply the personhood of God?

1. His personhood reminds us that we can get to know God more and more as with any person.

    Paul prays this in Ephesians 1:17 (NIV 1984): "I keep asking that the God of our Lord Jesus Christ, the glorious Father, may give you the Spirit of wisdom and revelation, *so that you may know him better.*"

2. His personhood reminds us that we must develop sensitivity to his person.

    Scripture says that we can grieve the Holy Spirit (Ephesians 4:30) and quench the Holy Spirit (1 Thessalonians 5:19). Therefore, like with any person, we must develop a sensitivity to God in order to please him in every way.

When a person is in a relationship, often one can tell when their partner or friend is mad even without a word. This is true because that person and has become sensitive to him or her. We must, similarly, develop this sensitivity to God.

Developing sensitivity to God has an objective side. It is developed by studying his Word. By doing this, we learn what does and does not please him. But there is a subjective side as well. At times, we may even sense God's feelings. Jeremiah said this: "I am as full of anger as you are, Lord, I am tired of trying to hold it in" (Jeremiah 6:11).

Jeremiah could feel God's anger at Israel. At times we may feel this as well. We may feel the Spirit of God grieving over a movie we are watching or disobedience in a friend's life. We may feel his love, joy, or peace. Paul said he longed for the Philippians with the very affections of Christ (Phil 1:8). He felt the way Christ felt about them. He had developed sensitivity to his Savior's emotions and so must we.

3.   His personhood reminds us that God is not a tool or an object to be used.

What does it mean that God is not a tool? See, a tool is only used for a specific purpose. We use a toothbrush to clean our teeth, but we don't have a relationship with a toothbrush. We only care about it to accomplish our purpose.

Sometimes, people treat one another like this. We network or talk to people only to open potential doors for a job or a promotion. Sometimes, people are willing to step over others or mistreat them to get what they want out of life. This is treating someone like a tool.

Sadly, many Christians treat God like a tool. He is just a genie in a lamp. When they want something, they pray to God. When they go through a trial, they come to him, but when things are okay, they ignore him. They are treating God like a tool, to get what they want, instead of as a person.

God is a person, and he wants to have a relationship with us. He sent his Son to die for this purpose, so we can have eternal life, which is knowing God (John 17:3).

God Is Independent

What does the independence of God mean? It essentially means that God does not need anything. He doesn't need anything to be who he is or contribute to who he is. Tony Evans said this about God's independence:

> This understanding can enhance our worship of God, because while God has a voluntary relationship to everything, He has a necessary

103

relationship to nothing. In other words, God relates to His creation because He chooses to, not because He needs to. For example, if you show up for worship at your church, that's good and God is glad to see you. But He will not be worse off if you stay home. He's not going to panic.[28]

We, on the other hand, are dependent. We are dependent on our parents for life and clothing as children, and when we are older, we are dependent upon friends, family, job, education, etc. In a sense, we need these things to make it in life or society.

But we serve a God who needs nothing because he is independent. Look at what Paul said to the Athenians in Acts 17:24–25:

The God who made the world and everything in it, who is Lord of heaven and earth, does not live in temples made by human hands, *nor is he served by human hands, as if he needed anything, because he himself gives life and breath* and everything to everyone.

Paul says, "nor is he served by human hands, as if he needed anything" (v. 25). What does Paul mean by "nor is he served by human hands"? Don't people serve God all the time? They serve him at church; they serve him at work; they serve in their personal worship.

Paul means at least two things by saying that God is not served by human hands. First, he simply means that God does not need anything. God is independent. But secondly, he means that God is not served by human hands because he is *the giver*. He says, "because he himself gives life and breath and everything to everyone" (v.25). What exactly does that mean?

We may get a good picture of this when small children buy their parent a gift. Did they buy the gift? Yes. But in another sense, the parent bought the gift because it was the parent's money. See, the parents are the ones who make money in the household. Similarly, Paul says we can't really serve him because he has given us all things. Can we really give God money on Sunday if he has already given it to us? In a sense, we can't. We can't because God is independent, and he is the true giver of all things. We can give only because he has given to us.

That is the wonderful thing about God. He doesn't need us, but he allows us and calls us to worship him, though he doesn't need anything.

Created for His Enjoyment

Well, one might ask, why did he create us then if he is independent? Was it because he was lonely or bored?

No, not at all. There are many things in life that I don't need. I don't need to look at ESPN to see who won the latest NBA game. That's something I do because I enjoy it. God made us because he enjoys us. Look at what he says about Israel and, through extension, the people of God of all times: "The LORD your God is with you, he is mighty to save. *He will take great delight in you, he will quiet you with his love, he will rejoice over you with singing*" (Zephaniah 3:17 NIV 1984).

It says he takes great delight in us and he will rejoice over us with singing. We often see people who are musically talented write or sing songs to people they care about. Our worship songs to God are commonly written this way. However, God also sings over us and delights in us. He delights in us, especially, when we are following him and walking in the unique giftings that he gave us. It brings him pleasure because we are fulfilling his purpose.

Scripture would say our high calling is to bring God both joy and pleasure. Colossians 1:16 says this:

> for all things in heaven and on earth were created in him—all things, whether visible or invisible, whether thrones or dominions, whether principalities or powers—*all things were created through him and for him.*

All things were made for him—to bring glory to God and to bring him pleasure.

A great illustration of this is seen in the story of Olympic runner, Eric Liddell. In 1924, he was competing in the Olympics and had decided this would be his last competition before he went into full-time missions. One person asked him, why not just stop running now and go into missions? He told the person, "I believe God made me for a purpose, but he also made me fast. And when I run I feel His pleasure."[29]

For each of us, God has given us certain gifts. For some, he made us intelligent, others athletic, others are great with their hands, and others are gifted at serving or teaching. When we do the things that God created us for, he takes great pleasure in us as well.

Creation's Dependence

The other side of God's independence is our dependence on him. Listen again to what Paul said to the Athenians: "nor is he served by human hands, as if he needed anything, *because he himself gives life and breath and everything to everyone*" (Acts 17: 25). We need God for everything, even life and breath.

Look at what else Paul says in Colossians 1:17: "He himself is before all things and *all things are held together in him.*" In talking about Christ, he says that he holds "all things" together. This means that not only does he give us life and breath, but he holds the trees, the plants, the oceans, the stars, and all the cosmos together. Everything is dependent upon him; we can do nothing apart from God.

I think we may get a clearer picture of the dependence of man in David's illustration of God being a shepherd in Psalm 23. Listen to Psalm 23:

The Lord is my shepherd, I lack nothing. He takes me to lush pastures, he leads me to refreshing water. He restores my strength. He leads me down the right paths for the sake of his reputation. Even when I must walk through the darkest valley, I fear no danger, for you are with me; your rod and your staff reassure me. You prepare a feast before me in plain sight of my enemies. You refresh my head with oil; my cup is completely full. Surely your goodness and faithfulness will pursue me all my days, and I will live in the Lord's house for the rest of my life.

Sheep are very interesting animals because they can't survive without a shepherd. They can't feed themselves; they can't protect themselves. Other animals can at least run away from predators but not sheep. They will idly stand by until their death. From this we get the phrase, "Like a lamb to the slaughter" (Is 53:7 NIV 1984). They are very fearful; one commentator said they are often fearful of running water or the dark. The shepherd must care for them like a baby. The shepherd would protect them with his rod and with his staff he would guide them. They are prone to go astray, and he must constantly bring them back.

Many have wondered if God made these dependent animals just as an illustration of how much humans need God. We are prone to fear: fear about the past, present, and future. We need a shepherd who calms our fear. We cannot direct our lives; we need a shepherd to guide us in the direction to go. We commonly go astray; we need a shepherd to save us from our wandering heart.

Our God is independent, and we are dependent upon him.

Applications

What are some applications we can take from this?

1. Understanding God's independence reminds us of God's love for us.

He didn't need to create us since he doesn't need anything, but God created us because he loves us. Paul believes this is a very important reality for Christians to understand. Look at what he prays in Ephesians 3:17–19:

that Christ may dwell in your hearts through faith, so that, because you have been rooted and grounded in love, you *may be able to comprehend with all the saints what is the breadth and length and height and depth,* and thus to know the love of Christ that surpasses knowledge, *so that you may be filled up to all the fullness of God.*

Paul prayed for the saints to know the depth and height of God's love. This is important because knowing that someone loves us will often radically change us. On earth, those who experience the greatest human love get married and spend the rest of their lives serving and getting to know one another.

When we know God's love, it should have a dramatic effect on us as well. Paul said this understanding would lead to our being filled with the "fullness of God." This means we would be controlled and empowered by him (cf. Eph 5:18).

No doubt, this is the reason Satan often attacks the love of God. In the Garden of Eden, Satan essentially was trying to make it seem like God did not really care about Adam and Eve. He said, "Did God really say you couldn't eat of every tree in the Garden?" He tried to make God's commands feel restrictive and domineering instead of loving. Then, he essentially calls God a liar. "You surely won't die if you eat from the tree. Instead, you will be like God."

Satan works overtime to keep us from knowing God's love. He plants doubt, anger, and fear in order to keep us from being transformed by it and saved by it. "For this is the way God loved the world: He gave his one and only Son, so that everyone who believes in him will not perish but have eternal life" (John 3:16).

Like Paul, we must pray for ourselves and others to have power to grasp God's love so that we may be transformed by it. God's independence reminds us about how much God loves us.

2.   Understanding God's independence reminds us of our need to be dependent.

Jesus said in Matthew 18:3 that in order for a person to enter the kingdom of God, they must become like a child. The word "child" in that context is used of a very young child, a toddler or an infant. He was saying that the person who enters the kingdom of God has learned dependence. An infant can't feed himself, clothe himself, guide himself, or protect himself. He is totally dependent upon his parents. In the same way, a person who is saved learns he can do nothing to get into the kingdom of God on his own; he is totally dependent upon God.

However, this is not only true in regards to salvation, but also in sanctification. In the next verse, Christ says he who becomes like this child is greatest in the kingdom of God (Matthew 18:4). The person who learns dependence upon this independent God shall be the greatest in the kingdom of God. This person knows his utter weakness and need for the Almighty.

How much do we need God? We can tell how much we need God by considering how much we pray, read the Bible, worship, or need to be around his people. This shows something of our dependence upon him. Some people can go weeks without reading his Word, which shows their lack of dependence, their lack of childlikeness.

In a very real sense we must learn to develop this. We must learn as a discipline to be like children in order to enter the kingdom. We can do nothing to save ourselves, and therefore, we must put our weight and faith fully on Christ. However, we must also learn this dependence to become great in the kingdom, essentially to grow.

God's independence reminds us of these things. It reminds us of his love for us and our dependence upon him. Let no one doubt how much he loves us, and let no one doubt how much we really need God.

God Is Immutable

Scripture would also teach that God is immutable. "Immutability means not having the ability to change."[30] This is a very important characteristic of God because it affects all his other characteristics. When we say that God is omniscient, that "he knows all things," it means he will always know all things. When we say he is loving, that means he will always be loving and always act in accordance with his love, even if that includes discipline. *Our God is always the same; he is unchangeable in his character.* Listen to a few texts that describe this:

> In earlier times you established the earth; the skies are your handiwork. They will perish, but you will endure. They will wear out like a garment; like clothes you will remove them and they will disappear. But you remain; your years do not come to an end.
> Psalm 102:25–27

As David looked at creation, he realized that this present earth and the way it operates will one day pass away. It will wear out like a garment or a piece of clothing and be discarded. But God, he remains the same. He does not corrupt or change; he will live and remain the same throughout eternity.

Listen to what God said through Malachi: "I, the Lord, do not go back on my promises" (3:6).

As we look at God, who is unchangeable, this certainly reflects a characteristic which we as humans do not share, for we are always changing. We are always growing in knowledge and wisdom. Our bodies are always changing with age or with every meal, but God never changes.

Sometimes, the fact that we are always changing makes it difficult to understand one another, even in the closest unions such as marriage. How can you really know someone completely if he or she is always changing? "Hold up, I thought you didn't like coffee." "I do now." "What? When did this happen?"

This may make it hard to know or understand one another, but it makes it easier to know God. He is the same yesterday, today, and forever (Hebrews 13:8).

Apparent Changes

God does not change, and therefore, we can trust that he will always act in accordance with his characteristics. Now with this said, some texts would seem to indicate that God changes. Let's look at a few:

> But the Lord saw that the wickedness of humankind had become great on the earth. Every inclination of the thoughts of their minds was only evil all the time. The Lord regretted that he had made humankind on the earth, and he was highly offended. So the Lord said, "I will wipe humankind, whom I have created, from the face of the earth—everything from humankind to animals, including creatures that move on the ground and birds of the air, for I regret that I have made them."
> Genesis 6:5-7

Genesis 6:6 says that God regretted making man. The KJV actually says he repented. Doesn't this seem like God changed his mind? He made men, and now, he is going to destroy them.

Certainly, we see God changing his mind, but only in accord with his characteristics. God is a holy God, and because he wants holiness, he will bring discipline or judgment. We see this characteristic throughout Scripture. One time he pronounced judgment on the city of Nineveh in the book of Jonah, and when they repented, he had mercy and removed the judgment (Jonah 3). This does not contradict God's immutability; it is a reflection of it. God is both holy and merciful. He always acts in accord with his characteristics. This is true because he is faithful and cannot deny himself (2 Tim 2:13). He does not change like the shifting shadows (James 1:17).

Unchangeable in Sovereign Plans

Not only is God unchangeable in his person but also in his sovereign plans. Listen to what he said in Psalm 33:11: "The Lord's decisions stand forever; his plans abide throughout the ages." His sovereign plans stand firm because our Lord does not change in his person and his characteristics. These plans include things like prophecy.

For example, Christ said he is coming back to take his people to himself (John 14:3). God said that in the end times, tremendous wars and natural disasters will occur right before Christ's coming (Matt 24:7, Rev 6:12-13). At his coming, people will be separated from one another and sent either into everlasting punishment or into everlasting life (Matt 25:46). We can trust these prophecies. His immutability means that we can trust the prophecies and plans he has shared with us in Scripture.

Unchangeable in Promises

Not only is God unchanging in his sovereign plans, but he is unchanging in his promises. Listen to what Numbers 23:19 says: "*God is not a man, that he should lie, nor a human being, that he should change his mind. Has he said, and will he not do it? Or has he spoken, and will he not make it happen?*"

How can we apply this?

This means we can trust every promise he has in Scripture because he is unchangeable. He is unchangeable in his person, in his plans, and his promises to us.

Does he promise to save you if you put your trust in the Son (Romans 10:13)? Then you can trust him. Does he promise to forgive your sins (1 John 1:9)? He will forgive. Does he promise to guide you throughout life as your shepherd (Psalm 23)? You can trust he will lead and guide you in the right paths because he is unchangeable; he is immutable.

This characteristic of God gives us great comfort. We can trust him because he doesn't change like man does.

God Is Good

Another characteristic of God is the goodness of God. What does the goodness of God mean? Tony Evans said this: "God's goodness can be defined as the collective perfections of His nature and the benevolence of His acts...God is good by nature and good in what He does."[31] Wayne Grudem defines it this way: "The goodness of God means that God is the final standard of good, and that all that God is and does is worthy of approval."[32]

God Is the Standard of Goodness

Essentially, this means that God is good in his nature, and everything that he does is good. We see this in how Christ responds to the rich man in Luke 18. The rich man approaches Jesus about how to inherit eternal life and calls Jesus good. Jesus responds with, "Why do you call me good? No one is good except God alone" (Luke 18:19).

Jesus declares that no one is good except for God alone. Christ says this to help the rich man recognize that Christ was actually God, and therefore, the only way to eternal life. In saying that only God is good, Christ essentially is saying that God is the definition of good. And therefore, it is by looking at God that we can determine if anything is truly good at all. This is very similar to how John declares that God is love (1 John 4:8). We cannot know what love is unless we know God. In the same way, we cannot know what is good unless we compare it to God. As Grudem said, "God is the standard of what is good and everything he does is worthy of approval."

In fact, *Scripture would declare that God's goodness is the sum total of his characteristics.* We see this in the story of Moses asking to see God's glory. Look at what Exodus 33:18–19 says:

> And Moses said, "*Show me your glory.*" And the Lord said, "*I will make all my goodness pass before your face*, and I will proclaim the Lord by name before you; I will be gracious to whom I will be gracious, I will show mercy to whom I will show mercy."
>
> .

God tells Moses that he will grant his request to see the LORD's glory. He will do this by causing his "goodness" to pass in front of him. What does God's goodness look like? It is described in Exodus 34:5–7:

> The Lord descended in the cloud and stood with him there and proclaimed the Lord by name. The Lord passed by before him and proclaimed: "The Lord, the Lord, the compassionate and gracious God, slow to anger, and abounding in loyal love and faithfulness, keeping loyal love for thousands, forgiving iniquity and transgression and sin. But he by no means leaves the guilty unpunished, responding to the

111

transgression of fathers by dealing with children and children's children, to the third and fourth generation."

The goodness of God is described in verses 6 and 7. It mentions his compassion, his grace, his patience (slow to anger), his love and faithfulness, and even his wrath. Everything that God does is good, and therefore, his goodness can summarize the rest of God's characteristics. We worship a God who is loving, patient, and compassionate simply because he is good. Even his wrath is a reflection of his goodness. Every person God loves, he disciplines (Hebrews 12:6). Everything God does is good.

This truth is a challenge to those who question God's goodness when they consider the many bad things that happen in life. They say, *"Why does God allow bad things if he is good? Why do innocent people die if God is good?"* It should be known that tsunamis, flooding, famine, government corruption, murder, family discord, etc., were never part of God's original plan. God did not create the earth with problems. When he finished his creation, he declared that it was very good (Genesis 1:31). It was not until sin came into the world that the earth developed its current problems. Therefore, the evil in creation must be attributed to someone other than God. He is sovereign and in control of everything, but evil cannot be attributed to him (cf. James 1:13). However, although God is not the author of evil, he nonetheless uses all things, including evil, for his glory.

God Is the Source of Good

> Every good and perfect gift is from above, coming down from the Father of the heavenly lights, who does not change like shifting shadows.
> James 1:17 (NIV 1984)

James says every good and perfect gift comes from above. When we look at family, friends, job, rain, sunshine, etc., they must all be attributed to God. He is the source of everything good. In fact, God gives these perfect gifts even to those who do not love him. Look at what Christ said in Matthew 5:45: "so that you may be like your Father in heaven, since he causes the sun to rise on the evil and the good, and sends rain on the righteous and the unrighteous."

God in his goodness gives rain and sunshine to the evil and good alike. Theologians have called this *common grace*. This is grace that God gives to all people, regardless of whether they accept him or not. Consider Acts 17:24–25:

> The God who made the world and everything in it, who is Lord of heaven and earth, does not live in temples made by human hands, nor is he

served by human hands, as if he needed anything, *because he himself gives life and breath and everything to everyone.*

Paul said to the Athenians, God gives "*life and breath and everything to everyone.*" He is constantly giving grace to people. He is constantly pouring out his goodness on the righteous and evil alike. Sometimes, people think of God as being stingy, as though we have to plead with him to give us good things. However, this is far from true. Look at how Christ described God's desire to give good things to his children:

> What father among you, if your son asks for a fish, will give him a snake instead of a fish? Or if he asks for an egg, will give him a scorpion? If you then, although you are evil, know how to give good gifts to your children, how much more will the heavenly Father give the Holy Spirit to those who ask him!
> Luke 11:11–13

Christ, while instructing his disciples on how to pray (Lk 11:1), encourages them to pray by teaching them about God's desire to give good gifts. He compares God's desire to give good gifts to a parent trying to feed his son. Typically, when you see parents trying to feed, especially, little children, the parent is not reluctant. The parent is running around, trying to get the child to take one more bite. They are trying to corral the child to open his mouth to eat what is good for him. Psalm 81:10 says, "…Open your mouth wide and I will fill it." It is the child who is reluctant in receiving the food, not the parent's reluctance in giving it. Jesus says if parents, who are evil, feed their children and give them good gifts, how much more will the heavenly Father give good gifts to those who ask him? God is not only the source of good things, but he desires to give his children good things, just like a parent does.

James 1:5 says this: "But if anyone is deficient in wisdom, he should ask God, who gives to all generously and without reprimand, and it will be given to him.*"* In describing God's desire to give wisdom to his children, especially when going through trials, he says God gives generously to those who ask him. In fact, James later says that many people have not received his gifts simply because they haven't asked (James 4:2). They are not willing to come to the source of all good things, and therefore, they receive nothing.

God is not only the standard of good things, but he is also the source of all good things, and therefore, we should seek his face for his blessing. Christ taught us in the Lord's Prayer to ask for our "daily bread" (Matt 6:11). Now, Scripture never teaches us that God wants to make us wealthy and healthy, but God is all about blessing us in order to better build his kingdom and bring glory to his name (cf. Gen 12:2-3). Those are the types of good things he wants to give. Jesus declared, "Blessed are those who hunger and thirst for righteousness, for they will be satisfied" (Matthew 5:6). God promises to fill our desire for truly good things—for things that are righteous.

God's Goodness Should Provoke Christians to Hedonism

What should the believer's response to God's goodness be? Paul said in 1 Timothy 4:4-5, "For every creation of God is good and no food is to be rejected if it is received with thanksgiving. For it is sanctified by God's word and by prayer."

Everything God created is good and is to be received with thanksgiving. Paul writes this in the context of teaching about false teachers who would forbid marriage and also certain foods (v. 3). Many Christians believe that if you are a Christian, you should not have any fun. Much of Christianity is full of all kinds of legalism, keeping Christians from things that God nowhere forbids in Scripture.

Let us remember that one of Satan's first temptations was to hinder the enjoyments of God's creation. He tried to implant the lie into the woman's head that "all the trees" of the garden were forbidden. In the same way, many Christians get snared by man-made laws that forbid them of the enjoyment of God's creation. Listen to what Paul told the rich people in Timothy's congregation:

> Command those who are rich in this world's goods not to be haughty or to set their hope on riches, which are uncertain, but on God *who richly provides us with all things for our enjoyment.*
> 1 Timothy 6:17

Paul told the rich people that God richly provides us with all things for our enjoyment. In a sense, Christians should have the most fun and pleasure in life. This is true because we see all these things as gifts from God. God wants us to enjoy food, he wants us to enjoy leisure, he wants us to enjoy the season of our youth, he wants us to enjoy work, etc. These are his gifts to us, created for our pleasure and enjoyment. Listen to what Solomon said, who was the wisest man on the earth:

> Then I realized that it is good and proper for a man to eat and drink, and to find satisfaction in his toilsome labor under the sun during the few days of life God has given him—for this is his lot. *Moreover, when God gives any man wealth and possessions, and enables him to enjoy them, to accept his lot and be happy in his work—this is a gift of God.* He seldom

reflects on the days of his life, because God keeps him occupied with gladness of heart.
Ecclesiastes 5:18–20 (NIV 1984)

Solomon said he realized (meaning this was something he did not previously understand) that it was good for man to eat, drink, and find satisfaction in his labor and that this was a gift from God (v. 18). He understood that wealth and possessions were given by God to be enjoyed (v. 19). These truths do not change the fact that Christians are called to be disciplined with their earthly treasures (Matt 6:19), and that in whatever we enjoy, we must not cause offense to other brothers (Romans 14:21). But in the confines of what is moral and loving, there is freedom and encouragement to enjoy. Christians are called to be hedonists as we enjoy God's gifts and always focus on the Giver of all good gifts.

God's Goodness Should Provoke Christians to Worship

How else should God's goodness affect us?
God's goodness should always provoke worship and thanksgiving. Because we realize where every good and perfect gift comes from, it should always prompt us to give glory to God. Look at what the Psalmist said:

> Give thanks to the Lord, for he is good, and his loyal love endures!
> Psalm 107:1

> Let them give thanks to the Lord for his loyal love, and for the amazing things he has done for people!
> Psalm 107:8

The believer should always respond with worship and thanksgiving to God since he is the giver of all good things. It should be noted, as we talk about God's goodness, that Scripture declares that God uses everything—all events— for the believer's good. Romans 8:28 says: "And we know that all things work together for good for those who love God, who are called according to his purpose."
Even though God gives a common grace, a common goodness, to all, he gives a special grace only to believers. For the believer, every event is working out to his good in order to make him into the image of Christ (cf. Romans 8:29). And for this reason, a believer should give thanks in every situation (1Thessalonians 5:18).

115

Like Job, the believer can give thanks even in difficulties because he knows God's hand and goodness are on it. Job declared, "The Lord gives, and the Lord takes away. May the name of the Lord be blessed!" (Job 1:21). Believers should respond to God's goodness by worshiping and saying, "Thank you."

How often do you tell God thank you?

God's Goodness Should Provoke Christians to Good Works

How else should God's goodness make the believer respond?

Not only should God's goodness provoke us to hedonism, thanksgiving, and worship, but it should also provoke us to practice good works. Listen to Christ's reasoning behind loving and blessing our enemy:

> But I say to you, love your enemy and pray for those who persecute you, *so that you may be like your Father in heaven*, since he causes the sun to rise on the evil and the good, and sends rain on the righteous and the unrighteous.
> Matthew 5:44–45

Christ essentially says, "Love your enemies and pray for them because your father also blesses both the good and evil. Do it because your father does it." God's goodness should draw his children to practice good works.

Galatians 6:10 says this: "So then, whenever we have an opportunity, let us do good to all people, and especially to those who belong to the family of faith." As the opportunities arise, let us do good to all people, but especially to those who are saved. Let us be zealous in our giving, let us be zealous in our praying, let us be zealous in acts of mercy because we have a Father who is always doing good. Let us, therefore, always do good as well.

What does God's characteristic of goodness mean?

God's goodness means that he is the standard of all that is good and that everything he does is ultimately good. Understanding this reality should make us seek to enjoy God's gifts. It should constantly draw us to worship, thanksgiving, and ultimately to practice good works, as children representing their good Father.

Conclusion

What can we know about God? He is spirit. He is a person, and therefore, we can relate to him and get to know him more. He is independent, and therefore, does not need a thing. However, we are dependent upon him for life, breath, and everything else. Also, he is immutable, unchangeable. This is a characteristic of

God we do not share, for we are always changing. But this means we can trust him. He will keep his promises and complete his plans because he does not change. Finally, we learned that God is good. He is the standard of good and everything good comes from him.

Review Questions

1. What does God being a "person" mean? How do we see this reflected in Scripture?

2. What does God being spirit mean and how should that affect our worship of him (cf. John 4:23)?

3. What does God's independence mean? In what ways are we and all creation dependent upon God, and how should this affect our daily lives?

4. What does God's immutability mean? In what ways does God's immutability comfort you?

5. What does the goodness of God mean? What should be our response to the goodness of God?

Prayer Prompts

- Pray that we would worship God in spirit with a right heart. Pray that God would reveal any areas in which our hearts are not pleasing to him (Psalm 139:23–24).

- Pray that we would have the spirit of wisdom and revelation to know God better (Ephesians 1:17). Pray that we would know his personhood and all his characteristics.

- Pray that we would be like little children (Matt 18:3–4) and that we would grow more and more in dependence upon God. Pray that he would deliver us from our pride and independence and that we would seek him through his Word and prayer.

Characteristics of God Part Two

What are some other characteristics of God?

We have looked at the fact that he is spirit; he does not have a human body. He is a person, meaning he demonstrates characteristics of personhood such as: personality, consciousness, anger, love, and jealousy. God is independent; he doesn't need anybody or anything. Finally, we saw that he is immutable. God doesn't change, and therefore, we can trust what he says and does.

What are other characteristics of God? We will look at four more in this chapter. God is eternal, omniscient, omnipresent, and omnipotent.

God Is Eternal

Another characteristic of God is that he is eternal. His eternality essentially means that he has no beginning and no ending. Everything else has a beginning but God does not. In fact, he is the one who created time. We see this in Genesis 1:1: "*In the beginning* God created the heavens and the earth." The question we should ask is, "In the beginning of what?" Moses, the author, is referring to time. When God created the earth, he also created time. Later in the Genesis narrative, he created the sun and moon specifically to track the time. It says, "Let there be lights in the expanse of the sky to separate the day from the night, and let them be signs to indicate seasons and days and years" (Gen 1:14). God is eternal, and he is the beginning of all things.

In fact, we see God's eternality in the covenant name he gave to Israel. Moses said,

> ..."If I go to the Israelites and tell them, 'The God of your fathers has sent me to you,' and they ask me, 'What is his name?'—what should I say to them?" God said to Moses, "I am that I am." And he said, "You must say this to the Israelites, 'I am has sent me to you.'"
> Exodus 3:13-14

"I am", or Yahweh, refers to the self-existent one, the one who always has been. I am because my parents were, but God just is; he is eternal. Jesus used this phrase to describe himself in his discussion with the Jews in John 8:57-58. It says, "'You are not yet fifty years old! Have you seen Abraham?' Jesus said to them, 'I tell you the solemn truth, before Abraham came into existence, I am!'" He was declaring himself to be the God of Israel (Ex 3:13–14), but he also was declaring that he always existed, as he had previously seen Abraham.

Jesus also declared his eternality in Revelation 1:8. Listen to what he says: "'I am the Alpha and the Omega,' says the Lord God—the one who is, and who was, and who is still to come—the All-Powerful!" Alpha and Omega are the first and last letters of the Greek alphabet. Christ was calling himself the beginning and the end. He was again declaring his eternality.

This characteristic is taught throughout the Scriptures. The Psalmist said this about God: "Even before the mountains came into existence, or you brought the world into being, *you were the eternal God*" (Psalm 90:2).

Reflected in the Way God Speaks about Time

Understanding God's eternality will help us better understand how he often speaks about time and events. Because he is eternal, he has a different view of time than us, and this often is reflected in his declarations.

Listen to what Peter says: "Now, dear friends, do not let this one thing escape your notice, that *a single day is like a thousand years with the Lord and a thousand years are like a single day*" (2 Peter 3:8). To God, a thousand years happens as fast as one day, but also, one day happens as slowly as a thousand years. His idea of time is very different from ours since he is eternal.

Not only does he see time differently, but he is outside of time. He sees the end from the beginning. Look at Isaiah 46:10 (NIV 1984): "I make known the end from the beginning, from ancient times, what is still to come. I say: My purpose will stand, and I will do all that I please." God stands outside of time, and therefore, he sees what happened in the past, what's happening right now, and what will happen at the end. His view is very different from ours.

Reflected in the Way God Speaks about Man

We see God's unique viewpoint in how he often speaks about man. Look at what he says to Jeremiah: "Before I formed you in the womb I knew you, before you were born I set you apart; I appointed you as a prophet to the nations" (Jeremiah 1:5 NIV 1984).

How can God know Jeremiah before he was born? Well, part of the reason is because God is outside of time. He sees Jeremiah before he was born and, at the same time, sees his end. He speaks blessing and purpose over his life before he was formed in the womb.

Look again at how he talks about all believers in Romans 8:29–30:

> *because those whom he foreknew he also predestined* to be conformed to the image of his Son, that his Son would be the firstborn among many brothers and sisters. *And those he predestined, he also called; and those he called, he also justified; and those he justified, he also glorified.*

In Romans 8:29-30, he says not only did he know and predestine believers before time (cf. Eph 1:4-5), but justified them and glorified them. Glorification specifically is an event which only happens at the rapture. It is then that we receive a glorified body. The believers in Rome that Paul was writing to had not yet died and certainly had not been glorified. However, Paul spoke about these events in the past tense. This is a reflection of God's eternality. They, as all believers, were predestined, called, justified, and glorified. These are words that only can be spoken by the Eternal One. They reflect his unique viewpoint. He sees the end from the beginning. In God's view, believers are already saved even before they are born. They are glorified in heaven with new bodies before they even died.

Certainly, we can get a very minute understanding of God's view in comparison to ours just by looking at a child and his father. The child drops his cookie and cries because it is lost, but the father does not cry because he knows he will simply buy the child another cookie. They have different views because the father has a broader view and more life experience than the child.

In an infinitely bigger way, God sees the end from the beginning. He knows what our present trials are meant to breed and develop in our lives and what their final end will be. He can speak comfort to us because he sees the end from the beginning. He looks at our situation from an eternal viewpoint.

Reflected in Prophecy

It should be added that this eternal viewpoint is also reflected in prophecy. Often when God gives a prophecy in Scripture, it can be confusing for us. Let me give you an example. Let's look at Isaiah's prophecy of Jesus's birth:

> *For to us a child is born, to us a son is given, and the government will be on his shoulders.* And he will be called Wonderful Counselor, Mighty God, Everlasting Father, Prince of Peace.

121

Isaiah 9:6 (NIV 1984)

In the first part of the verse, God prophesies about the coming messiah; however, he places Christ's first coming and second coming right next to one another. It says, "*For to us a child is born, to us a son is given, and the government will be on his shoulders.*" At Christ's first coming, he came as a child and a son, but the "government" being on his shoulders will not happen till his second coming, when he sets up his kingdom on the earth. This prophecy confused many of the Jews and that is why they rejected Christ. They were waiting for a conquering king, but Christ, at his first coming, came as a humble servant.

The confusion is taken away when we better understand God's eternality. God, who is outside of time, sees both of these events happening together, though there is at least two thousand years between the two comings up to this point. To God, a thousand years is like one day.

When we read the Scriptures that speak about God, we must be aware of his eternality lest we become confused. The fact that he is outside of time is seen in much of his speech and specifically his prophecies. We serve an everlasting God, an eternal God with no beginning and no end. When studying his revelation, we see this viewpoint as prevalent throughout Scripture.

Applications

How should we respond to God's eternality?

1.   Understanding God's eternality teaches us to be patient.

God does not operate according to our timetable. With Abraham, he promised him a nation and a land, but Israel did not become a nation for 400 years. Even now, they are still fighting for a land. In addition, the seed he promised Abraham wasn't born until he was 100 years old.

Scripture says many of the people of God did not receive what they were waiting for. Listen to Hebrews 11:13:

These all died in faith without receiving the things promised, but they saw them in the distance and welcomed them and acknowledged that they were strangers and foreigners on the earth.

God's timing is not our timing. David is still waiting for his seed to have an everlasting rule on the Davidic throne (2 Sam 7:13). Abraham is still waiting for his seed to have the land of Israel as an eternal inheritance (Gen 13:15). Understanding God's eternality should help us become more patient.

2. Understanding God's eternality should draw us to worship.

Our God is not like us. He is eternal and we are finite. This aspect of him should cause us to praise him. He is eternal.

God Is Omnipresent

Another characteristic of God is his omnipresence. This means "that God is everywhere present with His whole being at all times."[33] Listen to what David said about God:

> Where can I go from your Spirit? Where can I flee from your presence? If I go up to the heavens, you are there; if I make my bed in the depths, you are there. If I rise on the wings of the dawn, if I settle on the far side of the sea, even there your hand will guide me, your right hand will hold me fast.
> Psalm 139:7–10 (NIV 1984)

David said there was nowhere he could run from God's presence, not the heavens, not hell, not the sea, and not the sky. God was everywhere. In the same way, we cannot run from God because he is always present in all places, at all times.

Applications

How should God's omnipresence affect us?

1. God's omnipresence should give us a sense of accountability.

God is not just at church on Sunday or present when we read our Bible; he is there even when we sin and are in rebellion towards his plans for our lives.
We get a picture of this with Jonah, who runs from God's calling to preach repentance to the city of Nineveh. He goes out to the sea in a boat, but there God meets him in a storm. He was tossed into the sea by the crew to preserve their lives, but there God saves him by allowing him to be swallowed by a large fish. Jonah then fulfills God's original plan for him by calling Nineveh to repentance; however, he does it with wrong motives. Later, God meets with Jonah under the

shade of a vine in order to deal with the sin in his heart. There was no place to run from God, and this reality should give us a sense of accountability.

Listen to what James says, "Do not grumble against one another, brothers and sisters, so that you may not be judged. See, *the judge stands before the gates!*" (James 5:9). James commands these Jewish Christians, scattered because of persecution (James 1:1), to live without grumbling and complaining because the Judge was standing at the door. He challenges them to live holy lives because God was always near them, ready to discipline them.

God is omnipresent, he is everywhere, but he is in different places doing different things. He is one place to empower and comfort, and in another place to judge. Understanding this reality should create a sense of accountability in us.

2. God's omnipresence should give us encouragement to serve the Lord.

We see Christ speak of his presence as an encouragement to serve and do ministry. Look at what he tells his disciples in Matthew 28:19–20:

> Therefore go and make disciples of all nations, baptizing them in the name of the Father and the Son and the Holy Spirit, teaching them to obey everything I have commanded you. And *remember, I am with you always, to the end of the age.*

Christ gives his omnipresence as a comfort to the disciples and us, as we preach and share the gospel. If it is in front of a court or a classroom, if it's in a place where we feel scared or intimidated, we can take comfort from the fact that Christ is there with us to encourage and empower us.

It is probably this same type of encouragement we see given in the book of Philippians as the church is called to let their gentleness or care for others be known to all. Listen to what Paul says: "Let everyone see your gentleness. *The Lord is near!*" (Philippians 4:5).

Let this truth encourage us to be faithful in giving, serving, and ministering to one another because God's presence is near. He is near us to give us grace and strength. He is near to carry us and empower us to do his works. Our Lord is near.

3. God's omnipresence should give us comfort when discouraged.

The Psalmist said, "The Lord is near the brokenhearted; he delivers those who are discouraged" (Psalm 34:18). God is near us in our pain and near us in our distress in a special way. His omnipresence gives us accountability, gives us encouragement for ministry, and also comforts us in pain.

124

What about Hell?

What does God's omnipresence say about hell? Sometimes believers say *hell is the absence of God*. This is not true, for this would contradict the "omnipresence of God" and the "sovereignty" or "providence of God."

Colossians says he "holds all things together" (Col 1:17). Just as we cannot exist without God, neither can hell. He is even present there; he is present holding it together, but also specifically present for judgment. Consider Amos 9:1–4 and how it describes God being present to judge.

> I saw the sovereign One standing by the altar and he said, "Strike the tops of the support pillars, so the thresholds shake! Knock them down on the heads of all the people, and I will kill the survivors with the sword. No one will be able to run away; no one will be able to escape. Even if they could dig down into the netherworld, my hand would pull them up from there. Even if they could climb up to heaven, I would drag them down from there. Even if they were to hide on the top of Mount Carmel, I would hunt them down and take them from there. Even if they tried to hide from me at the bottom of the sea, from there I would command the Sea Serpent to bite them. Even when their enemies drive them into captivity, from there I will command the sword to kill them. I will not let them out of my sight; they will experience disaster, not prosperity.

When looking at God's presence, we must realize he is present everywhere. The question is, "What is he present for?" In hell, Scripture would say he is present to bring judgment instead of blessing. With those serving God in ministry, he is present to empower. With the brokenhearted, he is present to encourage.

How does God's presence affect you? Does it comfort you, does it scare you, or are you ambivalent to his presence? How can you grow to be more aware of God's presence? David was so aware of it he said, "I can't get away from you" (Psalm 139). Thank you, Lord, that you are always present.

God Is Omniscient

Another characteristic of God is his omniscience. If you break the word into two parts: "omni" means "all" and "science" means "knowledge." God has "all knowledge." A. W. Tozer's comments on God's omniscience are helpful. He wrote:

God knows instantly and effortlessly all matter and all matters, all mind and every mind, all spirit and all spirits, all being and every being, all creaturehood and all creatures, every plurality and all pluralities, all law and every law, all relations, all causes, all thoughts, all mysteries, all enigmas, all feeling, all desires, every unuttered secret, all thrones and dominions, all personalities, all things visible and invisible in heaven and in earth, motion, space, time, life, death, good, evil, heaven, and hell.

Because God knows all things perfectly, He knows no thing better than any other thing, but all things equally well. He never discovers anything, He is never surprised, never amazed. He never wonders about anything nor (except when drawing men out for their own good) does He seek information or ask questions.[34]

The Scripture teaches this in many ways. Look at what the writer of Hebrews says: "And no creature is hidden from God, but everything is naked and exposed to the eyes of him to whom we must render an account" (Hebrews 4:13).

Our God sees everything, and similar to his omnipresence, this is also meant to give us a sense of accountability. In fact, Solomon said this: "The eyes of the Lord are in every place, keeping watch on those who are evil and those who are good" (Proverbs 15:3). His eyes are everywhere, watching both the good and the wicked.

Different from Human Knowledge

What makes God's knowledge different from ours is the fact that everything we know has been taught to us. We learn by reading books, listening to our teachers, and looking at the Internet, but God intrinsically knows everything. Listen to 1 John 3:20: "if our conscience condemns us, that God is greater than our conscience and *knows all things.*"

Unlike us, he does not have to be taught because he innately knows everything. Listen to what Isaiah 40:13–14 says about him:

Who comprehends the mind of the Lord, or gives him instruction as his counselor? From whom does he receive directions? Who teaches him the correct way to do things, or imparts knowledge to him, or instructs him in skillful design?

He essentially says, "What school did God go to?" He didn't go to school. He knows everything there is to know.

Potential Events

In fact, his knowledge is so vast that not only does he know actual events but potential events. Look at what Jesus said to the cities that would not repent at his preaching and miracles:

> Woe to you, Chorazin! Woe to you, Bethsaida! If the miracles done in you had been done in Tyre and Sidon, they would have repented long ago in sackcloth and ashes.
> Matthew 11:21

Jesus said if the miracles that he performed in Korazin and Bethsaida, the cities of Israel, would have happened in Tyre and Sidon, they would still be standing today.

We should take great comfort in this. God knows what would have happened if you went to that university instead of this university, if you were raised in the U.S. instead of another country, if you married that person instead of this person. God knows all those things, and yet, chose or allowed you to be where you are (cf. Eph 1:11, Rom 8:28). This should give us great comfort, as we look over the events of our lives.

God Is All Wise

As we talk about God's omniscience, it should be noted that God is more than knowledgeable, he is all wise. This means *he always knows the best possible solution to every problem*. Look at what Paul calls God: "To the only wise God be glory forever through Jesus Christ! Amen" (Romans 16:27 NIV 1984).

He is the all wise God, and specifically for Christians, he uses this wisdom to guide every event in our lives for the good of bringing us into conformity with the image of his Son. Romans 8:28–29 says:

> And *we know that all things work together for good* for those who love God, who are called according to his purpose, because those whom he foreknew he also predestined to be conformed to the image of his Son, that his Son would be the firstborn among many brothers and sisters.

Were there possible better paths, better decisions we could have made? Certainly, in some cases. However, God, in his wisdom and sovereignty, chose to allow the events in our lives to happen, good and bad, for the purpose of making us look more like Christ.

127

This may be hard to believe as we look at some of the events and failures of our lives or other believers' lives, but it is true. God is all wise, and he uses that wisdom to make us more like his Son. This should give us great comfort and help us trust God more. Proverbs 3:5 says this: "Trust in the Lord with all your heart, and do not rely on your own understanding."

Intimate Knowledge

Not only does God know what potentially would have happened, but Scripture teaches he has an "intimate knowledge" of each person. He even knows the number of hairs on our head. Luke 12:7 says, "In fact, even the hairs on your head are all numbered. Do not be afraid; you are more valuable than many sparrows."

Listen to what David says:

"O LORD, you have searched me and you know me. You know when I sit and when I rise; you perceive my thoughts from afar. You discern my going out and my lying down; you are familiar with all my ways. Before a word is on my tongue you know it completely, O LORD.
Psalm 139:1–4 (NIV 1984)

He knows our thoughts, our sitting up, and our lying down. He is intimately involved in our lives because he loves us.

Applications

What does this mean for us? How can we apply the fact that God is omniscient?

1. God's omniscience means that we can be open with God in sharing our thoughts, fears, worries, and struggles.

In many of our relationships, we hide the truth. We often don't tell others how we are really feeling or share what is going on in our hearts for fear of rejection or misuse of the information. However, God already knows, and he understands our situation better than we do (Matt 6:8). Therefore, this should encourage us to share our most intimate concerns with God. Peter said, "by casting all your cares on him because he cares for you" (1 Peter 5:7).

God's omniscience is an encouragement for us to be transparent in our relationship with the Lord. He calls for us to cast our anxieties before him and to ask for our daily bread (cf. Matt 6:11).

128

2. God's omniscience should give us a sense of accountability, especially when we are tempted.

We may be able to hide our cheating, our lying, or our lustful thoughts from others, but we can't hide it from God. Not only does God know, but one day, he will even judge our "every worthless word" (Matthew 12:36). Listen again to what Hebrews 4:13 says: "And no creature is hidden from God, but everything is naked and exposed to the eyes of him to whom we must render an account."

God knows, and we will give an account to him for our sins. This should motivate us to live righteously and also to continually confess our sins daily before him. He promises to forgive the sins that we sincerely confess before him (1 John 1:9).

3. God's omniscience should continually draw us into prayer, as we seek him for daily wisdom.

Scripture teaches that God loves to give his children wisdom. James 1:5 says, "But if anyone is deficient in wisdom, he should ask God, who gives to all generously and without reprimand, and it will be given to him."

Solomon asked for wisdom, and God gave liberally. Solomon became the wisest man on earth (1 Kings 3). In fact, in Proverbs, he told us to seek after wisdom more than silver and gold (Prov 8:10–11). Solomon said this because God wants to give it; he wants to guide us into the right paths for our lives (Prov 3:6).

4. God's omniscience should continually draw us to the study of Scripture, for Scripture is the revelation of God's wisdom.

David said this about the Word of God: "The rules set down by the Lord are reliable and impart wisdom to the inexperienced" (Psalm 19:7).

Let us come daily to the Word of God so we can become wise. God's omniscience should continually draw us to seek the wisdom of the one who is all knowing and all wise.

God Is Omnipotent

What is another characteristic of God? Scripture would also teach that God is omnipotent, which means that God is all-powerful and able to do anything consistent with his own nature.[35] This is very important to us as Christians because when we look at how corrupt our nations are or how far away our friends or church communities are from God, we can take great comfort from this truth—God is all powerful. It simply means, "He's able" (Ephesians 3:20).[36] He is able to accomplish the impossible.

Power in Creation

Jeremiah said: "Oh, Lord God, you did indeed make heaven and earth by your mighty power and great strength. Nothing is too hard for you!" (Jeremiah 32:17).

Jeremiah declared that one of the greatest examples of God's power is the creation of the heavens and earth. He said, "Oh, Lord God, you did indeed make heaven and earth." However, it is not only the fact that he created the heavens and earth but, also, how he created them.

How did he create them? Scripture says that he just spoke. That is a lot of power. Some people on the earth speak and things get done. The president speaks and things start moving. But God speaks and the universe is created. That is how powerful God is. Listen to what David said as he meditated on God's power in Psalm 33:6–9:

> By the Lord's decree the heavens were made; by a mere word from his mouth all the stars in the sky were created. He piles up the water of the sea; he puts the oceans in storehouses. Let the whole earth fear the Lord! Let all who live in the world stand in awe of him! For he spoke, and it came into existence, he issued the decree, and it stood firm.

Ex Nihilo

But what is also so wonderful about God's creation of the earth is the fact that he created it ex nihilo. Ex nihilo is a Latin phrase which means "out of nothing." Now, if we were going to build a house, we would need bricks. If we were going to make a beautiful painting, we would need paint and canvas. But for God, he doesn't need any of those materials; he can make things out of nothing.

Listen to what Paul said about God's creative powers: "This happened because Abraham believed in the God who brings the dead back to life and who creates new things out of nothing" (Romans 4:17 NLT).

The writer of Hebrews said this: "By faith we understand that the worlds were set in order at God's command, so that the visible has its origin in the invisible" (Heb 11:3).

Our God can create out of nothing. You might say, "How is that possible? What about the law of thermodynamics? Energy is never created nor destroyed but only transferred." However, God is the one who created the laws of thermodynamics, and therefore, is not bound by it.

God is able. He is able to do more than we could ever ask or think (Eph 3:20). Christ said: "This is impossible for mere humans, but for God all things are possible" (Matthew 19:26).

Qualified by His Character

With God all things are possible; however, with that said, we need to qualify that statement. God's omnipotence is qualified by his character. Listen to what Paul said: "If we are unfaithful, he remains faithful, *since he cannot deny himself*" (2 Timothy 2:13).

This means that if we are faithless in trusting God, he will remain faithful because he cannot deny or disown himself, meaning his own characteristics. Man is fickle; we love this person today, and we hate the same person tomorrow. But God's characteristics are always the same; he is faithful. God is righteous, and he can never stop being righteous. He cannot disown himself.

Therefore, God's omnipotence is qualified by the rest of his characteristics. There are some things God cannot do. For example, he cannot lie (Titus 1:2), he cannot be tempted with evil (James 1:13), and he cannot deny himself (2 Tim 2:13). Also, he always works to bring glory to his name. Therefore, God's use of his infinite power is qualified by his other attributes.

What other ways do we see God's power?

We see his power in nature, as God destroyed the earth by flood in Genesis 6-7. We see his power over death, as he resurrected his own Son (Rom 8:11). We see his power over the devil, as the devil must get permission from him as seen in Job 1. We see his power to save, as he redeems souls all throughout the earth. His power is so great that Scripture says he sustains the earth by his Word. He is always holding everything together. Hebrews 1:3 says: "The Son is the radiance of his glory and the representation of his essence, and *he sustains all things by his powerful word.*"

Applications

How should we apply this reality in our lives?

1. In considering God's omnipotence, we should pray bigger and dream bigger.

It clearly should affect how we pray and how we live. Many have tiny prayers and tiny ambitions for their lives. They just want to live and make it through. Listen to what Matthew said about Jesus's hometown: "And he did not do many miracles there because of their unbelief" (Matthew 13:58).

Many people never see or experience God's mighty power. They never see God use them or others greatly to expand his kingdom, to lead people to Christ, or to encourage others. Why? It is because of their lack of faith.

It's hard to talk to some Christians because you wonder if they are worshiping the same God. "I can't serve. I can't talk to people about my faith. I am scared. I can't do this. I can't do that." Yeah, you can't, but what about God?

I fear many Christians are like the Jews from Christ's hometown. Because they knew Jesus and had been raised with him, they lost their wonder of him, and therefore, struggled with believing in him—struggled with their faith.

Listen to 2 Corinthians 9:8, "And God is able to make all grace overflow to you so that because you have enough of everything in every way at all times, you will overflow in every good work. "

Don't you want a God that can make all grace abound to you? He can make sure you always have what you need in finances, food, and other resources. He can make sure that you always abound in every good work. That's the life we should want. We should want an all-grace abounding life.

Paul gives this specific promise as an encouragement for believers to be faithful and to trust in God's goodness as they serve him, particularly in the area of giving (2 Cor 9:7). He wants us to know, "He is able." Look at what else Paul said: "Now to him who by the power that is working within us is able to do far beyond all that we ask or think" (Ephesians 3:20).

Our God can do more than we can ever ask or think. He is able. That is a God that we can and should believe in. That is the God we need, as we go through the trials and tribulations of life. That is the God we need, as we seek to see the nations know Christ. That is the God we need, as we pray for strongholds to be broken in our communities and our churches. We need to believe in a God that is able.

In fact, Scripture teaches that believing is the way to tap into this power. Jesus said this, "It was because of your little faith. I tell you the truth, if you have faith the size of a mustard seed, you will say to this mountain, 'Move from here to there,' and it will move; nothing will be impossible for you" (Matthew 17:20). Paul prays this in Ephesians 1:18–20 (NIV 1984):

> I pray also that the eyes of your heart may be enlightened in order that you may know the hope to which he has called you, *the riches of his glorious inheritance in the saints, and his incomparably great power for us who believe.* That power is like the working of his mighty strength,

which he exerted in Christ when he raised him from the dead and seated him at his right hand in the heavenly realms.

We need our eyes awakened to this great power as well. This great power is available only to those who "believe". Are you believing for God to work in your family, your church, your neighborhood, and your city? Are you trusting in God? Our God is able.
How else should we apply God's omnipotence?

2.   In considering God's omnipotence, we should be careful not to limit God.

Often when God calls us to do something, we try to limit him because we are focused on our inabilities. Moses, when he was called to lead Israel, began to question his abilities. He said, "I am slow of speech and slow of tongue." However, God confronted him with his omnipotence. "Who gave a mouth to man?" (Ex 4:10-12). Whatever God calls us to do, he will empower us to do. We should not limit God.
In addition, we should never give up on the most rotten sinner or the worst looking situation because he is able. We should never limit God.

3.   In considering God's omnipotence, we should always worship with thanksgiving.

His omnipotence is a wonderful characteristic, especially as you consider it in accordance with his love, grace, wisdom, and mercy. Our God is all-powerful, which is only fitting for one that is perfectly holy, wise, and gracious. We have seen a lot of power abused throughout history, but God never abuses his power. It is always used to the best and wisest end. For this reason, we should always worship and praise. Thank you, Lord!

God Is Merciful

Mercy by definition means "compassion or forbearance shown especially to an offender or to one subject to one's power."[37] Grudem defines it as "God's goodness toward those in misery and distress."[38] The Bible teaches us that God is a God of mercy. David said this in 1 Chronicles 21:13 (NIV 1984): "I am in deep distress. *Let me fall into the hands of the LORD, for his mercy is very great*; but do not let me fall into the hands of men."
How is God's mercy great? What examples do we see of this in Scripture?

133

One of the stories in the Bible that most clearly displays God's mercy is the story of Ahab. He, along with his wife, Jezebel, ruled Israel and caused them to sin against God more than any other king previously. They killed many of the prophets and hunted others, including Elijah.

One time, Ahab messed up so badly that God told him that he was going to kill him and his whole family, and that none of them would have proper burials. This was the worst king in the history of Israel. Listen to how Ahab responded and what God did in 1 Kings 21:25-29:

> (There had never been anyone like Ahab, who was firmly committed to doing evil in the sight of the Lord, urged on by his wife Jezebel. He was so wicked he worshiped the disgusting idols, just like the Amorites whom the Lord had driven out from before the Israelites.) *When Ahab heard these words, he tore his clothes, put on sackcloth, and fasted. He slept in sackcloth and walked around dejected.* The Lord said to Elijah the Tishbite, *"Have you noticed how Ahab shows remorse before me? Because he shows remorse before me, I will not bring disaster on his dynasty during his lifetime, but during the reign of his* son.

The worst king of Israel mourned before God, and God gave him mercy and favor because of it. Ahab, probably, will not be in heaven with us. No evidence indicates that he was a saved man, but because of his humility before God, the Lord had mercy on him. He did not give him what he deserved. This is amazing to consider.

Similarly, look at the display of God's mercy in the book of Amos:

> The sovereign Lord showed me this: I saw him making locusts just as the crops planted late were beginning to sprout. (The crops planted late sprout after the royal harvest.) When they had completely consumed the earth's vegetation, I said, "Sovereign Lord, forgive Israel! How can Jacob survive? He is too weak!" The Lord decided not to do this. "It will not happen," the Lord said. The sovereign Lord showed me this: I saw the sovereign Lord summoning a shower of fire. It consumed the great deep and devoured the fields. I said, "Sovereign Lord, stop! How can Jacob survive? He is too weak!" The Lord decided not to do this. The sovereign Lord said, "This will not happen either."
> Amos 7:1–6

The prophet Amos saw judgments coming to Israel, which prompted him to pray for mercy, and God relented from each of them. Another story showing God's great mercy is the story of the apostle Paul. Look at how Paul describes it:

even though I was formerly a blasphemer and a persecutor, and an arrogant man. But I was treated with mercy because I acted ignorantly in unbelief, and our Lord's grace was abundant, bringing faith and love in Christ Jesus
1 Timothy 1:13–14

As Paul said, he was shown mercy. The man, who hunted and killed Christians, by God's grace and mercy, became perhaps the greatest apostle.

In all these stories, we see that the character of God is merciful. He delights in forgiving people and being merciful to those who don't deserve it.

Applications

How should God being merciful affect us?

1. God's mercy should compel believers to seek God's forgiveness for their sins.

First John 1:9 says: "But if we confess our sins, he is faithful and righteous, forgiving us our sins and cleansing us from all unrighteousness."

This verse is abounding with mercy. When a believer confesses his sin, God forgives us for the specific sin and also cleanses us from *all* unrighteousness. When I confess known sin to God, he even forgives the sins I am unaware of. His mercy is abounding. He desires to give mercy to sinners.

Many saints walk around with condemnation about something they did or did not do in the past. This is because they don't truly have an understanding of God's great mercy. For that reason, they instead listen to and accept the condemnation of their flesh and the devil. Some have stopped going to church, some have stopped praying and reading their Bibles. They feel too guilty. Jesus took the penalty for our failures and our sins so that we could receive mercy. If we truly have a revelation of what Christ has done for us, we will run to the throne room of God constantly to receive grace and mercy in our time of need (Heb 4:16).

2. God's mercy should compel believers to pray for mercy over others.

If we understand God's mercy, it should cause us to seek and plead with him for mercy over others. At the cross, Jesus prayed, "Father, forgive them, for they don't know what they are doing" (Luke 23:34). He asked for mercy towards his persecutors. The Lord's Prayer says, "forgive us *our* debts" as it ushers us to

135

seek forgiveness for not only our sins but others (Matthew 6:12). In fact, listen to what Samuel said to Israel. "As far as I am concerned, far be it from *me to sin against the Lord* by ceasing to pray for you!" (1 Samuel 12: 23).

In 1 Samuel 12:19, the people asked Samuel to pray that they would not die for their sin of rejecting God and asking for a king. Samuel replied that he would not "sin" by failing to pray for them. We should see this as a duty from our Lord that we have been called to do, to pray for the sins of others, to pray for forgiveness, and to not sin by failing to do so.

This is often forgotten in our churches. If we truly understood this characteristic of God, we would plead with him for mercy on behalf of our nations, our communities, our families, friends, etc. The Lord's Prayer sets this as an abiding principle for the church: "Forgive us our sins." In fact, Scripture says that God seeks after people who will pray this way. Ezekiel 22:30 says this: "I looked for a man from among them who would repair the wall and stand in the gap before me on behalf of the land, so that I would not destroy it, but I found no one."

Do you ever ask for mercy over the sins of others? This is the same thing we saw the prophet Amos do for the nation of Israel (Amos 7:1-6). It is the same thing Moses did as he constantly asked God to forgive the nation of Israel for their sins (Ex 32:9-14). It is the same thing Stephen did as he asked for forgiveness over those stoning him (Acts 7:60). It is the same thing that Christ prayed for on the cross. "Father, forgive them, for they don't know what they are doing" (Lk 23:34). It is the same thing we must constantly do for those around us. God has called us to be priests that make intercession for people who are far away from God (1 Peter 2:9, 1 Tim 2:1-4).

3. God's mercy should compel believers to practice mercy.

The Beatitudes give mercy as a continuing attitude and action of the redeemed. Listen to Matthew 5:7: "Blessed are the merciful, for they will be shown mercy."

In the Beatitudes, Christ is teaching the attitudes that are within those who are truly part of the kingdom of God. With this specific attitude of mercy, Jesus gives a reciprocal promise. He says mercy will be given to those who have shown mercy. Those who practice mercy in their daily lives: forgiving others, giving to the poor, etc., will always receive mercy from God. But those who do not show mercy, God will show his justice. Matthew 6:15 says, "But if you do not forgive others, your Father will not forgive you your sins."

Certainly, this should be a warning to us. If we withhold mercy, God will withhold mercy from us—he will not forgive us. But even worse than withholding mercy, he will judge us for not being merciful as he is. Listen to the end of the Parable of the Unforgiving Servant:

Should you not have shown mercy to your fellow slave, just as I showed it to you?' And in anger his lord turned him over to the prison guards to torture him until he repaid all he owed. So also my heavenly Father will do to you, if each of you does not forgive your brother from your heart."
Matthew 18:33–35

Christ declared that torment awaited those who were not merciful. This torment is probably implemented by demons as seen with Saul and those in the early church who were handed over to Satan (cf. 1 Sam 16:14, 1 Cor 5:5, 1 Tim 1:20). How many Christians are under demonic torment because of a grudge they hold against somebody that hurt them or because they have been harsh towards others instead of merciful? This is a warning Christ gave to his apostles, and, certainly, we must heed it as well.

However, Scripture promises blessing to those who are merciful. Not only will they receive mercy but also other graces from God as well. Proverbs 19:17 says, "The one who is gracious to the poor lends to the Lord, and the Lord will repay him for his good deed." Proverbs 11:25 (NIV 1984) says, "A generous man will prosper; he who refreshes others will himself be refreshed." Reward and refreshment await those who relieve others of their pain through acts of mercy.

As we consider these promises, it should be a tremendous *encouragement to those serving in mercy ministries*. Mercy ministries often burn people out. However, God promises to reward and refresh us for our faithful service. Let us, especially, hold onto God's promise of refreshment. God refreshed Christ with the ministry of angels (Mark 1:13). He refreshed Elijah with food that was brought by ravens (1 Sam 17:4). David was strengthened in the Lord (1 Sam 30:6). We should hold on to God's promises.

Secondly, it also should be an *encouragement to those who are burnt out or too depressed to serve*. Sometimes, the best way to receive encouragement or relief is to have mercy on others, for then, God will have mercy on us. When discouraged, we often isolate ourselves and become consumed only with our problems. However, in ministering to others, God ministers to us. Christ promised that in taking on his yoke of service, we would find rest for our souls (Matt 11: 29). This is a challenge to the life of self-centeredness. It is a life about others that is full of refreshment and the blessings of God.

Understanding that this is a characteristic of God should cause us to practice the discipline of being merciful. By practicing mercy, we will look more like our Father who is great in mercy, and it also is the doorway to receiving tremendous blessings in our lives.

4.   God's mercy should compel believers to love mercy.

Listen to what Micah 6:8 (NIV 1984) says: "He has showed you, O man, what is good. And what does the LORD require of you? To act justly and *to love mercy* and to walk humbly with your God."

Micah says we must not only show mercy but love it. It is very possible for our acts of kindness and forgiveness toward others to have the wrong motive or simply to be done out of obligation. First Peter 4:9 says, "Show hospitality to one another without complaining."

God not only commands our actions but he commands our hearts. He commands us to love our neighbors as ourselves and to love him with all our heart, mind, and soul. God has called for us to love showing mercy because he loves showing mercy.

This is a wonderful characteristic of God that we must strive to show every day to those God has placed around us. God's mercy must also continually drive us to the feet of God in prayer to ask for mercy on us, our communities, our nations, and all those around us. Thank you, Lord, that you are God of mercy. Thank you, Lord, that you don't keep a record of sins, for who could stand your wrath (Psalm 130:3).

Conclusion

In order to know, understand, and better worship God, we must know his characteristics. We have seen that in order for us to understand how God speaks in Scripture, we must understand God's eternality. He is outside of time and knows the end from the beginning. He is omniscient; he knows all things and, in fact, is all wise. It is for this reason that we must continually seek his wisdom in every circumstance. God loves to give wisdom liberally and without partiality. He is omnipresent; he is in all places at all times. He is omnipotent, all-powerful. It is for this reason that we can pray to him and bring even our greatest problems before him. With man, many things are impossible, but with God, all things are possible. This should affect our prayers, it should affect our vision. We serve a God with unlimited resources. Finally, God is merciful, and we should be merciful as well.

Review Questions

1. What does God's eternality mean? How do we see God's eternality reflected in Scripture, and how should God's eternality affect our relationship with God?

138

2. What does God's omnipresence mean? How do we see this reflected in Scripture, and how should God's omnipresence affect us?

3. What does God's omnipotence mean? How do we see this reflected in Scripture, and how should it affect us?

4. What does God's omniscience mean? How do we see this reflected in Scripture, and how should it affect us?

5. Define the word *mercy*. In what ways do we see God's mercy reflected throughout the Scripture? In what ways is God calling us to demonstrate his mercy to the church and those around us?

Prayer Prompts

1. Pray that God would be great in mercy to your nation for its sins (Psalm 51:1). Pray a prayer of confession for specific sins and ask for God to bring revival.

2. Pray for God's power to be seen in a mighty way in the government, the school system, and the churches in your nation. Pray that God would draw people to himself.

3. Pray that God would pour out tremendous wisdom and power on your Christian leaders so that he may be glorified in the church. Pray for specific people as God puts them on your heart.

Characteristics of God Part Three

We have seen many of God's characteristics: he is a spirit, he is a person, he is independent, he is immutable, he is good, he is eternal, he is omniscient, he is omnipotent, he is omnipresent, and he is merciful. In this lesson, we will look at four more characteristics of God which are probably his most controversial characteristics. God is love, God is holy, God is wrathful, and God is sovereign.

God Is Love

Since love is a difficult concept to define, Grudem's comments are helpful. He says: "*God's love means that God eternally gives of himself to others.* This definition understands love as self-giving for the benefit of others. This attribute of God shows that it is part of his nature to give of himself in order to bring about blessing or good for others."[39] In fact, Scripture defines God as love, meaning he is the expression of love and all his characteristics flow out of this. Listen to what John said: "The person who does not love does not know God, because God is love" (1 John 4:8).

This means that it is impossible to truly know what love is unless we know God, for he epitomizes love. This is part of the reason that, looking at the world today, nobody has a good definition of love. For some, love is an emotion. If you watch any romantic comedy, without a doubt, there will always come the big question, "Do you love him?"

What does that mean?

Does it mean having butterflies in one's stomach? Does it mean two people have a good time together? We can only know what love is by looking at God. Moreover, since God is love, he was living out this love even before he created the world and everything in it. In John 17:24, Jesus says this: "Father, I want those you have given me to be with me where I am, so that they can see my glory that you gave me because you loved me before the creation of the world."

Before God created the world, he was living in a loving relationship with the Son and the Holy Spirit. In the Trinity, there has always been a perfect loving union between the members of the God-head.

141

We must ask the question then, "What is love?" We must know the characteristics of love in order to better understand God and to better love one another.

Scripture declares that since believers have experienced love, they naturally should demonstrate it to one another. John, who is often called the Apostle of Love and in his Gospel was identified as "the one Jesus loved" (John 13:23), said this in 1 John 4:11: "Dear friends, if God so loved us, then we also ought to love one another." Similarly, Jesus said this: "Everyone will know by this that you are my disciples—if you have love for one another" (John 13:35).

Supernatural love should mark believers. The world will know us by this love. In the New Testament, God's love is the word "agape." Because this love is so otherworldly, it was rarely used in secular Greek. However, this is the type of love that the world should see in Christians. They should see a love that doesn't make sense. It is sacrificial; it is forgiving; it blesses one's enemies; it is unconditional. It is a phenomenal love by which the world should be able to identify a believer.

What does this love look like—this agape love that defines God?

As the Trinity demonstrated love toward one another throughout eternity, Christians should also demonstrate this love. Its characteristics are as follows:

Agape Love Is Practical

God's love is practical. Listen to John again: "Little children, let us not love with word or with tongue but in deed and truth" (1 John 3:18).

Love is not just words, and it certainly is not just feelings. It is an act of the will. It is practical. Scripture does not say, "For God so loved the world that he felt all gushy inside." No, he so loved that he gave his only Son. It was practical. Look at what else the Apostle of Love says: "But whoever has the world's possessions and sees his fellow Christian in need and shuts off his compassion against him, how can the love of God reside in such a person?" (1 John 3:17).

Can this be true love John questions? How can a man love someone and not meet their needs? Surely, the love of God does not live in a man such as this. The fiancée of Solomon said something similar. Consider what she said: "He has taken me to the banquet hall, and his banner over me is love" (Song of Songs 2:4 NIV 1984).

The fiancée of Solomon declared that when they went out to eat, everybody could tell Solomon loved her. He pulled out the chair for her; he listened to her; he took care of her needs. She was the most important person in the room. His love was like a banner that everybody could see.

Sometimes, a female dates a guy who mistreats her, neglects her, and yet, still tells everybody how much they are in love. That is not love; love is practical. God's love is a giving love that provides for his people.

What else can we learn about God's love?

Agape Love Is Sacrificial

God's love is sacrificial. It cost him something. You can tell how much somebody loves you by how much they sacrifice for you. Is he or she willing to sacrifice time, money, hobbies, career, dreams, or friends for you? That is love. God so loved the world, he sacrificed himself. He sacrificed his Son. "For this is the way God loved the world: He gave his one and only Son" (John 3:16).

In fact, Christ demands that we love one another in the same sacrificial way. He said this: "I give you a new commandment—to love one another. Just as I have loved you, you also are to love one another" (John 13:34).

How did Christ love? He died for us, and therefore, we must be willing to die for one another as well. We see something of this sacrifice in the early church. In Acts 2, the wealthy sold all they had to take care of the poor (v. 44-45). This was a sacrificial love. It was a love that distinguished them from the world. It was agape.

Are we willing to sacrifice time, job, and career in order to love God and people? True love is sacrificial.

Agape Love Is Enduring

As a Reserve military chaplain, when talking to struggling married couples, I often ask them, "What happened? How did things get so bad?" Sometimes, I get the answer, "Oh, Chaplain, nothing happened. We just fell out of love." "You fell out of love? You woke up in the morning one day and it was just gone?"

This is how most people think about love. It is something elusive. It is here one day and gone tomorrow, but that is not what Scripture teaches us about true love. Agape love is everlasting. Look at what Scripture says about God's love:

> For I am convinced that neither death, nor life, nor angels, nor heavenly rulers, nor things that are present, nor things to come, nor powers, nor height, nor depth, nor anything else in creation will be able to separate us from the love of God in Christ Jesus our Lord.
> Romans 8:38–39

If you have been saved and have received God's love, life can't separate you from it, death can't separate you from it, and even demons can't separate you from it. The past, present, and future can't separate you from it. Nothing will be able to separate you from the love of God.

That is comforting. It tells us something about true love. It lasts. It lasts because it is an act of the will. I will marry you, and I am going to choose to love you forever, no matter what. That is God's love. It's enduring even through failures and hard times. Listen to what Paul says: "It is not glad about injustice, but rejoices in the truth. It bears all things, believes all things, hopes all things, endures all things" (1 Corinthians 13:6-7).

Love always perseveres. It is enduring. "And now these three remain: faith, hope, and love. But the greatest of these is love" (1 Corinthians 13:13).

Agape Love Is Selfless

First Corinthians 13:5 says, love "is not *self-serving.*"

See, most love is selfish. It is about what we can get out of somebody. If you call me, I will call you. If you give, I will give back. Human love is very selfish. If I don't get what I want, then I don't love you anymore. If you hurt me, it's over. On the contrary, true love is all about the benefit of the other person. It is not self-seeking. Philippians 2:3-5 says this:

> Instead of being motivated by selfish ambition or vanity, each of you should, in humility, be moved to treat one another as more important than yourself. Each of you should be concerned not only about your own interests, but about the interests of others as well. You should have the same attitude toward one another that Christ Jesus had

Our attitude must be the same as Christ. It must be selfless instead of selfish. This was the mindset that led Christ to die on the cross for the sins of the world. It was a mind that cared more about others and their benefit than his own. True love is selfless.

What else can we know about God's love?

Agape Love Is Unconditional

> But God demonstrates his own love for us, in that while we were still sinners, Christ died for us.
> Romans 5:8

God loved us while we were still sinners. He did not wait for us to clean ourselves up and to ask for forgiveness before he loved us. No, it was an unconditional and undeserved love. No strings were attached.

Our love is conditional. "I will love you if you do not cheat on me. I will love you as long as you treat me well, but when you fail me, we're done." However, we cheat on God all the time. In James 4:4, he called the church "adulterers," but that didn't stop his love for them. He would always love them unconditionally, with no strings attached. Our love must be unconditional as well.

> Therefore, be imitators of God as dearly loved children and live in love, just as Christ also loved us and gave himself for us, a sacrificial and fragrant offering to God.
> Ephesians 5:1-2

Agape Love Is Judicial

Some people have a hard time reconciling God's love and justice. But justice is an outworking of love. Listen to Hebrews 12:6: "For the Lord disciplines the one he loves and chastises every son he accepts."

Everybody he loves, he disciplines. For the believer, God will allow trials to happen in their lives to discipline them in order to make them more holy and righteous. Proverbs 13:24 says the same thing about parents: "The one who spares his rod hates his child, but the one who loves his child is diligent in disciplining him." Agape love is judicial.

Agape Love Is Emotional

Sometimes, believers talk as though agape love is only an act of the will. It is not; affections often come along with true love. However, emotions do not define love as many in the secular world would say. Listen to Philippians 1:8: "For God is my witness that I long for all of you *with the affection of Christ Jesus.*"

Paul said he loved the church with the affection of Christ. "Affection" was a physical word for the stomach or bowels. He loved the church with the same feeling Christ felt in his stomach for them. True love is emotional. "Rejoice with those who rejoice, weep with those who weep" (Romans 12:15).

Agape Love Is Wise

Paul said this:

And I pray this, that your love may abound even more and more in knowledge and every kind of insight so that you can decide what is best, and thus be sincere and blameless for the day of Christ.
Philippians 1:9–10

A person can love anything, even something that is bad for them. Love is so powerful it must be guided by *knowledge and depth of insight.* He essentially says, "I pray for your love to be wise so you can discern what is best."

Often "love" can lead us into things that are unhealthy for us and others, but agape love is a wise love. It is always seeking the best course of action for the other person and for ourselves.

I see that with my wife in parenting. Because my wife loves our daughter, she is very zealous in getting rid of anything that might be harmful. "Oh, that's plastic and it has chemicals; let's use something else instead." You often see this wise and discerning love with parents.

Agape love is not blind and it's not dumb. It's wise and discerning, seeking the best course of action for all.

Application

How should we apply the fact that God is loving to our lives?

1. God's love should comfort us and remove fear because God will always do what's best for us.

    Listen to Romans 8:31–32:

    What then shall we say about these things? If God is for us, who can be against us? Indeed, he who did not spare his own Son, but gave him up for us all—*how will he not also, along with him, freely give us all things?*

    God has already given his best in his Son; won't he graciously give us all things with Christ? Won't he provide whatever is beneficial since he has already given his best? If he closes the door for something, surely, it is out of love because he wants the best for us. Listen to what John said: "There is no fear in love, but perfect love drives out fear, because fear has to do with punishment. The one who fears punishment has not been perfected in love" (1 John 4:18).

    John says we should have no fear because of God's love. When love is perfected in our lives, it takes away fear. It takes fear away because we are convinced God loves us and is always working things out for our good (Rom 8:28).

2. God's love should produce the fruits of love in our lives.

Those who have truly received love should naturally demonstrate it to others. We often see this with children who are unruly. When children come from a background lacking love or filled with abuse, they often are abusive, unforgiving, and cold. But those raised in love, often are very loving.

Scripture says this should be true of every believer as well. Look at what John says:

> Dear friends, let us love one another, because love is from God, and everyone who loves has been fathered by God and knows God. The person who does not love does not know God, because God is love. 1 John 4:7–8

Everyone who loves like we have talked about is born of God and knows God. Whoever doesn't love is not from God. No matter what our background is, if we have been born again, the love of God has been shed abroad in our hearts (Rom 5:5), and it will be our tendency to love, forgive, serve, and bless others. Yes, we are not perfect yet, but we should be growing in this because we have experienced love.

Are you demonstrating love?

God Is Holy

What does God's holiness mean? John MacArthur said this:

> God is holy. Of all the attributes of God, holiness is the one that most uniquely describes Him. In reality, this is a summarization of all His other attributes. The word holiness refers to His separateness, His otherness, the fact that He is unlike any other being. It indicates His complete and infinite perfection. Holiness is the attribute of God that binds all the others together. Properly understood, it will revolutionize the quality of our worship.[40]

God's holiness is a summary of all his other characteristics. In fact, when the angels see God in heaven, they constantly declare his holiness. Isaiah 6:3 says this: "They called out to one another, 'Holy, holy, holy is the Lord who commands armies! His majestic splendor fills the entire earth!'"

The fact that they say it three times means that it is emphatic; it is something very important that we do not want to miss. This is not only important because it is a primary characteristic of God, but it is also important because God commands us to be holy like him. Look at what he says in Leviticus 11:44: "for I am the Lord your God and you are to sanctify yourselves and be holy because I am holy."

What exactly does it mean for God to be holy?

Holiness is a word that essentially means "set apart" and is closely connected to his righteousness. God's holiness is a picture of how righteous he is in every way.

Holiness Affects Man's Relationship with God

In fact, holiness is such a special characteristic of God that it affects our ability to be in his presence. When Adam sinned, he was kicked out of the garden, kicked out of the presence of God. Because Adam was not holy anymore, he could not dwell in God's presence.

With Israel, God set up a very elaborate system of sacrifices, washings, and cleansings in order for the people of Israel to live in the presence of God. They needed to be different from all the other nations around them because God dwelled in the midst of them. These regulations were meant to demonstrate that God was holy, set apart from everything common.

When Moses first met God on the mountain, God said to him, "Take your sandals off your feet, for the place where you are standing is holy ground" (Ex 3:5). God's holiness is such a defining characteristic it must affect how we relate to him. Listen to what David said: "If I had harbored sin in my heart, the Lord would not have listened" (Psalm 66:18).

David said that a person who is living in unrepentant sin, which primarily is a matter of the heart, affects the power of their prayers. God will not listen to the prayers of a person who wants to hang on to his sin and, yet, be intimate with God at the same time.

In fact, this is what the writer of Hebrews said: "Pursue peace with everyone, and holiness, *for without it no one will see the Lord*" (Hebrews 12:14).

He says, without holiness, no one will see God. Ultimately, without a righteous life, no one can have a relationship with God.

Atonement

Well, how does this work and how can man then come into God's presence since every man has sinned (Romans 3:23)?

In the Old Testament, God set up a sacrificial system to teach man about something called *substitution*. Because God is holy and righteous, he must punish sin. Therefore, God would symbolically punish the sins of man on a sacrificed lamb so the people could enter his presence and worship him.

In fact, many scholars see "substitution" implied in the very first death. After Adam sinned, God immediately killed an animal and clothed Adam and Eve (Gen 3:20). The wages of sin is death (Romans 6:23), and therefore, someone had to die for Adam's sin. From the very beginning, God showed mercy to man by providing a substitute.

However, the sacrificial animal could never take away the sins of the world; it was only a symbol of a future reality. When John the Baptist saw Jesus, he said this: "Look, the Lamb of God who takes away the sin of the world!" (John 1:29).

Jesus was the perfect lamb that all the sacrificial lambs always symbolized. He was man's substitute. It was only through his righteous life and death that man could be holy, and therefore, truly have a relationship with a holy God. In fact, the death of Christ was applied to all the ancient saints who died before Christ lived. Listen to what Paul said:

> God presented him as *a sacrifice of atonement*, through faith in his blood. He did this to demonstrate his justice, because in his forbearance he had left the sins committed beforehand unpunished— he did it to demonstrate his justice at the present time, so as to be just and the one who justifies those who have faith in Jesus.
> Romans 3:25–26 (NIV 1984)

Revelation 13:8 says the same thing: "and all those who live on the earth will worship the beast, everyone whose name has not been written since the foundation of the world *in the book of life belonging to the Lamb who was killed.*"

Christ's death was applied to ancient saints from the very beginning of mankind. The sacrificial lamb was only a symbol of how God was going to save people through substitution.

Justified by Christ's Death

Because of Christ's death, God justified us, meaning he made us "just as though we never sinned." Romans 5:1 says: "Therefore, since we have been declared righteous by faith, we have peace with God through our Lord Jesus Christ."

We can be made as though we have never sinned because of Christ's death, but it is because of his sinless life that righteousness can be applied to our account as we put our faith in him (Rom 3:26). Paul said this: "God made the one who did not know sin to be sin for us, so that in him we would become the righteousness of God" (2 Cor 5:21).

Not only did Jesus take the punishment for our sins, but he became sin and gave us his righteousness. In a sense, every time God sees us, he sees the righteousness of his Son. We have been made holy by the Son. This is the only way we can have a relationship with a holy God (Hebrews 12:14).

Holiness Identifies Believers

In the same way "holiness," being set apart, is a primary characteristic of God, it has now become a primary characteristic of every believer. In fact, in Scripture we are often identified by this holiness. We see this in the commonly used title "saints."

In Scripture, believers often are called "saints" which means "holy ones" because they are now set apart as positionally holy in Christ. We are holy because Christ's righteousness has been accredited to our account. Listen to how Paul commonly greeted Christians with this title:

> From Paul, an apostle of Christ Jesus by the will of God, to the *saints* [in Ephesus], the faithful in Christ Jesus.
> Ephesians 1:1

> Give greetings to all the *saints* in Christ Jesus. The brothers with me here send greetings. All the saints greet you, especially those who belong to Caesar's household.
> Philippians 4:21-22

Our identity is tied to Christ's righteousness and not to our failures. That is why God calls us saints, set apart ones. We must learn to identify ourselves and others in accordance with Christ's work and not ours. This would greatly change how we view ourselves and others. It also would change how we approach God. Our identification with Christ's righteousness should encourage us to approach the throne of grace with boldness to receive mercy and grace in our time of need (cf. Heb 4:16). We are set apart from the rest of the world as saints in order to know, enjoy, and represent God.

Holiness Should Be the Practice of Believers

Not only are we saints who are set apart as holy, but we must now seek practical holiness in our daily lives. It is both a matter of our position as saints and also a matter of daily practice. Listen to what Peter says: "but, like the Holy One who called you, become holy yourselves in all of your conduct, for it is written, 'You shall be holy, because I am holy'" (1 Peter 1:15–16).

Because God is holy, we must always seek to be holy in all our conduct. We must be separate from the world and godly in the same way our Lord is. If a person's profession of faith does not lead to a lifestyle of practicing holiness, then this person's position might not be that of a saint before God. *Position always leads to practice.* Listen to what Christ said in Matthew 7:21: "Not everyone who says to me, 'Lord, Lord,' will enter into the kingdom of heaven—*only the one who does the will of my Father* in heaven."

Those who have truly been saved and set apart will do "the will" of the Father. We should not think that the substitution we have encountered through God's grace is without effect. It affects how God sees us, and it radically changes the life of every true believer. Paul said this: "So then, if anyone is in Christ, he is a new creation; what is old has passed away—look, what is new has come!" (2 Corinthians 5:17).

The believer's position in Christ changes him or her into a new creation. They now desire righteousness where they previously did not, and they start to practice a life that is pleasing to God. This does not mean they will never sin, for that will not happen until the believer has a new body, without the indwelling presence of sin. But the true believer has received a new nature that compels him to seek to live a life of holiness (cf. Rom 8:13-14, 2 Cor 5:14).

Application

How does the believer grow in holiness?

1.   We must grow in holiness by studying God's Word.

How do we practice this practical righteousness? We practice it not only by knowing who God is and who we now are, but by growing in the knowledge of his Word (2 Pet 2:3). Listen to how Jesus prayed: "They are not of the world, even as I am not of it. *Sanctify them by the truth; your word is truth*" (John 17:16–17 NIV 1984).

We are set apart to be different by the Word, that's how God sanctifies us. Why then do many Christians not live holy lives? Much of it can be attributed to not living and abiding in God's Word. This is how he trains us; this is also how he gives us strength to be righteous. Many have problems stepping away from bad relationships or the entrapment of habitual sins. This power comes through his Word. Listen to what Paul said: "Every scripture is inspired by God and useful for teaching, for reproof, for correction, and for training in righteousness, that the person dedicated to God *may be capable and equipped for every good work*" (2 Tim 3:16–17).

Most Christians are not equipped. To be equipped means to be ready and empowered. This happens as we get into God's Word.

2. We must grow in holiness by the practice of righteousness.

James 1:27 says:

Pure and undefiled religion before God the Father is this: to care for orphans and widows in their misfortune and to keep oneself unstained by the world.

Religion that our Father accepts practices righteous deeds. Holiness has a positive element of righteous works such as caring for orphans and widows.

3. We must grow in holiness by keeping ourselves from sin and the world.

James 1:27 says:

Pure and undefiled religion before God the Father is this: to care for orphans and widows in their misfortune and *to keep oneself unstained by the world.*

The negative element of holiness is keeping oneself from the pollution of the world. We must not be conformed to this world, but transformed by the renewing of our minds (Romans 12:2). God is holy, and therefore, we must be holy.

God Is Wrathful

Very close to God's holiness is his wrath. Because he is holy, he cannot tolerate sin. We often don't like to talk about his wrath, but the Scripture is full of the wrath of God. "In fact, the Bible has more to say about God's wrath than it does about His love."[41] What exactly is the wrath of God? Tony Evans defines the wrath of God as: "His necessary, just, and righteous retribution against sin." [42]

Examples

What examples do we see of God's wrath?

We see his wrath in cursing creation after Adam's sin in the Garden of Eden (Gen 3:17). We see his wrath in destroying the earth by water in the Genesis flood (Gen 6 and 7). We see his wrath in the destruction of Sodom and Gomorrah (Gen 19). We see his wrath throughout the OT in the discipline of Israel for not obeying him; they were persecuted by their enemies and eventually exiled from the land.

Oftentimes, people try to say his wrath is only seen in the Old Testament and not in the New, but this is not true. It is clearly seen throughout the New Testament as well. In the early church, Ananias and Sapphira were both killed for lying about the profit made from selling their land (Acts 5:1-10). In Corinth, people were sick and dying because God judged them for dishonoring the Lord's Supper (1 Cor 11:30).

We see his wrath through church discipline as the apostles and the early church handed people over to Satan, which seemed to mean kicking them out of the church (1 Cor 5:5, 1 Tim 1:20). Scripture says that, "God is a just judge; he is angry throughout the day" (Psalm 7:11).

How do we see God's wrath every day?

1. God's wrath is seen in handing people over to the sin they desire and allowing them to reap the consequences of it.

Sometimes, in order to teach a child, a parent will allow his son or daughter to experience the consequences of disobedience. How does God do that with the world? Consider what Romans 1:18 says: "*For the wrath of God is revealed* from heaven against all ungodliness and unrighteousness of people who suppress the truth by their unrighteousness."

It says the wrath of God is being revealed. But how is it revealed? As we read the chapter, it tells us about how God allows people to practice idolatry, sexual immorality, homosexuality, and all types of other sin. He gives a society over to their desires. Some of the worst discipline is to live in a corrupt society, with corrupt leadership, and corrupt people around us. God essentially says, "Okay, fine. Do what you want." Look at how the wrath of God is displayed in this text:

> And just as they did not see fit to acknowledge God, God gave them over to a depraved mind, to do what should not be done. They are filled with every kind of unrighteousness, wickedness, covetousness, malice. They are rife with envy, murder, strife, deceit, hostility. They are gossips, slanderers, haters of God, insolent, arrogant, boastful, contrivers of all sorts of evil, disobedient to parents, senseless, covenant-breakers,

153

heartless, ruthless. Although they fully know God's righteous decree that those who practice such things deserve to die, they not only do them but also approve of those who practice them.
Romans 1:28–32

Sometimes we experience God's wrath when he gives us over to the sin we desire, and we, therefore, experience the consequences of that sin.

2. God's wrath is seen in regular discipline for sin.

We see this especially with Christians. Hebrews 12:10 says, "For they disciplined us for a little while as seemed good to them, but he does so for our benefit, that we may share his holiness." God disciplines his children so that they can grow in holiness.

David said this: "It was good for me to suffer, so that I might learn your statutes" (Psalm 119:71). It was through affliction that David learned God's Word and learned how to obey it. God often disciplines people like a parent to deter them from sin and to promote righteousness. Certainly, we see this with government, which is a reflection of God's authority. Romans 13:1–4 says this:

> Let every person be subject to the governing authorities. For there is no authority except by God's appointment, and the authorities that exist have been instituted by God. So the person who resists such authority resists the ordinance of God, and those who resist will incur judgment (for rulers cause no fear for good conduct but for bad). Do you desire not to fear authority? Do good and you will receive its commendation, for it is God's servant for your good. But if you do wrong, be in fear, for it does not bear the sword in vain. It is God's servant to administer retribution on the wrongdoer.

Through government, God commends the righteous and punishes the wrongdoer. This is to be done in reverence of God who is the ultimate authority.

We will ultimately see God's disciplinary wrath during the tribulation period. Sometimes, it is called the "wrath of the Lamb" or the wrath of Christ (Rev 6:16).

> Then the kings of the earth, the very important people, the generals, the rich, the powerful, and everyone, slave and free, hid themselves in the caves and among the rocks of the mountains. They said to the mountains and to the rocks, "Fall on us and hide us from the face of the one who is

154

seated on the throne and from the *wrath of the Lamb,* because the great day of their wrath has come, and who is able to withstand it?"
Revelation 6:15–17

Revelation 3:10 describes the tribulation further. It says, "Because you have kept my admonition to endure steadfastly, I will also keep you from the hour of testing that is about to come on the whole world to test those who live on the earth."

The tribulation will be a time of trial the whole world will go through. God will bring his wrath on the earth in retribution for all the sins that have been committed.

3. God's wrath is seen in "eternal wrath."

John 3:36 says, "The one who believes in the Son has eternal life. The one who rejects the Son will not see life, but *God's wrath remains on him."*

The wrath of God abides on the unbeliever. Mankind is under a form of wrath right now for not believing in the Son, but one day, this will become an eternal wrath. Revelation 20:15 says this: "If anyone's name was not found written in the book of life, that person *was thrown into the lake of fire."*

This judgment is eternal. It will be the final display of God's wrath, as rebellious mankind, Satan, and his angels are tormented throughout eternity (Matt 25:41). This wrath will have varying degrees of punishment based on the amount of knowledge one had and also the amount of rebellion one committed. Look at how Christ described this:

> That servant who knew his master's will but did not get ready or do what his master asked will receive a severe beating. But the one who did not know his master's will and did things worthy of punishment will receive a light beating. From everyone who has been given much, much will be required, and from the one who has been entrusted with much, even more will be asked.
> Luke 12:47–48

Those who know God's will and do not obey it, will have a greater judgment and those who don't know God's will and disobey, will have a less strict judgment. There will be varying degrees of punishment in hell in the same way that there will be varying degrees of reward in heaven (1 Cor 3:12-15).

This seems to be exactly what the author of Hebrews is describing in Hebrews 10, as he mentions those who had received the knowledge of the truth but rejected it. Listen to what he says:

155

For if we deliberately keep on sinning after receiving the knowledge of the truth, no further sacrifice for sins is left for us, but only a certain fearful expectation of judgment and a fury of fire that will consume God's enemies. Someone who rejected the law of Moses was put to death without mercy on the testimony of two or three witnesses. *How much greater punishment do you think that person deserves who has contempt for the Son of God, and profanes the blood of the covenant that made him holy, and insults the Spirit of grace?* For we know the one who said, "Vengeance is mine, I will repay," and again, "The Lord will judge his people." *It is a terrifying thing to fall into the hands of the living God.* Hebrews 10:26–31

Those who had received the truth and then ultimately rejected it through apostasy will receive a greater punishment from God.

Applications

How should we respond to the wrath of God?

1. God's wrath should create a holy fear in us.

Scripture says, "For our God is indeed a devouring fire" (Heb 12:29). He is not only a God of love but of wrath, and therefore, we should fear and revere him.
Hebrews 12:28–29 says,

So since we are receiving an unshakable kingdom, let us give thanks, and through this let us *offer worship pleasing to God in devotion and awe.* For our "God is indeed a devouring fire".

2. God's wrath should encourage us to cleanse ourselves from every form of sin.

Second Corinthians 7:1 says,

Therefore, since we have these promises, dear friends, let us cleanse ourselves from everything that could defile the body and the spirit, *and thus accomplish holiness out of reverence for God.*

We must pursue holiness because we fear God. Those who do not fear God, will not.

3. God's wrath should be modeled.

An aspect of God's wrath should be modeled by believers. Not all anger is sinful. Sometimes, it is sinful for us to not be angry about things that are happening in the world. To not be angry would be to fall short of the glory of God (Romans 3:23). In Mark 11, Christ went into the temple, used a whip and flipped tables because the leaders were cheating people and dishonoring God. He said, "Is it not written: 'My house will be called a house of prayer for all nations'? But you have turned it into a den of robbers!" (Mark 11:17).

A righteous anger must be developed in the life of those who follow Christ and who are seeking to imitate him (Eph 5:1).

How do we discern if we have a righteous anger or a selfish anger (James 1:19-20)?

Certainly, we can learn to distinguish by a careful study of Christ. When people were being cheated and God was being dishonored, he was like a lion. He pulled out the whip and was aggressive with a righteous anger. But when he was dishonored, he was like a lamb to the slaughter. Let's look at 1 Peter 2:21–23:

> For to this you were called, since *Christ also suffered for you, leaving an example for you to follow in his steps.* "He committed no sin nor was deceit found in his mouth". When he was maligned, *he did not answer back; when he suffered, he threatened no retaliation, but committed himself to God who judges justly.*

When Christ was treated unjustly, he turned the other cheek, and was silent. But when others were mistreated, he demonstrated righteous anger. Certainly, there is a place for defending our rights and going to the authorities. Paul himself appealed to Caesar when he was being mistreated in prison (Acts 25:11). We have that right as well, but there is also a time to be silent and submit to harsh treatment (1 Cor 6:7). We must through prayer and wise counsel discern those times.

However, we also must discern when to be righteously angry. Anger is a characteristic of God that has been given to us in order for us to seek justice in the same way he does. It is needed to fight against religious corruption, unethical law practices, trafficking, abortion, racism, etc., and it is even needed for us to faithfully pray against these things. We must develop a holy anger for it is a characteristic of God.

157

God Is Sovereign

Is God in control of all things and if so to what extent? This is one of the most controversial aspects of the characteristics of God. Christians are divided on this issue. Some declare if God is totally in control of everything, humans are just robots with no free will.

What exactly does the Scripture say about God being in control of everything, and how does this correspond with free will and the presence of evil and Satan in the world?

Scriptures Teaches God's Sovereignty

God is in control of all things. Listen to what Ephesians 1:11 says: "In Christ we too have been claimed as God's own possession, since we were predestined according to the one purpose of him *who accomplishes all things according to the counsel of his will.*"

It does not say that God works some things according to the counsel of his will, but *all things*. Everything somehow is moving in line with God's plan, including my writing this, and your reading and thinking about it. Everything is working in conformity with the plan of God. This is a mystery, but it is clearly taught in Scripture.

How do we see this sovereignty expressed and explained in Scripture?

Romans 8:28 tells us something about his purposes in controlling all events. It says, "And we know that *all things work together for good for those who love God*, who are called according to his purpose." God controls events in such a way that they always work to the good of his children.

For this reason, the doctrine of the sovereignty of God gives Christians great confidence since nothing happens outside of his control. We know that Satan isn't in control, the government isn't in control, terrorists aren't in control— God is. He is even in *control of trials*. Scripture says he holds the temperature gauge on our trials so that we are never tempted above what we are able. Look at 1 Corinthians 10:13:

> No trial has overtaken you that is not faced by others. And God is faithful: *He will not let you be tried beyond what you are able to bear,* but with the trial will also provide a way out so that you may be able to endure it.

How else do we see God's sovereignty throughout Scripture?

We see God in *control of each man's time on the earth*. Listen to what David said, "Your eyes saw me when I was inside the womb. All the days ordained for me were recorded in your scroll before one of them came into existence" (Psalm 139:16).

What about a chance death or a sickness that takes somebody away? David said these were "ordained." The word "ordained" eliminates the possibility of chance. It means God is in control of our days on the earth and that they were written out beforehand.

We see God clearly described as *in control of nature*. What did Christ teach in Matthew 6 about nature? Jesus said that God clothes the lilies of the field and he feeds the birds of the air.

> Look at the birds in the sky: They do not sow, or reap, or gather into barns, yet your heavenly Father feeds them. Aren't you more valuable than they are? And which of you by worrying can add even one hour to his life? Why do you worry about clothing? Think about how the flowers of the field grow; they do not work or spin.
> Matthew 6:26–28

This might seem strange to us for we know all these things happen naturally. Natural processes happening in the world allow these things to happen. However, Scripture would say these things are not happening apart from God's sovereignty; he is actually working in his creation and never losing control.

We also see this in what Paul taught about Christ in Colossians 1:17: "He himself is before all things and *all things are held together in him."*

Is God a clockmaker that winds up creation and allows it to continually work on its own? Or is he somehow vitally involved and always in control of it? Paul says Christ is always holding everything together, and, in Acts, he even declares that each breath of man comes from God. "Nor is he served by human hands, as if he needed anything, because *he himself gives life and breath and everything to everyone*" (Acts 17:25).

What else does Scripture say God controls?

Scripture declares that God is in *control of random events* such as the rolling of dice. "The dice are thrown into the lap, but their every decision is from the Lord" (Prov 16:33).

It even declares that *God is in control of kings* and that he turns their hearts in whatever direction he wills. "The king's heart is in the hand of the Lord like channels of water; he turns it wherever he wants" (Prov 21:1).

God is in control of *disasters*. Look at what Amos says: "If an alarm sounds in a city, do people not fear? *If disaster overtakes a city, is the Lord not responsible?*" (3:6). Sometimes the disasters are directly a judgment for sin as seen in the Genesis flood and sometimes not as with Job and Joseph. Either way, Scripture would say that God is in control of these events.

159

God is in control of trials, each person's time on the earth, nature, random events, the heart of kings, and even disasters.

God's Control over Men and Evil

What about the decisions of men and evil?

Yes, Scripture also teaches that God is in control of the decisions of men and evil. In fact, it would seem to indicate that God is the first cause of these things even though he cannot be blamed because of the secondary causes. Theologians have called this the *law of concurrence*.[43] It is possible for something to have many causes. The bird has food because he went and caught the food, but God ultimately provided it for him. Satan tempted man, but God was in control as seen in the story of Job. There are many causes. Wayne Grudem's comments are helpful:

> In this way it is possible to affirm that in one sense events are fully (100 percent) caused by God and fully (100 percent) caused by the creature as well. However, divine and creaturely causes work in different ways. The divine cause of each event works as an invisible, behind-the-scenes, directing cause and *therefore could be called the "primary cause" that plans and initiates everything that happens* (emphasis mine).[44]

In one sense, Scripture shows God as being the first cause of events simply because nothing can happen apart from his sovereign purpose and his sustaining power (cf. Eph 1:11, Heb 1:3). God sustains "all things by his powerful word" (Heb 1:3). However, again, Scripture would teach this without placing the blame on God for sin or evil (James 1:13). The sovereignty of God and, yet, human responsibility is a mystery, but Scripture teaches them both. It is a paradox—two seemingly contradicting realities.

Pharaoh's Hardened Heart

Let's consider a familiar passage with Pharaoh, the king of Egypt. Moses asks Pharaoh to let the people of Israel go even though God had already predicted that he would harden Pharaoh's heart (Ex 4:21). Then later, the narrator gives two seemingly conflicting statements. It says that Pharaoh hardened his own heart in Exodus 8:15. "But when Pharaoh saw that there was relief, *he hardened his heart* and did not listen to them, just as the Lord had predicted." And later, it says that God hardened his heart in Exodus 14:8. "*But the Lord hardened the heart of*

Pharaoh king of Egypt, and he chased after the Israelites. Now the Israelites were going out defiantly."

Which is the first cause, God or Pharaoh? It teaches that both were responsible in some way or another. But since God is the sovereign, he is ultimately in control, and therefore, the first cause (cf. Prov 21:1).

Why does God harden his heart? This is what Paul says about the event in Romans 9:17–18:

> For the scripture says to Pharaoh: "For this very purpose I have raised you up, that I may demonstrate my power in you, and that my name may be proclaimed in all the earth." So then, God has mercy on whom he chooses to have mercy, and he hardens whom he chooses to harden.

Paul quotes a verse in Exodus saying God hardened Pharaoh's heart for his purposes, which was that his name might be proclaimed throughout all the earth. God was the first cause. In fact, we see that when Israel later entered Jericho, the people there were afraid. They had heard about God parting the Red Sea and his destruction of the Egyptians (Josh 2:10). Pharaoh's sin was used to bring glory to God.

This might give us an answer to the question, "If God is in control, why did he allow sin in the first place?" In some way or another, God's characteristics and his glory are more powerfully displayed with the reality of sin. Like a diamond against a black cloth—God's beauty is more clearly displayed against the darkness. If there was no sin, then we would never fully know the concept of God's holiness and his anger against sin. We would never fully know his characteristics of patience, grace, or mercy.

Now, the reality of God's sovereignty, as seen in his hardening Pharaoh's heart, might naturally provoke men to anger or resentment. Paul, in fact, expected that some reading his teachings about Pharaoh and God's sovereignty might respond that way. They would say, "How can God hold us accountable or blame us if he is in control of everything?" Look at his reply:

> You will say to me then, "Why does he still find fault? For who has ever resisted his will?" But who indeed are you—a mere human being—to talk back to God? "Does what is molded say to the molder, "Why have you made me like this?" Has the potter no right to make from the same lump of clay one vessel for special use and another for ordinary use?
> Romans 9:19–21

161

Paul simply replies to their confusion with the doctrine of God's sovereignty. The Lord is God, he is the Creator, and he does what he wants. Who are you to say to the Creator, why did you make me like this?

God's Kingship

Listen to what David says in Psalm 47:2: "For the sovereign Lord is awe-inspiring; he is *the great king who rules the whole earth!*"

See, this concept of God being king over the whole earth is very hard, especially for westerners, to accept because we have never had a king. But a true monarchy is not a democracy, where people get to choose. In a true monarchy, the king is in total control and does what he wishes. This is what Psalm 115:3 says: "Our God is in heaven! *He does whatever he pleases!*"

Now with that said, we can take comfort in all the other characteristics of God. He is all wise; he is good; he is righteous. He works all things out for the good. There is no better person to be in total control. That should comfort us.

With that said, God's sovereignty somehow works together with man's free will, as we saw in the case of Pharaoh. God hardened Pharaoh's heart, and yet, Pharaoh hardened his own heart. Scripture says that even though God was in control and the first cause, Pharaoh was responsible—he made a choice.

We make choices every day, and if we sin, we are to blame. But somehow with that reality, Scripture would say God was in control. The mystery is in how these two truths can coexist. It doesn't make sense to us; however, we can be sure they make perfect sense to God.

This again reflects the *law of concurrence*; there are at least two causes. God acted and man acted. Which is the primary cause? Scripture would say God is, and therefore, there is a sense in which his will is always done (Eph 1:11).

God's Sovereignty and Satan

Now, here is the next question, we have looked at God's sovereignty in considering man's free will and specifically sin, but what about God's sovereignty over Satan? The Bible also teaches that God is in control of Satan. Let's look at a story with David in 2 Samuel 24:1: "*The Lord's anger again raged against Israel, and he incited David against them, saying*, 'Go count Israel and Judah.'"

This is the narrative of David counting all the soldiers in Israel and God punishing Israel because of David's pride. In the 2 Samuel narrative, it says God "incited David against them." However, when you look at the parallel passage in Chronicles, it gives a different cause behind David's census. It says in 1 Chronicles

21:1 (NIV 1984): "*Satan rose up against Israel and incited David* to take a census of Israel."

It says Satan incited David. Which one did it, God or Satan? They both did, but again, Scripture would say God is sovereign; he is the ruler who is always working out his plans on the earth. Therefore, he is the first cause. Satan is the second cause. Scripture would teach that God is the cause because nothing can happen apart from his sovereignty. However, the paradox is that Scripture would also teach that God cannot be blamed and that he tempts no man (James 1:13). It would attribute blame both to Satan and David for they both chose to sin. This is a mystery. In some way, God's sovereignty over all things does not relinquish the blame of demons or mankind.

We see a similar case in the story of Job. In chapter 1, Satan asked God for permission to touch Job, but when Job had lost everything, Job declared God was the cause of his loss. Look at what he says:

> He said, "Naked I came from my mother's womb, and naked I will return there. *The Lord gives, and the Lord takes away.* May the name of the Lord be blessed!" In all this Job did not sin, nor did he charge God with moral impropriety.
> Job 1:21–22

Job sees God in control of his loss and worships him. The author quickly adds, "In all this Job did not sin, nor did he charge God with moral impropriety."

In addition, we see another story that teaches this truth in Micaiah's vision that was shared with both King Ahab and King Jehoshaphat. Listen to the prophecy:

> Micaiah said, "That being the case, hear the word of the Lord. I saw the Lord sitting on his throne, with all the heavenly assembly standing on his right and on his left. *The Lord said, 'Who will deceive Ahab, so he will attack Ramoth Gilead and die there?'* One said this and another that. *Then a spirit stepped forward and stood before the Lord. He said, 'I will deceive him.'* The Lord asked him, 'How?' He replied, 'I will go out and be a lying spirit in the mouths of all his prophets.' The Lord said, '*Deceive and overpower him. Go out and do as you have proposed.'* So now, look, the Lord has placed a lying spirit in the mouths of all these prophets of yours, but the Lord has decreed disaster for you."
> 1 Kings 22:19-23

In this prophecy, God is pictured as looking for someone to entice King Ahab so he can be led to his destruction for all the evil that he had previously committed. Apparently, a demon approaches the Lord and says that he will entice Ahab by being a lying spirit in the mouth of his prophets. God tells him to "Go and do it" and that he would be successful. Who enticed Ahab? The demonic spirit did. Who was in control? God was.

Scripture clearly declares that God is in control of all things (Eph 1:11), and yet, there can be other causes such as Satan or man. Wayne Grudem gives a very insightful conclusion to our look at how Scripture teaches God's control over both man's sin and the devil. Listen to what he says:

> We must remember that in all these passages it is very clear that Scripture nowhere shows God as directly doing anything evil but rather as bringing about evil deeds through the willing actions of moral creatures. Moreover, Scripture never blames God for evil or shows God as taking pleasure in evil and Scripture never excuses human beings for the wrong they do. However we understand God's relationship to evil, we must never come to the point where we think that we are not responsible for the evil that we do, or that God takes pleasure in evil or is to be blamed for it. Such a conclusion is clearly contrary to Scripture.[45]

With this said, there are different views on this subject. The one detailed here is primarily the Calvinistic view that is believed in many denominations, but primarily in the reformed camp such as Presbyterians and Reformed Baptists. Calvinists are in every denomination; however, Arminianism is stronger in Methodist denominations and some Pentecostals.

Wayne Grudem states the Arminian position this way:

> Those who hold an Arminian position maintain that in order to preserve the *real human freedom* and *real human choices* that are necessary for genuine human personhood, God cannot cause or plan our voluntary choices. Therefore they conclude that God's providential involvement in or control of history must *not* include *every specific detail* of every event that happens, but that God instead simply *responds* to human choices and actions as they come about and does so in such a way that his purposes are ultimately accomplished in the world.[46]

However, it's difficult to come to that doctrinal conclusion because so many Scriptures address God's sovereignty and speak of "all" circumstances, not just some, in his control. One Scripture says, "In Christ we too have been claimed as God's own possession, since we were predestined *according to the one purpose of him who accomplishes all things according to the counsel of his will*" (Ephesians 1:11).

Everything is working in conformity to his plan and purpose. They are not just happening and then he fixes them.

"And we know that *all things* work together for good for those who love God, who are called according to his purpose" (Romans 8:28).

David said, "Your eyes saw me when I was inside the womb. *All the days ordained for me were recorded in your scroll before one of them came into existence*" (Psalm 139:16).

The author of Hebrews said, "The Son is the radiance of his glory and the representation of his essence, and he *sustains all things by his powerful word*, and so when he had accomplished cleansing for sins, he sat down at the right hand of the Majesty on high" (Hebrews 1:3).

"I am the one who forms light and creates darkness; *the one who brings about peace and creates calamity. I am the Lord, who accomplishes all these things* (emphasis mine)" (Isaiah 45:7).

"Is it not from the mouth of the Most High that everything comes—both calamity and blessing?" (Lamentations 3:38).

Mundane events like eating and drinking are under his control; random events, our future, and both disaster and good things come from him. His sovereignty is absolute, total, and comprehensive. If God ceased to be in control, he would cease to be God. His sovereignty is just as much a characteristic of him as his omniscience or omnipresence.

With all that said, we must always realize an aspect of mystery comes with this doctrine. If we try to explain it without recognizing the paradox—the apparent contradiction—then we are oversimplifying God for our own understanding. Some aspects of God we cannot fully comprehend. God is the first cause of all things but only in such a way that he cannot be blamed for evil. How this works, we cannot be fully sure, but we must teach it and uphold God's right as the potter to do whatever he wants since he is king (cf. Rom 9:19-21, Psalm 47:2).

Application

What are some encouragements from the fact that God is sovereign?

1.   We can have comfort in the fact that there are no accidents.

Nothing happens outside of his will. Even our mistakes and the greatest evils somehow fit into God's sovereign plan (Eph 1:11).

2.   We can have comfort in the fact that God can hear and respond to our prayers.

Why pray if God is not sovereign and in control of all things? It is his sovereignty that gives us confidence that he can change things or make things better. We get to talk to the God who is controlling everything and ask for his perfect will to be done on the earth. Though he is sovereign, he has chosen to work through the prayers of his people. Ezekiel 22:30 says, "I looked for a man from among them who would repair the wall and stand in the gap before me on behalf of the land, so that I would not destroy it, but I found no one."

3.   We can have comfort in failure and difficult circumstances.

We can be comforted no matter how bad a situation is, or how badly we have failed, or what Satan has done. God is ultimately in control. We can see Joseph's comfort and also how he comforted his brothers in referring to their sin of selling him into slavery in Genesis 50:20. When his brothers asked for forgiveness, he responded with, "As for you, you meant to harm me, but God intended it for a good purpose, so he could preserve the lives of many people, as you can see this day." He saw God in control, and therefore, he took comfort and held no grudges. He also was calling for his brothers to take comfort in God's sovereignty, as he used even their bad intentions for good.

A person who doesn't understand and trust God's sovereignty will be a person who holds tremendous grudges and may find themselves very fearful or anxious at times. They also may find it impossible to accept God's forgiveness for their failures. God's sovereignty gives us confidence and brings comfort to our lives.

Conclusion

Why is knowing the characteristics of God important? It is important so we can worship him and serve him properly. The more you know him, the more your worship will be enhanced and the better you can please him (John 4:23).

What characteristics of God have we studied in the last few chapters?

1.   God is spirit.
2.   God is a person.
3.   God is immutable.
4.   God is independent.
5.   God is good.
6.   God is eternal.
7.   God is omnipresent.

8. God is omniscient.
9. God is omnipotent.
10. God is merciful.
11. God is loving.
12. God is holy.
13. God is wrathful.
14. God is sovereign.

Review Questions

1. What are characteristics of God's love? What aspect of God's love was most challenging to you and why?

2. What does God's holiness mean? How do we see God's holiness demonstrated throughout Scripture? In what ways should we demonstrate holiness?

3. What does God's wrath mean? In what events in Scripture do we see God's wrath? In what ways should Christians demonstrate God's wrath?

4. In what ways do we see God's sovereignty taught in the Scriptures? Why is God's sovereignty such a controversial doctrine? What is the main difference between a Reformed understanding of God's sovereignty and an Arminian one? Which one do you lean toward?

Prayer Prompts

- Pray for the church and small groups to increase and overflow in love for one another (1 Thess 3:12). Pray that the members of the church would demonstrate this love by serving one another, forgiving one another, and being patient with one another so that Christ will be glorified (John 13:35).

- Pray for Christians to trust God's sovereignty in all things, especially in trials. Pray for believers to be free of worry, fear, and anxiety as they trust God with their past, present, and future (Prov 3:5). Pray that God would guard their hearts and minds and give them peace that passes all understanding (Phil 4:6).

- Pray for God to move in the areas of religious and government corruption, unjust laws, trafficking, abortion, the persecution of Christians in many nations of the world, etc., even as Christ moved to correct injustice in the temple (John 2:14-17). Pray that Christians would faithfully pray over these issues (1 Timothy 2:1-2) and get involved as God leads (Matt 5:13).

- Pray that Christians would be holy as God is holy (1 Peter 1:16). Pray for them to separate from ungodly relationships, ungodly practices, and ungodly entertainment so that we can be lights to the world as Christ desired (Matt 5:14). Pray that Christians would be zealous for good works in order to honor Christ (Titus 2:14).

Names of God

As we are seeking to know God more, one of the greatest ways to know God is by the names given him in Scripture. In the ancient Hebrew culture, a name meant so much more than just what you called somebody; it reflected a person's character. Satan means "opposer" or "adversary," and Devil means "accuser" or "slanderer." This tells us a lot about Satan's role as he opposes God and man and seeks to accuse both. We also see that Jacob in the Bible meant "heel grabber" or "trickster." He lived out his name as he tricked his brother and stole his birthright. He also tricked his uncle Laban and took his lambs. Names are a reflection of character in the Bible.

Wayne Grudem said this about God's names: "The many names of God in the Scripture provide additional revelation of His character. These are not mere titles assigned by people but, for the most part, His own descriptions of Himself. As such they reveal aspects of His character."[47]

Ryrie adds: "In a broad sense, then, God's 'name' is equal to all that the Bible and creation tell us about God. When we pray, 'Hallowed be your *name*' as part of the Lord's Prayer (Matt. 6:9), we are praying that people would speak about God in a way that is honoring to him and that accurately reflects his character."[48]

The names of God give Christians tremendous comfort because they reveal aspects of his nature and character. Proverbs 18:10 says this: "The name of the LORD is a strong tower; the righteous person runs to it and is set safely on high." The person who understands God's names will better understand his character, and therefore, have a tremendous source of strength and protection while enduring the trials of life.

Therefore, in this lesson, we will look at a few of the names of God. First, we will look at Old Testament names and then New Testament names.

Old Testament Names

Yahweh: LORD

YHWH, often pronounced Yahweh, is the most frequently used name of God in the Old Testament, and it is commonly translated as LORD, with all capitals.[49] Mark Driscoll said this about the name:

> In the Old Testament the most sacred name for God is Yahweh. Yahweh is a distinctly proper name for the God of the Bible. Because it is sacred, it is never used to refer to any pagan gods; neither is it used in regard to any human. It is reserved solely for the one true God alone. The name Yahweh appears some 6,823 times in the Old Testament, as he is the focus and hero of the Scriptures.[50]

Yahweh is the personal and intimate name for himself that God gave to Israel when he made a covenant with them to be their God as he delivered them from Egypt.

It was also the name used by Eve (Gen 4:1), Noah (Gen 9:26), and Abraham (Gen 12:6). Look at Genesis 4:1: "Now the man had marital relations with his wife Eve, and she became pregnant and gave birth to Cain. Then she said, 'I have created a man just as the Lord did!'"

But it was with Moses and Israel that it took on a greater significance. When Moses was told to set Israel free, he asked God what name he should call him and God replies by saying, "I AM." "God said to Moses, 'I am that I am.' And he said, 'You must say this to the Israelites, 'I am has sent me to you'" (Exodus 3:14).

This name was considered so sacred to Israel that they would never pronounce the name. It was too holy. Instead, they used the name "Adonai,"—Lord—when reading the name Yahweh. In fact, around the ninth century AD[51], the vowels of Adonai were combined with YHWH to make the artificial name "Jehovah," which became the spoken way of saying Yahweh for the Jews.[52] Jehovah was popularized in early English translations of the Bible such as the KJV—though it is not the correct way to pronounce the Divine name.[53]

What does the name Yahweh mean?

1. The name Yahweh means that God is eternal.

John 8:57-58 says: "Then the Judeans replied, 'You are not yet fifty years old! Have you seen Abraham?' Jesus said to them, 'I tell you the solemn truth, before Abraham came into existence, *I am*!'"

Jesus used the name to refer to his preexistence, his eternality. Yahweh means God has always existed.

2. The name Yahweh means God is unchangeable.

God's name is "I Am." It is not "I Was" or "I Will Be" because God does not change. We can put our full trust in God because he is the same yesterday, today, and forever. He does not change. He is "I Am."

3. The name Yahweh represents a covenant relationship.

Yahweh is forever attached with God's covenant with Israel. Therefore, it demonstrates God's intimacy and that he is a personal God. Yahweh also has a personal relationship with us and he will never leave nor forsake us. Look at what Paul says in Romans 8:38–39:

> For I am convinced that neither death, nor life, nor angels, nor heavenly rulers, nor things that are present, nor things to come, nor powers, nor height, nor depth, nor anything else in creation will be able to separate us from the love of God in Christ Jesus our Lord.

Nothing can separate us from the love of God because he is in covenant with us. This covenant was cut and sealed with the blood of Christ, and therefore, God will remain faithful to us. We are in covenant with him. He is our Yahweh.

Next, we will look at compound forms of the name Yahweh.

Yahweh Jireh: The Lord Will Provide

In Genesis 22, God commands Abraham to sacrifice his son, Isaac. However, when it was time to offer Isaac to the Lord, God provided a ram in the thicket. Genesis 22:14 shows Abraham's response, "And Abraham called the name of that place '*The Lord provides.*' It is said to this day, 'In the mountain of the Lord provision will be made.'"

Abraham names the place of provision Yahweh Jireh, which means "The LORD Provides." Those who are in covenant relationship with God shall lack no provisions because he will provide.

We get another great picture of the Lord's faithfulness to provide in Matthew 6. The disciples were worried about their futures. What would they and their families eat, drink, and wear?

Christ told them to stop worrying because God knew that they had need of these things. He comforted them with how God provides for the birds of the air and the lilies of the field. Consider what Christ says in Matthew 6:26 and verse 30:

Look at the birds in the sky: They do not sow, or reap, or gather into barns, yet your heavenly Father feeds them. Aren't you more valuable than they are? ... And if this is how God clothes the wild grass, which is here today and tomorrow is tossed into the fire to heat the oven, won't he clothe you even more, you people of little faith?

Jesus called the disciples to stop worrying based on the fact that God would provide. He provides for the birds of the air and he clothes the lilies of the field. Will God not provide for us as well?

Our world is filled with uncertainty about the economy, future employment, retirement, the education system, etc. God wants us to know that his name is Yahweh Jireh; he is faithful and he will provide.

Yahweh Nissi: The Lord Is My Banner

The name Yahweh Nissi is given in the context of warfare. The Amalekites and Israel were at war and as long as Moses had his hands raised, they were winning. Moses's hands being raised seemed to represent his prayers and, therefore, dependence upon the God of Israel. Philip Ryken said this:

> The Israelites generally stood when they prayed, lifting their hands to offer their praises and their petitions up to God. For example, when God brought an end to the plague of hail, Moses said to Pharaoh, "I will spread out my hands in prayer to the LORD" (Exod. 9:29). Hannah and Jehoshaphat both stood at the temple to pray (1 Sam. 1:9–11; 2 Chron. 20:5, 6). The psalmist said, "in your name I will lift up my hands" (63:4b).[54]

We also can discern Moses was praying and depending on God by the fact that Moses builds an altar after the battle was won and calls it Yahweh Nissi, which means the Lord is my banner. "Moses built an altar, and he called it 'The Lord is my Banner'" (Exodus 17:15).

Typically, when armies went to battle, the flag would go out in front of them, representing the power and spirit of the nation. Similarly, when Israel fought, God went before them. He led the way; he was their banner. However, this is not just true for Israel. It is true for us. Our God always goes before us. He makes our paths straight, and he fights our battles. Look at what Paul said to the Ephesians: "Finally, be strengthened in the Lord and in the strength of his power. Clothe yourselves with the full armor of God so that you may be able to stand against the schemes of the devil" (Eph 6:10-11).

Like Moses keeping his hands up in dependence upon God, we must also depend on God daily. Isaiah 40:31 says, "But those who wait for the Lord's help find renewed strength; they rise up as if they had eagles' wings, they run without growing weary, they walk without getting tired." Like Moses, we must wait on the Lord and rely on him. He will fight our battles. The Lord is our banner, and he goes before us to bring us victory.

Yahweh Rapha: The Lord Who Heals

Yahweh Rapha is a name used of God by Israel while they were in the wilderness. While journeying, they encountered bitter water at a place called Marah (Ex 15:23). However, God told Moses to throw wood into the water, and as the wood entered the water, it would heal the water. After this, God told Israel if they obeyed him he would be their healer. Listen to what he says in Exodus 15:26:

> He said, "If you will diligently obey the Lord your God, and do what is right in his sight, and pay attention to his commandments, and keep all his statutes, then all the diseases that I brought on the Egyptians I will not bring on you, *for I, the Lord, am your healer.*"

God also heals us. It is part of his character; God is a healer. When Christ came to the earth, he healed the sick, the blind, the lame, and, even more than that, he healed the hearts of people. People who were separated from God and under his wrath, Christ reconciled through his death. He healed the terminal sickness of our souls and drew us back to God. Thank God that he is a healer and that he still heals today.

In fact, we see in James 5:14–15 that God teaches the sick to call the elders of the church to pray over them so that they may be healed. Listen to what he says:

> Is anyone among you ill? He should summon the elders of the church, and they should pray for him and anoint him with oil in the name of the Lord. And the prayer of faith will save the one who is sick and the Lord will raise him up—and if he has committed sins, he will be forgiven.

Certainly, healing is at the discretion of God. Not everybody will receive physical healing in this life. Sin is in our bodies, and therefore, they decay and get old. But one day, the great healer will raise our bodies from the dead (Rom 8:11), and we will experience no more sickness and no more pain. Our God is a healer. He is Yahweh Rapha, the God who heals us.

Yahweh Shamma: The Lord Is There

Yahweh Shamma is the name given to the New Jerusalem, a future city that was prophesied by Ezekiel through a vision. This name speaks of God's special presence with the people of God. Look at what Ezekiel shares in his vision: "The circumference of the city will be six miles. The name of the city from that day forward will be: *'The Lord Is There.'*" (Ezekiel 48:35).

The Israelites at this point were discouraged because they had been exiled by Babylon and their city and temple had been destroyed. However, God gave Ezekiel a vision about a future city that would be far better than any previous city. In that vision, he said that the name of the city will be "The Lord is there." This would have been tremendously encouraging to Ezekiel and the Israelites because earlier in Ezekiel's prophecies God's presence had left the temple and the city of Israel before it was destroyed (chapters 8-11).

It seems that there will be a future glorious city and a temple in Israel that are marked by the presence of God eternally. However, this truth of God being present with his people is still true today. God has indwelled every believer and he will abide in them forever. Look at what Paul said in 1 Corinthians 6:19–20:

> Or do you not know that your body is the temple of the Holy Spirit who is in you, whom you have from God, and you are not your own? For you were bought at a price. Therefore glorify God with your body.

Christ indwells every individual believer, and in a special sense his presence comes when the believers are gathered together. Matthew 18:20 says, "For where two or three are assembled in my name, I am there among them."

The Lord's presence is there. He is with us and that's what makes the gathering of the saints special. The gathering of the saints is about God's presence. We thank you, Lord, that you will be with us always, even to the ends of the earth (Matt 28:19). Thank you that you are Yahweh Shamma, the Lord is there.

Yahweh Roi: The Lord Is My Shepherd

Yahweh Roi is the name that David uses of God in Psalm 23. He says, "The Lord is my Shepherd, I lack nothing" (Psalm 23:1).

We can be sure that as David was caring for his sheep, feeding them, and protecting them, he thought about how God did the same for him. Similarly, the Lord is our Shepherd and we shall not want (Psalm 23:1). This speaks of the weakness of his children. We are prone to wander, and we cannot protect ourselves. Therefore, we need a shepherd that leads, provides, and protects us; a shepherd that gives us rest and makes sure that we lack nothing. God is that shepherd.

In fact, what makes our shepherd so wonderful is that he even died for us. Shepherding during David's time could be very dangerous. Shepherds were exposed to extreme temperatures, wild animals such as lions and wolves, and even robbers. A shepherd that did not really care for the sheep would simply run away when attacked. But good shepherds were willing to give their lives for the sheep. Look at what Christ said about himself: "I am the good shepherd. The good shepherd lays down his life for the sheep" (John 10:11).

Our Lord is not just a shepherd. He is the good shepherd. He provides for us, cares for us, and even gave his life for us. He is our Yahweh Roi. Thank you, Lord.

Yahweh Tsidkenu: The Lord Our Righteousness

Yahweh Tsidkenu was the name given by God in the book of Jeremiah for the messiah. It means "The Lord Our Righteousness." The character of the messiah that Israel was waiting for was righteousness. He would gather Israel from all the lands of the earth and he would rule over them. He would be a righteous shepherd and they would call him, "The Lord Our Righteousness." Listen to what Jeremiah said:

> The days are coming," declares the LORD, "when I will raise up to David a righteous Branch, a King who will reign wisely and do what is just and right in the land. In his days Judah will be saved and Israel will live in safety. This is the name by which he will be called: The LORD Our Righteousness.
> Jeremiah 23:5-6 (NIV 1984)

Jesus, the messiah, is the righteousness of the nation of Israel. He is the one that will eventually turn them from their sins and give them a new heart to follow him (cf. Romans 11:26). However, this is what Christ has already done for us. Christ took our sins while on the cross and gave us his righteousness. Second Corinthians 5:21 says: "God made the one who did not know sin to be sin for us, so that in him we would become the righteousness of God."

It is on the basis of Christ's righteousness that we are justified before God. But Christ does not just give us his forensic righteousness in order to be saved; he also leads us practically into new righteousness every day as we are

175

conformed to his image. He is the good shepherd that leads us into righteousness for his name's sake (Psalm 23:3). The Lord is our righteousness.

Yahweh Shalom: The Lord Is Peace

Yahweh Shalom is the name given by Gideon to the Lord. In the context, Gideon sees the Angel of the Lord and cries out that he would die, but the angel said, "Peace! Do not be afraid. You are not going to die" (Judges 6:23 NIV 1984). Listen to the story in Judges 6:22–24 (NIV 1984):

> When Gideon realized that it was the angel of the LORD, he exclaimed, "Ah, Sovereign LORD! I have seen the angel of the LORD face to face!" But the LORD said to him, "Peace! Do not be afraid. You are not going to die." *So Gideon built an altar to the LORD there and called it The LORD is Peace...*

To see God face to face meant death (Ex 33:20), and therefore, Gideon was afraid. However, the angel comforts him and speaks peace to him. Gideon accepts the Lord's words and builds an altar to proclaim that the Lord is Yahweh Shalom—The Lord is Peace.

Similarly, we do not have to be afraid of the eternal wrath of God. Christ bore the wrath of God so we could have a right relationship with him. Listen to what Romans 5:1 says: "Therefore, since we have been declared righteous by faith, *we have peace with God through our Lord Jesus Christ.*"

Christ has brought peace in our relationship with God where before there was only enmity (Rom 5:10). But not only do we have "peace with God," we also are given the "peace of God." This is a peace that God gives regardless of circumstance in order to guard the hearts and minds of those he loves (Phil 4:6-7). Jesus said this: "Peace I leave with you; my peace I give to you; I do not give it to you as the world does. Do not let your hearts be distressed or lacking in courage" (John 14:27). In this world, we will have troubles and difficulties, but in the midst of these Christ wants us to have his supernatural peace. Therefore, we must let this peace rule in our hearts as we enjoy intimacy with Christ. Colossians 3:15 (NIV 1984) says, "Let the peace of Christ rule in your hearts, since as members of one body you were called to peace. And be thankful." How do we let this peace rule? Philippians 4:6-7 gives us the answer:

> Do not be anxious about anything. Instead, in every situation, through prayer and petition with thanksgiving, tell your requests to God. And the

peace of God that surpasses all understanding will guard your hearts and minds in Christ Jesus.

God promises that if we practice these disciplines he will guard our hearts with his peace.

Like Gideon who accepted God's word of peace while facing the prospect of death, we must in obedience choose not to be anxious as we trust God's words to us. The Lord is our peace, not the economy, not our family situation, not the government. Our peace is in the Lord.

Yahweh Sabaoth: The Lord of Hosts or the Lord Almighty

The name Yahweh Sabaoth pictures God as the ruler of the angels, the armies of heaven. We see this image throughout the Scripture. Look at what the Sons of Korah said in Psalm 46:7 (KJV): "*The LORD of hosts* is with us; the God of Jacob is our refuge. Selah."

The phrase "Lord of hosts" pictures God as a warrior and one who fights for us and protects us. We get a good picture of this when Elisha is protected by an army of angels that are surrounding his house (2 Kings 6:16-17). Certainly, we can be sure that God is always protecting us with angels. They are spirits sent to serve those who will inherit salvation (Hebrews 1:14). The Psalmist said this about angels: "For he will order his angels to protect you in all you do" (Psalm 91:11).

He said that God will guard you with his angels in all your ways. This includes one's eating, drinking, sleeping, working, etc. God, the "Lord of hosts," is always protecting his saints. In fact, Jesus warns his disciples to not offend or look down on God's children because of this reality. He says, "See that you do not disdain one of these little ones. *For I tell you that their angels in heaven always see the face of my Father in heaven*" (Matthew 18:10).

The angels of the Lord of hosts are always watching the Master, listening to his words. They are ready to respond at any injustice or offense against his little ones. We thank you, God, that you are the Lord of hosts and that you are always protecting your saints.

Elohim

Elohim is a general name translated "God" in the Bible. It is the second most used name of God in the Old Testament. "El" comes from a root that means strong or power, and therefore, has the connotation of "Strong One" or "Mighty Leader."[55]

177

Because Elohim's root means power or might, the name will commonly be used in verses that demonstrate the power or awesomeness of God. For example, look at Jeremiah 32:27: "I am the Lord, *the God of all humankind.* There is, indeed, nothing too difficult for me"

He is the "Strong One" of all mankind and nothing is too hard for him. We also see this in Deuteronomy as Moses used it to describe God's greatness over all other gods. Deuteronomy 10:17 says, "For the Lord your God is *God of gods and Lord of lords*, the great, mighty, and awesome God who is unbiased and takes no bribe."

Our God is Elohim, the mighty God. No one is stronger than him and nothing is impossible for him (Matt 19:26).

Trinitarian Implications

One of the interesting things about the word "Elohim" is that it is a plural noun that always is used with a singular verb. For instance, we see this in the first verse of the Bible. "In the beginning *God created* the heavens and the earth" (Genesis 1:1).

The noun "God" is plural and the verb "created" is singular. Because of this, many have seen implications of Trinitarian doctrine in the use of Elohim. The word "Elohim" would then not only be a reference to God's strength, but it would also imply his "plurality" and yet "oneness." He is plural, but at the same time one. "Listen, Israel: The Lord is our God, the Lord is *one!*" (Deuteronomy 6:4).

El: God

As mentioned, El is the root of Elohim and is commonly used for the God of Israel; however, the word is also used of false gods like Molech or Baal. The context determines who is referred to when the word is used. Though Elohim is more commonly used to refer to God, the root El is also at times used in Hebrew poetry in conjunction with other adjectives about God.

Let's look at some compound words that come from "El".

El Shaddai: God Almighty

El Shaddai is used when God promises to give Abraham a son at the age of ninety-nine. Listen to the narrative in Genesis 17:1 (NIV 1984): "When Abram was ninety-nine years old, the LORD appeared to him and said, 'I am *God Almighty*; walk before me and be blameless.'"

God was declaring to Abraham, through his name, that he was about to do something impossible. He was about to demonstrate his power in the supernatural birth of his son, Isaac. The almighty God would give Abraham a son, even though he and his wife, Sarah, were past the age of child bearing.

However, this is not the only time we see God Almighty accomplish things that are impossible. The Scripture is full of his mighty works. He created the heavens and the earth with spoken words. He delivered Israel from the oppression of Egypt, parted the Red Sea so they could walk through it, and then closed the Red Sea to destroy the army of the Egyptians that was chasing after them. He is God Almighty.

When Christ came on the earth, he spoke peace into raging storms. He multiplied bread and fish to feed the multitudes. The Almighty God did what was impossible. In fact, the greatest work that El Shaddai has done is to save sinful man. Christ said this in reference to the possibility of a rich man being saved.

> Again I tell you, it is easier for a camel to go through the eye of a needle than for a rich man to enter the kingdom of God." When the disciples heard this, they were greatly astonished and asked, "The disciples were greatly astonished when they heard this and said, "Then who can be saved?" Jesus looked at them and replied, "*This is impossible for mere humans, but for God all things are possible.*"
> Matthew 19:24–26

Christ declared the impossibility of a rich man being saved through the illustration of a camel trying to go through the eye of a needle. He widened this impossible illustration to include all mankind. The disciples said, "Then who can be saved?" (v. 25). He replied, "*This is impossible for mere humans, but for God all things are possible*" (v. 26).

It is impossible for man to save himself. This is what every religion has tried to accomplish from the beginning of time. Like the rich man who sought to justify himself through his works (Matt 19:17–20), the religions of the world have sought salvation through prayer, through works of kindness, through sacrifice, etc. Because of their works, they have assumed that they can merit salvation before a holy God. However, Christ says that this is impossible. Man cannot save himself. It is something only God can do. Salvation is monergistic, a work that can only be done by God. Even man's faith is a gift from God in salvation (Eph 2:8–9).

The God who did something impossible in allowing Abraham and his wife Sarah, who were past childbearing age, to give birth, is the same God that reaches into the deadness of our sin and brings new life (Eph 2:1–5). He saves us and makes us new creations in Christ (2 Cor 5:17).

179

In fact, he promises us that if we will only call upon the name of the Lord, we shall be saved (Rom 10:13). He makes a promise to us, even as he made to Abram. He promises that he will be our God Almighty, our El Shaddai, if we commit to him.

Certainly, this name reminds us of the importance of prayer. It reminds us that we have a God that can meet all our needs, as we bring them before him. Nothing is impossible for El Shaddai.

> Now to him who by the power that is working within us is able to do far beyond all that we ask or think, to him be the glory in the church and in Christ Jesus to all generations, forever and ever. Amen.
> Ephesians 3:20–21

El Elyon: Most High or Most High God

The name El Elyon means "the Most High." "El Elyon is the name that designates God as the sovereign ruler of all the universe."[56] It emphasizes God's supremacy and sovereignty over everything. We see this name used in reference to Abraham and his defeat of four kings in Genesis 14. Even though Abraham only had 318 trained men and a few allies (Gen 14:14, 24), he took on the four kings and their armies and defeated them. The King of Salem, Melchizedek, in response to this victory, blessed Abraham. Look at what he said: "Worthy of praise is the *Most High God*, who delivered your enemies into your hand" (Gen 14:20).

Melchizedek blessed Abraham by blessing God. He said that El Elyon, *God Most High*, delivered Abraham from his enemies. This victory was so spectacular that it was clear that it could have only been done through the Most High God.

The name El Elyon should comfort us because it teaches that God is in control everything. There is nothing on the earth that happens apart from his control. He is the sovereign over all things. Similarly, look at what Nebuchadnezzar says about the Lord Most High.

> But at the end of the appointed time I, Nebuchadnezzar, looked up toward heaven, and my sanity returned to me. I extolled the *Most High*, and I praised and glorified the one who lives forever. For his authority is an everlasting authority, and his kingdom extends from one generation to the next. All the inhabitants of the earth are regarded as nothing. He does as he wishes with the army of heaven and with those who inhabit the earth. No one slaps his hand and says to him, 'What have you done?'
> Daniel 4:34–35

Nebuchadnezzar, the most powerful king on the earth at that time, said the Most High does what pleases him both in heaven and on earth. "No one slaps his hand and says to him, 'What have you done?'"

God is El Elyon, the Most High God. As talked about in studying his sovereignty, we see his sovereignty over random events. Scripture says even the roll of the dice is of the Lord (Prov 16:33). He is in control of calamity (Isaiah 45:6–7). He is in control of every temptation (1 Cor 10:13). He is in control of every good and perfect gift we receive (James 1:17). He is even in control of Satan (Job 1:12). Ephesians 1:11 says this about God: "In Christ we too have been claimed as God's own possession, since we were predestined according to the one purpose of him who *accomplishes all things according to the counsel of his will.*" He works all things according to the counsel of his will.

Like Nebuchadnezzar realized, because he is the Most High God that is in control of all things, he is worthy of praise. He is worthy of glory and of honor. Let us adore him as the Psalmist does. "I will be glad and rejoice in you; I will sing praise to your name, O Most High" (Psalm 9:2 NIV 1984).

El Roi: The God Who Sees

Hagar, Abraham's wife's servant, called the Lord, El Roi, "The God who sees." The context of this is that Hagar had been mistreated by her master, Sarah, and therefore, ran away from Abraham's household with her child Ishmael. Hagar was alone by a spring in the desert, and it was there that the angel of the Lord appeared to her. He commanded her to return to Abraham's household and to submit to Sarah (Gen 16:9). He also promised that God was going to increase Hagar's descendants and that they would be too numerous to count (v.10). Hagar responded to the angel by blessing the Lord and calling him El Roi. Listen to what Genesis 16:13 says: "So Hagar named the Lord who spoke to her, 'You are the God who sees me,' for she said, 'Here I have seen one who sees me!'"

Hagar recognized God's faithfulness in watching over her and her child. Similarly, El Roi, the omniscient one, sees and knows all things and is always watching us. But this watch is not a casual stare, it is a watch of love, in the same way that every parent watches and enjoys their children. It is a watch that brings his protection and favor. Look at what the Psalmist said: "*For the LORD watches over the way of the righteous,* but the way of the wicked will perish" (Psalm 1:6 NIV 1984).

Does not God watch over the wicked as well? Yes, but, his watch is for the purpose of discipline and judgment. God watches the righteous in order to bless them and provide for them. In fact, like with Hagar, God promises to bless to the thousandth generation of those who love him. Listen to what Exodus 20:5–6 says:

> You shall not bow down to them or serve them, for I, the Lord, your God, am a jealous God, responding to the transgression of fathers by dealing with children to the third and fourth generations of those who reject me, and *showing covenant faithfulness to a thousand generations of those who love me and keep my commandments.*

We should consider that his favor over us reaches to our families and even to our children's children. God is our El Roi. He is the God that sees us and watches over us and our various affairs.

El Echad: The One God

Malachi declared that God is the "one God." Listen to Malachi 2:10: "Do we not all have one father? Did not *one God* create us? Why do we betray one another, in this way making light of the covenant of our ancestors?"

This is a declaration of monotheism, the belief in one God. This was very unique in the time of the ancient Jews because almost everybody was polytheistic. They believed in many gods and even accepted the gods of others as true gods. However, the God of the Bible claims to be the "one God," the only God. In fact, this was the great schema or declaration of Israel. Listen to what Deuteronomy 6:4 says: "Listen, Israel: The Lord is our God, the Lord *is one!*" To Israel, God was the one God and every other god was false.

Today, a similar attack on the monotheism of Scripture is pluralism. People are proclaiming that there are many ways to God, and some proclaim that the gods in all the different religions are the same god. However, Scripture clearly teaches that there is one God and that the only way to him is through Christ. Listen to what Jesus said: *"I am the way, and the truth, and the life. No one comes to the Father except through me"* (John 14:6).

El Echad, the God of the Scripture is the "one God." There are no other gods and there is only one way to God. The only way to have a relationship with the God of the Bible is through his Son, Jesus Christ.

Adonai: Lord, Master, or Owner

Adonai is the third most used name of God in the Old Testament, and it is a plural noun similar to "Elohim."[57] Therefore, many scholars see this as another implication of the Trinity in the Old Testament. The name could be translated,

"Lord" or "Master." Listen to Psalm 8:1 (NIV 1984): "O LORD, our *Lord*, how majestic is your name in all the earth! You have set your glory above the heavens."

O LORD, our "Lord" how majestic is your name. This was a declaration that not only was Yahweh God, but he also was the master of all people. This is important to say for many recognize the God of the Bible as God but will not take him as Lord and Master of their lives. James confronted scattered Hebrew Christians about the impossibility of this type of faith being salvific. Listen to what he says in James 2:19: "You believe that God is one; well and good. Even the demons believe that—and tremble with fear."

James says it is possible to believe in God, be monotheistic, and yet not truly be saved. The demons have orthodox theology as well, but they do not have orthopraxy—they do not submit to him as Lord and Master of their lives. They live a life of rebellion against his Lordship.

Christ proclaimed that if anybody was going to follow him as a disciple, they must make him the Lord of their lives. Listen to what he said in Luke 14:26–27:

> If anyone comes to me and does not hate his own father and mother, and wife and children, and brothers and sisters, and even his own life, he cannot be my disciple. Whoever does not carry his own cross and follow me cannot be my disciple.

Christ was declaring the need for absolute Lordship in order to be one of his followers. Every type of love must pale in comparison to our love for Christ. In the same way, David proclaimed that God was both Yahweh and also Lord of his life. "O LORD, our *Lord*, how majestic is your name in all the earth! You have set your glory above the heavens" (Psalm 8:1 NIV 1984).

Is God really the Lord of your life? Orthodox theology that doesn't lead to orthopraxy does not save. To truly believe in God means to follow him as Lord and Master of our lives. Let us adore him as God, and follow and submit to him as Master.

Emmanuel: God with Us

Emmanuel (or Immanuel) was one of the names used for Jesus, the messiah. It means "God with us" or "God among us." Listen to the prophecy in Isaiah 7:14: "For this reason the sovereign master himself will give you a confirming sign. Look, this young woman is about to conceive and will give birth to a son. You, young woman, will name him *Immanuel*."

This wonderful name is rich with theology. It speaks of the incarnation. The God of heaven came down to earth in the form of a baby. The "all powerful" God became weak and vulnerable. The "all knowing" God became a child that grew in stature and wisdom. It is the greatest miracle in the Bible, and it is this name that speaks grace and comfort to us.

God became a man not only so he could save us (Hebrews 2:14) but also so he could understand and sympathize with us. Listen to what Hebrews 4:15-16 says:

> For we *do not have a high priest incapable of sympathizing with our weaknesses, but one who has been tempted in every way* just as we are, yet without sin. Therefore let us confidently approach the throne of grace to receive mercy and find grace whenever we need help.

We have a God that understands weakness. He has been hungry. He has been thirsty. He has been lonely. He has been weary unto death. And, it is for these reasons that we can approach the "throne of grace" in search of mercy and grace in our time of need. He is Emmanuel, God with us—the God that understands.

The writer of Hebrews says that it is this reality that should draw us to prayer with confidence. He understands. He is our counselor, and yet, he is more than a counselor because most counselors can only listen. Emmanuel is God, and therefore, he can give grace. He can minister to whatever problems we have in our lives. The name Emmanuel tells us that God cares, understands, and that he wants to give grace.

New Testament Names

We will also look at the names of God used in the New Testament.

Theos: God

Theos is the most common name used of God in the New Testament.[58] It is not only used of God the Father but also of Christ. Look at these verses:

> To them belong the patriarchs, and from them, by human descent, came the Christ, who is *God* over all, blessed forever! Amen.
> Romans 9:5

In the beginning was the Word, and the Word was with *God*, and the Word was fully God.
John 1:1

Kurios: Lord

Kurios can mean Lord, sir, master, or owner. The word represents "authority and supremacy."[59] To call God "Lord" means that we not only recognize his authority, but that we will also submit to it. Romans 10:9 says, "because if you confess with your mouth that Jesus is *Lord* and believe in your heart that God raised him from the dead, you will be saved."

As said previously, we must not only recognize that Jesus is God, but he must also be Lord of our lives. Anything less falls short of saving grace (Eph 2:8–9).

Despotes: Master or Lord

The name "despotes" emphasizes "the idea of ownership, whereas *kurios* emphasizes authority and supremacy."[60] A despot is a king, ruler, or master with absolute power. In the Scriptures, it was commonly used in reference to slave masters. Look at 1 Timothy 6:1: "Those who are under the yoke as slaves must regard their own *masters* as deserving of full respect. This will prevent the name of God and Christian teaching from being discredited."

The word *master* in this text is the word "despotes." Similarly, Scripture often calls God and Christ despotes, ones with absolute power. We see this in Revelation 6:10 as the martyrs in heaven call God their despot as they pray to him. Listen to the text: "They cried out with a loud voice, 'How long, *Sovereign Master*, holy and true, before you judge those who live on the earth and avenge our blood?'"

Christ also is called the despot in 2 Peter 2:1:

> But false prophets arose among the people, just as there will be false teachers among you. These false teachers will infiltrate your midst with destructive heresies, even to the point of denying *the Master* who bought them. As a result, they will bring swift destruction on themselves.

This not only represents the absolute authority of God, but it also shows that we are his servants. Paul, in fact, often called himself a slave or servant of Christ (Phil 1:1). A despot typically owned many slaves whom he had absolute power over. Therefore in the Scriptures, we commonly see this analogy of God

185

being a household owner and believers being his servants. Consider Luke 12:35–38:

> "Get dressed for service and keep your lamps burning; be like people waiting for their master to come back from the wedding celebration, so that when he comes and knocks they can immediately open the door for him. Blessed are those slaves whom their master finds alert when he returns! I tell you the truth, he will dress himself to serve, have them take their place at the table, and will come and wait on them! Even if he comes in the second or third watch of the night and finds them alert, blessed are those slaves!

As servants, we must always be aware that we have a master in heaven, and that we are not our own. We have been bought with a price (1 Cor 6:20) and everything that we own is his. Therefore, we must always recognize that we are but humble stewards of the resources of God. We will be held accountable for how we steward our time, family, friendships, careers, and even the Word of God. Look at what Paul said about stewardship of the Word of God:

> One should think about us this way—as servants of Christ and *stewards of the mysteries of God*. Now what is sought in stewards is that one be found faithful. So for me, it is a minor matter that I am judged by you or by any human court. In fact, I do not even judge myself. For I am not aware of anything against myself, but I am not acquitted because of this. The one who judges me is the Lord.
> 1 Corinthians 4:1–4

Paul here says we are stewards of the mysteries of God. God has given us his Word and we must study it, obey it, teach it, and protect it. One day, the judge, the master, the despot will come and judge us according to our faithfulness. Have we been faithful stewards?

The believer that will be found faithful, not only with the Word of God, but with all things God has given, will understand that everything he owns is not his. He has a despot, an owner that will one day hold him accountable for his stewardship. We must be ready for our despot to return.

Abba: Father or Dearest Father

Something new to New Testament thinking was the revelation of God as Father. "Whereas the word 'Father' is used of God only fifteen times in the Old Testament,

186

it occurs 245 times of God in the New."[61] The name Abba shows the intimacy and care of God for his children. It can be translated "Father" or "Dearest Father." This was probably the Aramaic name that Jesus taught his disciples to use in the Lord's Prayer. "So pray this way: Our *Father* in heaven, may your name be honoured" (Matt 6:9).

We should also notice that this is one of the ministries of the Holy Spirit in the life of a believer. The Holy Spirit comes into a believer's life and brings intimacy with God. He enables us to call God "Abba." Romans 8:15 says this: "For you did not receive the spirit of slavery leading again to fear, but you received the Spirit of adoption, by whom we cry, "*Abba, Father.*"

Most of us only have one person in our life that we call father. That person will go out of his way to provide for us, to make sure we have all that we need. We can share our most intimate secrets with that person. When a person is truly born again, the Spirit of God creates this intimacy in the believer's life. He gives him a desire to pray and to call upon his Abba.

Again, this reminds us of the exclusive intimacy we have with God, but it also is a reminder of how much our God desires to provide for us. Listen again to what Christ said about our Father:

> What father among you, if your son asks for a fish, will give him a snake instead of a fish? Or if he asks for an egg, will give him a scorpion? If you then, although you are evil, know how to give good gifts to your children, how much more will the heavenly Father give the Holy Spirit to those who ask him!
> Luke 11:11–13

We must know how committed God is to listen to our prayers and also to provide for all of our needs. He is our Abba. Where earthly fathers have failed because they have been infected by sin, we can be sure that God will not. He is our perfect Abba, and he desires for us to cast our cares upon him for he cares for us (1 Peter 5:7).

Conclusion

What can we take from the names of God?

1.   Understanding the names of God should help us worship him better.

The names of God were often used as a way to give praise and honor to God throughout the Scripture. They enabled the worshiper to reflect on a specific characteristic of God's goodness. Judges 6:22–24 (NIV 1984) demonstrates this:

> When Gideon realized that it was the angel of the LORD, he exclaimed, "Ah, Sovereign LORD! I have seen the angel of the LORD face to face!" But the LORD said to him, "Peace! Do not be afraid. You are not going to die." *So Gideon built an altar to the LORD there and called it The LORD is Peace.*

When Gideon was afraid, God comforted him. He built an altar to worship God, and, there, he called him "the Lord is Peace," Yahweh Shalom. The names of God were used to help people worship.

Similarly, David said this: "I will be glad and rejoice in you; *I will sing praise to your name, O Most High*" (Psalm 9:2 NIV 1984). When David reflected on God's sovereignty, he called him the "Most High," El Elyon. He is the God who is over all things.

When David wanted to focus on God's care and provision, he said the Lord is my Shepherd, Yahweh Roi. "The Lord is my shepherd, I lack nothing" (Psalm 23:1).

He is our shepherd; he is our strong one; he is our daddy dearest; he is our banner who will represent us in battle; he is the Lord of hosts who sends his angels to fight for us. He is our Elohim, the God who exists in three persons and yet is one. He is the God who sees us in our pain. He is the God who sees and knows our problems. He is the Almighty God, and nothing is impossible for him. As we reflect on his names, our expression of worship can find more fullness. Let us worship his name, for he is wonderful.

2. Knowing the names of God should help our prayer life.

Many times, these names are used in the midst of prayer. Listen again to Genesis 16:13: "So Hagar named the Lord who spoke to her, *'You are the God who sees me,'* for she said, *'Here I have seen one who sees me!'*" Hagar speaks to God in prayer and calls him the "God who sees me."

Similarly, Jesus taught us to use the name "Abba" in prayer, Daddy Dearest. When we do this we reflect on our intimacy with God and his desire to provide for us as his children. We should use God's names in the midst of prayer.

3. Knowing the names of God should help us be more secure and less shaken in the midst of trials.

Listen again to Proverbs 18:10: "The name of the Lord is like a strong tower; the righteous person runs to it and is set safely on high."

The name of the Lord again refers to God's characteristics. As we reflect on Yahweh Jireh, the Lord who will provide, and Yahweh Rapha, the Lord who heals, we should find great comfort in the difficulties of life. "The name of the Lord is a strong tower; the righteous person runs to it and is set safely on high."

Review Questions

1. Why are names important in Scripture? What can we learn about God from the names given to him in Scripture?

2. Many believe that there are no references to the Trinity in the Old Testament. What Old Testament names show implications of the Trinity?

3. Which name or names of God were most comforting to you and why?

4. In what ways can you use the names of God in order to enhance your worship and prayer life?

Prayer Prompts

- Pray that God would "honor his name" by revealing his characteristics to us personally, to our church community, and to the world (Matt 6:9). As you pray this, pray some of his names and ask for him to reveal these specific character traits.

- Pray that God's name would bring comfort and strength to saints who are going through trials or being persecuted. Name individuals and communities who you know are struggling. Pray that they may know his character better (Prov 18:10).

- Pray that God would provide for the needs of everyone in your small group and in your church as a good shepherd does (Psalm 23). As you pray, bring people's needs before God.

The Trinity

What is the doctrine of the Trinity? It should be noted that the word Trinity is never given in the Bible; it was originally used by the church father Tertullian (AD 155–220)."[62] "The word *trinity* means 'tri-unity' or 'three-in-oneness.' It is used to summarize the teaching of Scripture that God is three persons yet one God."[63] Essentially, the doctrine of the Trinity teaches these three things:

1. There is one God
2. God is three individual persons and each is fully God.
3. God is a unity (three-in-oneness)

The Westminster Confession of Faith (1647) summarizes these statements this way: "In the unity of the God-head there be three persons, of one substance, power, and eternity: God the Father, God the Son, and God the Holy Ghost."[64]

These truths seem to contradict one another. How can there be one God and, yet, three individual persons that are also fully God? It is not something that we necessarily fully understand, but it is something that the Bible teaches. J. I. Packer said this:

> The historic formulation of the Trinity...seeks to circumscribe and safeguard this mystery (not explain it; that is beyond us), and it confronts us with perhaps the most difficult thought that the human mind has ever been asked to handle. It is not easy; but it is true.[65]

Let's investigate each of these statements regarding the doctrine of the Trinity.

One God

Where do we see the teaching that we have one God? We see it throughout the Old Testament. In fact, this was the teaching that at that time separated Judaism from other religions. Monotheism during ancient times was unique, as most nations accepted many gods.

We see this in Deuteronomy 6:4–5: "Listen, Israel: *The Lord is our God, the Lord is one! You must love the Lord your God* with your whole mind, your whole being, and all your strength."

The great declaration of the Jewish religion was that God was one Lord, and on that basis, he should be loved with all one's mind, being, and strength. He was the only one worthy of worship because he was the only God. In fact, we see this reiterated by implication in the Ten Commandments through the prohibition against idols.

> "I, the Lord, am your God, who brought you from the land of Egypt, from the house of slavery. *"You shall have no other gods before me. "You shall not make for yourself a carved image or any likeness of anything that is in heaven above or that is on the earth beneath or that is in the water below.* You shall not bow down to them or serve them, for I, the Lord, your God, am a jealous God, responding to the transgression of fathers by dealing with children to the third and fourth generations of those who reject me.
> Exodus 20:2–5

The implication is that God is the only God, and therefore, the Israelites should not worship other gods or make any idols before him. God is one.

We also see this teaching throughout the New Testament. James declares this in James 2:19: "You believe that *God is one*; well and good. Even the demons believe that—and tremble with fear."

James says even demons believe in monotheism. Paul similarly teaches this in 1 Corinthians 8:4: "With regard then to eating food sacrificed to idols, we know that '*an idol in this world is nothing,*' and that '*there is no God but one.*'"

Paul teaches that there is only one God and that all other deities or idols are nothing at all. They are false. There is only one God in the world.

The teaching of the entire Scripture is very clear; there is only one God, and therefore, we should not worship any other. And because he is the only God, the Creator, we should love him with all our heart, soul, and might. Nobody else deserves our devotion and the best of our affections except God.

Three Individual Persons

But that is not the only thing the Scripture teaches about the Trinity. It also teaches that God is three separate persons.

Where do we see this? We have seen this in every place that speaks of God, Jesus, and the Holy Spirit as uniquely and fully God. We will consider a few Scriptures that teach this.

God the Father Is Fully God

Typically, when the term "God" is used in Scripture, it is referring to God the Father. We obviously see numerous verses about God, and therefore, there really is no discussion about whether or not God the Father is God. Genesis 1:1 says, "In the beginning God created the heavens and the earth." Jesus taught the disciples to pray to the Father in the Lord's Prayer (Matt 6:9). God the Father is uniquely and fully God.

Jesus Is Fully God

We also see throughout the Scriptures that Jesus is God. One of the initial prophecies about Jesus was that he would be called Mighty God. Isaiah 9:6 (NIV 1984) says this:

> For to us a child is born, to us a son is given, and the government will be on his shoulders. And he will be called Wonderful Counselor, *Mighty God*, Everlasting Father, Prince of Peace.

In the book of Titus, Paul called Jesus God as well. He said, "As we wait for the happy fulfillment of our hope in *the glorious appearing of our great God and Savior, Jesus Christ*" (Titus 2:13).

It should be noted that not only does the Bible teach that Jesus is God, but that he is fully God. He is not fifty percent man and fifty percent God, but one hundred percent God and one hundred percent man, even though we may not be able to fully comprehend how this is possible. Listen to what Colossians 2:9 says about Jesus: "For in him all the fullness of deity lives in bodily form."

Christ is fully God. In addition, Hebrews 1:3 says this:

> *The Son is the radiance of his glory and the representation of his essence,* and he sustains all things by his powerful word, and so when he had accomplished cleansing for sins, he sat down at the right hand of the Majesty on high.

Christ being fully God is an important doctrine that has been constantly attacked throughout the centuries. Mormons and Jehovah's Witnesses both teach that Jesus is a created being. Mormons believe he originally was an angel, and Jehovah's Witnesses see him as only the Son of God, a created being, and not God.

These interpretations do not agree with sound doctrine; the Son of God is fully God. When Jesus was born, it was his humanity that came into being but he has always eternally existed as God (John 1:1, 8:58).

The Holy Spirit Is Fully God

Not only are the Son and Father fully God, but the Holy Spirit is fully God as well. This boggles the mind. However, Scripture clearly declares this reality. Look at Acts 5:3–4:

> But Peter said, "Ananias, why has Satan filled *your heart to lie to the Holy Spirit* and keep back for yourself part of the proceeds from the sale of the land? Before it was sold, did it not belong to you? And when it was sold, was the money not at your disposal? How have you thought up this deed in your heart? *You have not lied to people but to God!*"

Peter equates lying to the Holy Spirit as lying to God. Similarly, in 1 Corinthians 3:16, Paul calls the church the "temple of God," and then he says that the Holy Spirit indwells us, equating the Holy Spirit to God. Listen to the text: "Do you not know that *you are God's temple and that God's Spirit lives in you*?"

It is very clear that even though the Scripture says that we have only one God, it also says that the Holy Spirit is God, the Father is God, and that Jesus is God.

Distinct

The Bible also teaches that the three persons of the God-head are distinct. Look at Matthew 3:15–17 at Jesus' baptism:

> So Jesus replied to him, "Let it happen now, for it is right for us to fulfill all righteousness." Then John yielded to him. After *Jesus was baptized*, just as he was coming up out of the water, the heavens opened and he saw *the Spirit of God descending like a dove and coming on him*. And a voice from heaven said, "*This is my one dear Son; in him I take great delight.*"

In this verse, we see the Trinity's distinctness. Jesus comes out of the water from his baptism, the Holy Spirit descends upon him like a dove, and God speaks saying, "This is my one dear Son; in him I take great delight." Though they are one, we see them clearly operating individually and separately.

This is also an important doctrine of the Trinity to understand for there are many false teachings concerning it. One such false teaching is called *modalism*. Instead of God being three distinct persons that are unified, God is seen as being one person showing up or revealing himself in different modes. In the Old Testament, God revealed himself as God the Father. In the Gospels, God revealed himself as Jesus. In the book of Acts till now, God has revealed himself through the Spirit. It would be similar to me saying I am a husband at home, a pastor at church, and a professor in the classroom. I am the same person, but I wear three different hats.

But that is not what Scripture teaches. In Matthew 3:15-17, Christ is baptized, the Holy Spirit descends, and God speaks. They are all God but independent and distinct.

Unity of God

We have seen that we have only one God and that this God manifests himself in three unique and separate persons: Jesus the Son, the Holy Spirit, and God the Father. But we also see clear teaching that they are unified, that they are three in one. This is especially important in order to protect us from the false understanding of the Trinity called *tritheism*. Tritheism does not err in teaching the independence and distinct nature of the God-head. It errs in teaching that there is no unity at all. The Father, the Son, and the Holy Spirit are three distinct powerful gods that are not unified. However, Scripture clearly contradicts this. We have one God that is three separate persons that are fully God and are yet somehow unified. How do we see this throughout the Scripture?

Unity in the New Testament

John 10:29-30 says this: "My Father, who has given them to me, is greater than all, and no one can snatch them from my Father's hand. *The Father and I are one.*" Christ clearly declares to his disciples that he and the Father are one. Similarly, John 14:9–10 says this:

> Jesus replied, "Have I been with you for so long, and you have not known me, Philip? *The person who has seen me has seen the Father!* How can you say, 'Show us the Father'? Do you not believe that *I am in the Father, and the Father is in me?* The words that I say to you, I do not speak on

my own initiative, but the Father residing in me performs his miraculous deeds.

Jesus said to Philip, "The person who has seen me has seen the Father" (v. 9). Christ was in the Father and the Father was in him. There is unity within the God-head. They are separate and distinct, but they are also unified.

How else do we see this unity in Scripture?

Great Commission

We also see this unity in the Great Commission. Matthew 28:19–20 says this:

> Therefore go and make disciples of all nations, baptizing them in the *name of the Father and the Son and the Holy Spirit*, teaching them to obey everything I have commanded you. And remember, I am with you always, to the end of the age.

What is interesting about the Great Commission is that Christ gave God a singular "name" (v.19), but then gave the three persons of God-head next: Father, Son, and Holy Spirit. He gives a singular name to refer to three distinct persons. This is a great evidence of their unity—their three in oneness.

Close Relationship

We also see some evidence for their unity in how they are often closely put together in many of the blessings or descriptions given in the epistles. We see this often in the writings of Paul. In 2 Corinthians 13:13, he says this: "The grace of the Lord Jesus Christ and the love of God and the fellowship of the Holy Spirit be with you all." In this passage, Jesus, God, and the Holy Spirit are associated with one another and seen ministering with one another. Jesus gives grace, God gives love, and the Holy Spirit brings fellowship. This hints at the unity of their relationship in the Trinity. We see this also with Peter's greeting in 1 Peter 1:1–2:

> From Peter, an apostle of Jesus Christ, to those temporarily residing abroad (in Pontus, Galatia, Cappadocia, the province of Asia, and Bithynia) who are chosen according to the foreknowledge of God the Father by being set apart by the Spirit for obedience and for sprinkling with Jesus Christ's blood. May grace and peace be yours in full measure!

196

God knows every believer intimately through his foreknowledge, the Spirit sanctifies believers by making them holy, and Christ cleanses them through his blood. Their close ministry together also hints at their unity.

Where else do we see this unity?

Unity in Works

We see this unity in statements that declare that Jesus, God, and the Holy Spirit are doing the same works. We will consider several examples of this.

Creation

Scripture teaches that God the Father created the earth: "In the beginning God created the heavens and the earth" (Genesis 1:1).

But it also teaches that Christ created all things. Listen to this: *"for all things in heaven and on earth were created in him—all things, whether visible or invisible, whether thrones or dominions, whether principalities or powers—all things were created through him* and for him" (Colossians 1:16).

John says the same thing: "In the beginning was the Word, and the Word was with God, and the Word was fully God. The Word was with God in the beginning. *All things were created by him, and apart from him not one thing was created that has been created*" (John 1:1–3).

Not only do we see the distinctness of Christ as he was "with God," but also the unity as he "was fully God" and made all things. God made all things, and yet, Christ made all things. Christ, the Word, is the Creator.

Similarly, the Bible teaches that the Holy Spirit was a part of the creation process, especially in the creation of humanity.

We see the Holy Spirit's involvement from the very beginning of creation as it speaks of him "moving over the surface of the water" (Gen 1:2). We also can discern his involvement as God breathed the breath of life into man's lifeless body (Gen 2:7). The word for *breath* in the Hebrew can also be translated *Spirit*. The Spirit was involved in creation. We see further evidence of this in how wisdom literature speaks of the Spirit's current work in creating. Job 33:4 says: "The Spirit of God has made me; the breath of the Almighty gives me life."

Job claims that the Spirit of God created him. This would mean that not only was the Spirit involved in the initial creation of man, but also that the Spirit is necessary for the creation of every human today.

The Psalmist said the same thing about the *creatures of the earth* (cf. Psalm 104:25, 30). "When you send your life-giving breath, they are created, and you replenish the surface of the ground" (Psalm 104:30).

197

How can God and Jesus have created all things, and yet, as Job said, the Spirit of God created him and David said the Holy Spirit creates animals? This can only be true if they are unified, if they are all equally God.

Dwelling in Our Hearts

We also see the same works ascribed to them in their indwelling of the hearts of believers. The Holy Spirit, the Father, and the Son are said to indwell the hearts of believers. Look at these verses: "Or do you not know *that your body is the temple of the Holy Spirit* who is in you, whom you have from God, and you are not your own?" (1 Corinthians 6:19).

Paul calls believers the temple of the Holy Spirit in 1 Corinthians 6:19, but in 1 Corinthians 3:16, he calls them the temple of God. "Do you not know that you are God's temple and that God's Spirit lives in you?" (1 Corinthians 3:16). God the Father and God the Holy Spirit both indwell the believer.

In Ephesians 3:16–17, we also see the Bible teaching that Christ indwells believers. "I pray that according to the wealth of his glory he may grant you to be strengthened with power through his Spirit in the inner person, *that Christ may dwell in your hearts through faith*."

What other works do we see shared among the God-head?

Protecting Salvation

We see all three persons working to keep the salvation of the believer. Listen to this text:

> I give them eternal life, and they will never perish; no one will snatch them from my hand. My Father, who has given them to me, is greater than all, and no one can snatch them from my Father's hand. The Father and I are one.
> John 10:28–30

We see here that Jesus has the believers in his hand in order to keep them from perishing (v. 28). But God also has the believers in his hand as well for the same purpose (v. 29). Jesus then declares this is possible because they are one (v. 30).

We also see the Holy Spirit working to keep the salvation of believers. "And do not grieve the Holy Spirit of God, by whom *you were sealed for the day of redemption*" (Eph 4:30). The Holy Spirit seals every believer until the day of redemption. He is protecting them so they will not be lost and eternally condemned. We are in God's hand, Jesus' hand, and also in the grip of the Holy Spirit.

We see the unity of God in his works.

Unity in the Old Testament

Do we also see the unity of God in the Old Testament? Are there any ways that we see the doctrine of the Trinity?

In the Old Testament, the doctrine of the Trinity is never clearly taught, but many passages suggest or imply Trinitarian doctrine.

What are these passages?

Plurality in Hebrew Words for God

As mentioned before, we may see an implication of the Trinity in the name Elohim. Elohim, which can be translated as God, is a plural noun that is typically used with a singular verb. Genesis 1:1 says, "In the beginning *God created* the heavens and the earth." Here, God (Elohim) is plural while the word created (bara) is singular, representing both God's plurality and oneness.

Similarly, the Hebrew word "Adonai" (Lord) is also a plural noun that receives a singular verb. The Hebrew God is plural yet singular, as shown in the use of the names Elohim and Adonai.

Plurality in the Creation of Mankind

It should also be noted that when God made mankind, he did not make one human. He made two, which says something about God since man was made in his "image." The image of God is seen in a plurality. Genesis 1:27 (NIV 1984) says this: "So God created man in his own image, in the image of God he created him; *male and female he created them."*

When he says, "in the image of God he created him," "him" is referring to man as a collective (mankind). He then describes how he created mankind as both "male and female." We may see the plural nature of God hidden in the fact that he made mankind, "male and female."

The singularity of the plural God may also be discerned in that the male and female would come together and be "one flesh," a plural becoming singular. Listen to Genesis 2:24 (NIV 1984): "For this reason a man will leave his father and mother and be united to his wife, and they will become *one flesh."*

In what other ways is the Trinity implied in the Old Testament?

Plurality in the Plural Pronouns

We also see an implication of the Trinity in the plural pronouns used for God. Genesis 1:26 says this:

> Then God said, "Let us make humankind in *our* image, after *our* likeness, so they may rule over the fish of the sea and the birds of the air, over the cattle, and over all the earth, and over all the creatures that move on the earth."

God says, "Let *us* make humankind in *our* image, after *our* likeness." Who could he be referring to when he says "us" and "our"?

It does not seem to be referring to angels, as Scripture never clearly teaches that angels are made in the image of God. It must be himself that God is referring to by the plural pronouns. In the beginning there was a conversation among the members of the God-head about the creation of man.

This plural language is also seen in other sections of Scripture. Genesis 11:5–7 (NIV 1984) says:

> But the LORD came down to see the city and the tower that the men were building. The LORD said, "If as one people speaking the same language they have begun to do this, then nothing they plan to do will be impossible for them. Come, *let us go down* and confuse their language so they will not understand each other.

When God came down to the tower of Babel and confused the language of the people, he again referred to himself in plurality. "*Let us go down* and confuse their language." It doesn't say the Lord came down with his angels. It only says, "the LORD" came down and said, "Let us."

We see this also in Isaiah 6:8. It says, "I heard the voice of the sovereign master say, '*Whom will I send? Who will go on our behalf?*' I answered, 'Here I am, send me!'"

Right before commissioning Isaiah to prophesy to the nation of Israel, God refers to himself first in singular, "Whom will *I* send," and then in plural, "Who will go on *our* behalf." Again, this is probably an implication of the Trinity—God's plurality, and yet, oneness.

God Distinguished from God in Passages

There are also passages in the Old Testament where one person is called God or Lord, and yet distinguished from another person called God or Lord in the

200

same scenario. This shows the distinctness of the individual persons in the God-head. Psalm 110:1 (NIV 1984) says this, "*The LORD says to my Lord*: 'Sit at my right hand until I make your enemies a footstool for your feet.'"

Psalm 110:1 has messianic expectations. The Jews believed that David, who was the author of this passage, was talking about a conversation between God (LORD) and the messiah (Lord). God told the messiah to come and sit at his right hand till all his enemies were made a "footstool" for his feet. But interestingly, David calls them both "Lord." Jesus uses this passage to try to help the Pharisees recognize that the messiah would also be God. Consider their discussion in Matthew 22:41–46:

> While the Pharisees were assembled, Jesus asked them a question: "What do you think about the Christ? Whose son is he?" They said, "The son of David." He said to them, "How then does David by the Spirit call him 'Lord,' saying, 'The Lord said to my lord, "Sit at my right hand, until I put your enemies under your feet"'? If David then calls him 'Lord,' how can he be his son?" No one was able to answer him a word, and from that day on no one dared to question him any longer.

It is clear from this text that David believed in the plurality of God. He declared that not only was God, LORD (Yahweh), but the messiah was also Lord (Adonai). A father or grandfather in the Hebrew context would never call a son "Lord." It was a patriarchal culture, and therefore, that would never happen. David, the grandfather of the coming messiah, only did this because he believed that the messiah was God and at the same time separate from God. The Pharisees could not explain this, and it is impossible for a Jewish person to explain it today unless he or she recognizes the plurality of God (cf. Isaiah 9:6).

We see the same thing happen in Malachi. The Lord God refers to the coming messiah as Lord. Malachi 3:1 (NIV 1984) says this: "'See, I will send my messenger, who will prepare the way before me. Then suddenly *the Lord you are seeking will come to his temple*; the messenger of the covenant, whom you desire, will come,' *says the LORD Almighty.*"

Yahweh (the LORD) distinguishes himself from the messiah in this passage by saying the "Lord" is coming to his temple. Malachi prophesied that the messiah was God but, at the same time, distinct from God. There are many implications of the Trinity in the Old Testament, even though they are not explicitly explained.

Therefore, the Bible teaches that there is only "one" God, but also teaches that God is three distinct persons. It also clearly teaches that these three distinct persons are a unity (three-in-oneness). Scripture teaches Trinitarian doctrine.

Roles in the Trinity

Another aspect of Trinitarian doctrine is the fact that there are roles within the Trinity. This is even implied by the familial names in the God-head. God is called God the Father (Matt 6:9) and Jesus is called God the Son (1 John 4:15). Scripture teaches that a son should submit to his father (Colossians 3:20), and this happens in the God-head as well. This submission is clearly seen throughout Scripture. John 3:16 says: "For this is the way God loved the world: He gave his one and only Son, so that everyone who believes in him will not perish but have eternal life." God sends his Son into the world, and the Son obeys.

We also see Christ's submission to the Father. Christ said this, "For I have come down from heaven not to do my own will but the will of the one who sent me" (John 6:38). He obeys the father throughout his life and gives his life in obedience to him. Listen to Christ's prayer to the Father right before his crucifixion: "Father, if you are willing, take this cup away from me. Yet not my will but yours be done" (Luke 22:42).

We even see that Christ's purpose in redemption is to bring glory to the Father eternally. First Corinthians 15:24–28 says,

> Then comes the end, when he hands over the kingdom to God the Father, when he has brought to an end all rule and all authority and power. For he must reign until he has put all his enemies under his feet. The last enemy to be eliminated is death. For "he has put everything in subjection under his feet". But when it says "everything" has been put in subjection, it is clear that this does not include the one who put everything in subjection to him. And when all things are subjected to him, then the Son himself will be subjected to the one who subjected everything to him, so that God may be all in all.

Finally, Scripture teaches that the Holy Spirit submits both to the Father (John 14:26) and to the Son (John 16:7, 15:26). Jesus told the disciples that he would send the Holy Spirit and also that the Father would send him. John 14:26 says, "But the Advocate, the Holy Spirit, whom the Father will send in my name, will teach you everything, and will cause you to remember everything I said to you."

John 15:26 says, "When the Advocate comes, whom I will send you from the Father—the Spirit of truth who goes out from the Father—he will testify about me."

There is perfect submission in the God-head. Jesus obeys and submits to the Father and seeks to bring glory to him (cf. John 17:4). The Holy Spirit seeks to bring glory to both the Son and to the Father (cf. John 16:14, 1 Cor 2:12). There is a perfect unity in their oneness.

It should also be added that there is perfect love in the Trinity. First John 4:8 says this: "The person who does not love does not know God, because God is love."

What did God do before the creation of man and angels? He lived in a perfect loving relationship with God the Son and God the Holy Spirit. And in this perfect loving relationship, there was submission and authority.

It is, therefore, no surprise that human relationships, which are meant to reflect the image of God, are built both on love and submission. Children love their parents and submit to their authority (cf. Eph 6:1). Wives love their husbands and also submit to them (cf. Eph 5:22). All human relationships should be built on love and submission as seen in the God-head. Human relationships fall apart from lack of love or lack of submission. This is true of the husband and wife relationship, the child and parent relationship, and also in work relationships.

We were made in the image of God, and therefore, we are called to reflect both love and submission.

Importance of the Doctrine of the Trinity

Why is the doctrine of the Trinity important? Wayne Grudem gives six reasons:

> First, the atonement is at stake. If Jesus is merely a created being, and not fully God, then it is hard to see how he, a creature, could bear the full wrath of God against all of our sins. Could any creature, no matter how great, really save us? Second, justification by faith alone is threatened if we deny the full deity of the Son. (This is seen today in the teaching of the Jehovah's Witnesses, who do not believe in justification by faith alone.) If Jesus is not fully God, we would rightly doubt whether we can really trust him to save us completely. Could we really depend on any creature fully for our salvation? Third, if Jesus is not infinite God, should we pray to him or worship him? Who but an infinite, omniscient God could hear and respond to all the prayers of all God's people? And who but God himself is worthy of worship? Indeed, if Jesus is merely a creature, no matter how great, it would be idolatry to worship him—yet the New Testament commands us to do so (Phil. 2:9–11; Rev. 5:12–14). Fourth, if someone teaches that Christ was a created being but nonetheless one who saved us, then this teaching wrongly begins to attribute credit for salvation to a creature and not to God himself. But this wrongfully exalts the creature rather than the Creator, something

Scripture never allows us to do. Fifth, the independence and personal nature of God are at stake: If there is no Trinity, then there were no interpersonal relationships within the being of God before creation, and, without personal relationships, it is difficult to see how God could be genuinely personal or be without the need for a creation to relate to. Sixth, the unity of the universe is at stake: If there is not perfect plurality and perfect unity in God himself, then we have no basis for thinking there can be any ultimate unity among the diverse elements of the universe either. Clearly, in the doctrine of the Trinity, the heart of the Christian faith is at stake. Herman Bavinck says that "Athanasius understood better than any of his contemporaries that Christianity stands or falls with the confession of the deity of Christ and of the Trinity." He adds, "In the confession of the Trinity throbs the heart of the Christian religion: every error results from, or upon deeper reflection may be traced to, a wrong view of this doctrine."[66]

Certainly, we can see why this is such an important doctrine—one worth teaching and defending.

Applications

What are applications one can take from the doctrine of the Trinity?

1.   The Trinity reminds us of why we should not make any idols of God.

Nothing in the world is like the God of the Bible. Nothing can accurately demonstrate the doctrine of the Trinity. It is a paradox. How can we make an idol of something that cannot be fully comprehended or demonstrated? Nothing is like the God of Scripture. He is the one and only God, and therefore, he deserves all our love and worship.

2.   The Trinity reminds us of our need for community.

If God is a Trinity that has forever lived in communion, and humans are made in his image, how much more do we need continual fellowship? When God made man he did not make him to be alone; he made two which would become "one flesh." Man was never meant to be independent. We need friends, family, church members, etc., for we were meant to grow and develop in community. This comes from being made in the image of God.

3. The Trinity reminds us of the order that should be seen in human relationships.

There is order in the Trinitarian relationship. The Son submits to the Father, the Spirit submits to both the Son and the Father, and all this is done in love (1 John 4:8). Therefore, we see the need for this order in our human relationships. We see this order in various ways.

This order is seen in citizens submitting to the government and its officials. Romans 13:1 says:

> Let every person be subject to the governing authorities. For there is no authority except by God's appointment, and the authorities that exist have been instituted by God.

This order is seen in employees submitting to employers. Colossians 3:22 says, "Slaves, obey your earthly masters in every respect, not only when they are watching—like those who are strictly people-pleasers—but with a sincere heart, fearing the Lord."

This order is also seen in congregants submitting to the leadership of the church. Hebrews 13:17 says,

> Obey your leaders and submit to them, for they keep watch over your souls and will give an account for their work. Let them do this with joy and not with complaints, for this would be no advantage for you.

This order is seen in children obeying their parents. Colossians 3:20 says, "Children, obey your parents in everything, for this is pleasing in the Lord."

This order is seen in wives submitting to their husbands. "Wives, submit to your husbands, as is fitting in the Lord" (Colossians 3:18).

In fact, Paul uses the authority in the God-head as a reflection of the roles between a husband and wife. First Corinthians 11:3 says this: "But I want you to know that *Christ is the head of every man*, and *the man is the head of a woman*, and God is the head of Christ."

It should be noted that the word "woman" should probably be translated "wife." Women are not called to submit to every man, but only to their husbands (Col 3:18). Paul teaches the husband's headship over the wife by comparing the husband to God and the wife to Christ. The wife is meant to submit to her husband in the same way that Christ submits to God.

Now, this may sound chauvinist and sexist and some have declared it so. However, it is not chauvinist or sexist because God created the sexes, and he made the husband and wife relationship to reflect the order in the Trinity. Christ is not less than God the Father. They are coequal, but there is order in their relationship. In the same way, the husband and wife are coequal, but there is order in their relationship as it reflects the image of God.

As we consider all these areas of authority given by God, which reflect the Trinity, it is important to remember that all these relationships must be centered in love (1 John 4:8). Submission in the God-head happens in a loving relationship. It should be the same for citizens and government officials, employees and employers, church members and leadership, children and parents, and husbands and wives. Without love and submission, society will fall apart.

What else does the Trinity teach us?

4. The Trinity reminds us that the authorship of Scripture is Divine.

Paradoxical doctrines in the Bible, such as the Trinity, are a form of evidence for its divine origin. Man would never make up doctrines such as this. They would make up doctrines one could fully understand and comprehend; however, the Bible is full of paradoxes.

How can Jesus be one hundred percent God and one hundred percent man? That doesn't make any sense. How can God be in control of everything, yet man still have free-will? How can God be three in one? These are mysteries.

However, they make perfect sense if the Bible has been written by an infinite God. A finite mind could never fully comprehend something "infinite" such as God. Therefore, if Scripture is truly divine, then one should expect to find such mysteries as the Trinity in it. We should expect to not "fully comprehend" an infinite God.

Review Questions

1. What are three essential statements about the Trinity?

2. In what ways do we see the doctrine of the Trinity throughout Scripture? What implications of the Trinity do we see in the Old Testament?

3. What are some false ways of looking at the Trinity that have been taught throughout church history?

4. What are some applications we can take from the "authority" and "love" seen in the Trinity? Where is God calling you to model the God-head in demonstrating these characteristics better?

5. Why do you think paradoxes like the Trinity are so common in the Scripture? What are some other seemingly doctrinal paradoxes? How do you reconcile this with your faith?

Prayer Prompts

- Pray that we would experience the unity, fellowship, and love of the Trinity within our small groups and churches (John 17:21–23). Ask for the removal of all division and the reconciliation of people who are estranged.

- Pray that the church would demonstrate the order of the Trinity in all of our affairs: as children submit to parents, wives to husbands, members to church leaders, and citizens to leaders of government, so that God will be glorified (Romans 13:1).

- Pray that we may experience the "grace of the Lord Jesus Christ, the love of God and the fellowship of the Holy Spirit" in our homes, churches, and individual lives (2 Corinthians 13:14).

Study Group Tips

Leading a small group using the Bible Teacher's Guide can be done in various ways. One format for leading a small group is the "study group" model where each member prepares and shares in the teaching. This appendix will cover tips for facilitating a weekly study group.

1. Each week the members of the study group will read through a select chapter of the guide, answer the reflection questions (see Appendix 2), and come prepared to share in the group.

2. Prior to each meeting, a different member can be selected to lead the group and share question 1 of the reflection questions, which is to give a short summary of the chapter read. This section of the gathering could last from five to fifteen minutes. This way, each member can develop their gift of teaching. It also will make them study harder during the week. Or each week the same person could share the summary.

3. After the summary has been given, the leader for that week will facilitate discussions through the rest of the reflection questions and also ask select review questions from the chapter.

4. After discussion, the group will share prayer requests and pray for one another.

The strength of the study group is the fact that the members will be required to prepare their responses before the meeting, which will allow for easier discussion. In addition, each member will be given the opportunity to teach which will further equip their ministry skills. The study group model has distinct advantages.

Reflection Questions

Writing is one of the best ways to learn. In class, we take notes and write papers and all these methods are used to help us learn and retain the material. The same is true with the Word of God. Obviously, all of the authors of Scripture were writers. This helped them better learn the Scriptures and also enabled them to more effectively teach it. In studying God's Word with the *Bible Teacher's Guide*, take time to write so you can similarly grow both in your learning and teaching.

1. How would you summarize the main points of the text/chapter? Write a brief summary.

2. What stood out to you most in the reading? Did the contents trigger any personal memories or experiences? If so, please share them.

3. What follow-up questions did you have about the reading? What parts did you not fully agree with?

4. What applications did you take from the reading, and how do you plan to implement them into your life?

5. Write several commitment statements: *As a result of my time studying God's Word, I will...*

6. What are some practical ways you can pray as a result of studying the text? Spend some time ministering to the Lord through prayer.

Walking the Romans Road

How can a person be saved? From what is he saved? How can someone have eternal life? Scripture teaches that after death each person will spend eternity either in heaven or hell. How can a person go to heaven?

Paul said this to Timothy:

> You, however, must continue in the things you have learned and are confident about. You know who taught you and how from infancy you have known the holy writings, which are able to give you wisdom for salvation through faith in Christ Jesus.
> 2 Timothy 3:14-15

One of the reasons God gave us Scripture is to make us wise for salvation. This means that without it nobody can know how to be saved.

Well then, how can a people be saved and what are they being saved from? A common method of sharing the good news of salvation is through the Romans Road. One of the great themes, not only of the Bible, but specifically of the book of Romans is salvation. In Romans, the author, Paul, clearly details the steps we must take in order to be saved.

How can we be saved? What steps must we take?

Step One: We Must Accept that We Are Sinners

Romans 3:23 says, "For all have sinned and fall short of the glory of God." What does it mean to sin? The word sin means "to miss the mark." The mark we missed is looking like God. When God created mankind in the Genesis narrative, he created man in the "image of God" (1:27). The "image of God" means many things, but probably, most importantly it means we were made to be holy just as he is holy. Man was made moral. We were meant to reflect God's holiness in every way: the way we think, the way we talk, and the way we act. And any time we miss the mark in these areas, we commit sin.

Furthermore, we do not only sin when we commit a sinful act such as: lying, stealing, or cheating. Again, we sin anytime we have a wrong heart motive.

213

The greatest commandments in Scripture are to "Love the Lord your God with all your heart and to love your neighbor as yourself" (Matt 22:36-40, paraphrase). Whenever we don't love God supremely and love others as ourselves, we sin and fall short of the glory of God. For this reason, man is always in a state of sinning. Sadly, even if our actions are good, our heart is bad. I have never loved God with my whole heart, mind, and soul and neither has anybody else. Therefore, we have all sinned and fall short of the glory of God (Rom 3:23). We have all missed the mark of God's holiness and we must accept this.

What's the next step?

Step Two: We Must Understand We Are Under the Judgment of God

Why are we under the judgment of God? It is because of our sins. Scripture teaches God is not only a loving God, but he is a just God. And his justice requires judgment for each of our sins. Romans 6:23 says, "For the payoff of sin is death."

A wage is something we earn. Every time we sin, we earn the wage of death. What is death? Death really means separation. In physical death, the body is separated from the spirit, but in spiritual death, man is separated from God. Man currently lives in a state of spiritual death (cf. Eph 2:1-3). We do not love God, obey him, or know him as we should. Therefore, man is in a state of death.

Moreover, one day at our physical death, if we have not been saved, we will spend eternity separated from God in a very real hell. In hell, we will pay the wage for each of our sins. Therefore, in hell people will experience various degrees of punishment (cf. Lk 12:47-48). This places man in a very dangerous predicament—unholy and therefore under the judgment of God.

How should we respond to this? This leads us to our third step.

Step Three: We Must Recognize God Has Invited All to Accept His Free Gift of Salvation

Romans 6:23 does not stop at the wages of sin being death. It says, "For the payoff of sin is death, but the gift of God is eternal life in Christ Jesus our Lord." Because God loved everybody on the earth, he offered the free gift of eternal life, which anyone can receive through Jesus Christ.

Because it is a gift, it cannot be earned. We cannot work for it. Ephesians 2:8-9 says, "For by grace you are saved through faith, and this is not from yourselves, it is the gift of God; it is not from works, so that no one can boast."

Going to church, being baptized, giving to the poor, or doing any other righteous work does not save. Salvation is a gift that must be received from God. It is a gift that has been prepared by his effort alone.

How do we receive this free gift?

Step Four: We Must Believe Jesus Christ Died for Our Sins and Rose from the Dead

If we are going to receive this free gift, we must believe in God's Son, Jesus Christ. Because God loved us, cared for us, and didn't want us to be separated from him eternally, he sent his Son to die for our sins. Romans 5:8 says, "But God demonstrates his own love for us, in that while we were still sinners, Christ died for us." Similarly, John 3:16 says, "For this is the way God loved the world: He gave his one and only Son, so that everyone who believes in him will not perish but have eternal life." God so loved us that he gave his only Son for our sins.

Jesus Christ was a real, historical person who lived 2,000 years ago. He was born of a virgin. He lived a perfect life. He was put to death by the Romans and the Jews. And he rose again on the third day. In his death, he took our sins and God's wrath for them and gave us his perfect righteousness so we could be accepted by God. Second Corinthians 5:21 says, "God made the one who did not know sin to be sin for us, so that in him we would become the righteousness of God." God did all this so we could be saved from his wrath.

Christ's death satisfied the just anger of God over our sins. When God saw Jesus on the cross, he saw us and our sins and therefore judged Jesus. And now, when God sees those who are saved, he sees his righteous Son and accepts us. In salvation, we have become the righteousness of God.

If we are going to be saved, if we are going to receive this free gift of salvation, we must believe in Christ's death, burial, and resurrection for our sins (cf. 1 Cor 15:3-5, Rom 10:9-10). Do you believe?

Step Five: We Must Confess Christ as Lord of Our Lives

Romans 10:9-10 says,

> Because if you confess with your mouth that Jesus is Lord and believe in your heart that God raised him from the dead, you will be saved. For with the heart one believes and thus has righteousness and with the mouth one confesses and thus has salvation.

215

Not only must we believe, but we must confess Christ as Lord of our lives. It is one thing to believe in Christ but another to follow Christ. Simple belief does not save. Christ must be our Lord. James said this: "...Even the demons believe that – and tremble with fear" (James 2:19), but the demons are not saved—Christ is not their Lord.

Another aspect of making Christ Lord is repentance. Repentance really means a change of mind that leads to a change of direction. Before we met Christ, we were living our own life and following our own sinful desires. But when we get saved, our mind and direction change. We start to follow Christ as Lord.

How do we make this commitment to the lordship of Christ so we can be saved? Paul said we must confess with our mouth "Jesus is Lord" as we believe in him. Romans 10:13 says, "For everyone who calls on the name of the Lord will be saved."

If you admit that you are a sinner and understand you are under God's wrath because of them; if you believe Jesus Christ is the Son of God, that he died on the cross for your sins, and rose from the dead for your salvation; if you are ready to turn from your sin and cling to Christ as Lord, you can be saved.

If this is your heart, then you can pray this prayer and commit to following Christ as your Lord.

Dear heavenly Father, I confess I am a sinner and have fallen short of your glory, what you made me for. I believe Jesus Christ died on the cross to pay the penalty for my sins and rose from the dead so I can have eternal life. I am turning away from my sin and accepting you as my Lord and Savior. Come into my life and change me. Thank you for your gift of salvation.

Scripture teaches that if you truly accepted Christ as your Lord, then you are a new creation. Second Corinthians 5:17 says, "So then, if anyone is in Christ, he is a new creation; what is old has passed away – look, what is new has come!" God has forgiven your sins (1 John 1:9), he has given you his Holy Spirit (Rom 8:15), and he is going to disciple you and make you into the image of his Son (cf. Rom 8:29). He will never leave you nor forsake you (Heb 13:5), and he will complete the work he has begun in your life (Phil 1:6). In heaven, angels and saints are rejoicing because of your commitment to Christ (Lk 15:7).

Praise God for his great salvation! May God keep you in his hand, empower you through the Holy Spirit, train you through mature believers, and use you to build his kingdom! "He who calls you is trustworthy, and he will in fact do this" (1 Thess 5:24). God bless you!

Coming Soon

Praise the Lord for your interest in studying and teaching God's Word. If God has blessed you through the BTG series, please partner with us in petitioning God to greatly use this series to encourage and build his Church. Also, please consider leaving an Amazon review and signing up for free book promotions. By doing this, you help spread the "Word." Thanks for your partnership in the gospel from the first day until now (Phil 1:4-5).

Available:
First Peter
Theology Proper
Building Foundations for a Godly Marriage
Colossians
God's Battle Plan for Purity
Nehemiah
Philippians
The Perfections of God
The Armor of God
Ephesians
Abraham
Finding a Godly Mate
1 Timothy
The Beatitudes
Equipping Small Group Leaders
2 Timothy
Jacob

Coming Soon:
The Sermon on the Mount

About the Author

Greg Brown earned his MA in religion and MA in teaching from Trinity International University, a MRE from Liberty University, and a PhD in theology from Louisiana Baptist University. He has served over fourteen years in pastoral ministry, and currently serves as chaplain and professor at Handong Global University, teaching pastor at Handong International Congregation, and as a Navy Reserve chaplain.

Greg married his lovely wife, Tara Jayne, in 2006 and they have one daughter, Saiyah Grace. He enjoys going on dates with his wife, playing with his daughter, reading, writing, studying in coffee shops, working out, and following the NBA and UFC. His pursuit in life simply put is "to know God and to be found faithful by Him."

To connect with Greg, please follow at http://www.pgregbrown.com/

Notes

[1] James I. Packer. *Knowing God* (Great Britain: Hodder and Stoughton, 1973), Kindle Edition.

[2] James I. Packer. *Knowing God* (Great Britain: Hodder and Stoughton, 1973), Kindle Edition.

[3] James I. Packer. *Knowing God* (Great Britain: Hodder and Stoughton, 1973), Kindle Edition.

[4] Wayne A. Grudem. *Systematic Theology: An Introduction to Biblical Doctrine.* (Leicester, England; Grand Rapids, MI: Inter-Varsity Press; Zondervan Pub. House, 2004), 149.

[5] Charles C. Ryrie. *Basic Theology: A Popular Systematic Guide to Understanding Biblical Truth* (Chicago, IL: Moody Press, 1999), 31.

[6] Millard J. Erickson, M. J. *Christian Theology* (2nd ed). (Grand Rapids, MI: Baker Book House, 1998.), 201.

[7] http://www.merriam-webster.com/dictionary/divine (accessed March 12, 2014)

[8] http://www.merriam-webster.com/dictionary/transcendent (accessed March 12, 2014)

[9] Daryl Aaron. *Understanding Theology in 15 Minutes a Day* (Grand Rapids, MI: Baker Book Group 2012), Kindle edition.

[10] Harold L, Wilmington. *Wilmington's Bible Handbook* (Carol Stream, IL. Tyndale House Publisher, 1981), 775.

[11] John R. Stott. *God's New Society: The Message of Ephesians.* The Bible Speaks Today (Downers Grove, IL: InterVarsity Press, 1979). 160.

[12] Wayne A. Grudem. *Systematic Theology : An Introduction to Biblical Doctrine* (Leicester, England; Grand Rapids, Mich.: Inter-Varsity Press; Zondervan Pub. House, 1994), 81.

[13] Walter A. Elwell. *Entry for 'Theophany.* Evangelical Dictionary of Theology (Grand Rapids, Michigan: Baker Pub Group, 1997). LOGOS Bible Software.

[14] Warren, Wiersbe. *The Bible Exposition Commentary* (Vol. 2, p. 75). (Wheaton, IL: Victor Books. 1996) Logos Bible Software.

[15] Wayne A. Grudem; Elliot Grudem. *Christian Beliefs: Twenty Basics Every Christian Should Know*. (Grand Rapids: MI: Zondervan, 2009), Kindle Edition.

[16] Wayne A. Grudem. *Systematic Theology: An Introduction to Biblical Doctrine* (Leicester, England; Grand Rapids, MI: Inter-Varsity Press; Zondervan Pub. House, 2004), 127.

[17] http://www.bibleinfo.com/en/questions/how-many-bible-promises-are-there (accessed June 19, 2014)

[18] Wayne A. Grudem, W. A. *Systematic Theology: An Introduction to Biblical Doctrine* (Leicester, England; Grand Rapids, MI: Inter-Varsity Press; Zondervan Pub. House, 2004), 90.

[19] Charles C. Ryrie. *Basic Theology: A Popular Systematic Guide to Understanding Biblical Truth* (Chicago, IL: Moody Press, 1999), 92.

[20] Charles C. Ryrie. *Basic Theology: A Popular Systematic Guide to Understanding Biblical Truth* (Chicago, IL: Moody Press, 1999), 92.

[21] Millard J. Erickson. *Christian Theology* (2nd ed). (Grand Rapids, MI: Baker Book House, 1998), 246.

[22] MacDonald, William. *Believer's Bible Commentary: Old and New Testaments*. (A. Farstad, Ed.). Nashville: Thomas Nelson, 1995), 1287.

[23] Gleason Archer and Gregory C. Chirichigno, *Old Testament Quotations in the New Testament: A Complete Survey*. (Eugene, Oregon: Wipf & Stock Pub, 2005), Kindle edition.

[24] Josh Mcdowell. *New Evidence that Demands a Verdict*. (Nashville, TN: Thomas Nelson, 1999), Kindle edition.

[25] Millard J. Erickson. *Christian Theology* (2nd ed.). (Grand Rapids, MI: Baker Book House, 1998), 291.

[26] Charles C. Ryrie. *Basic Theology: A Popular Systematic Guide to Understanding Biblical Truth* (Chicago, IL: Moody Press, 1999), 39.

[27] Wayne A. Grudem. *Systematic Theology: An Introduction to Biblical Doctrine* (Leicester, England; Grand Rapids, MI: Inter-Varsity Press; Zondervan Pub. House, 2004), 167.

[28] Evans, Tony. *Theology You Can Count On.* (Chicago, IL: Moody Publishers, 2008), Kindle edition.

[29] Chariots of Fire (1981 feature film)

[30] Evans, Tony. *Theology You Can Count On* (Chicago, IL: Moody Publishers, 2008), Kindle edition.

[31] Evans, Tony. *Theology You Can Count On.* ((Chicago, IL, Moody Publishers, 2008), Kindle edition.

[32] Wayne A. Grudem, *Systematic Theology: An Introduction to Biblical Doctrine* . (Leicester, England; Grand Rapids, Mchigan: Inter-Varsity Press; Zondervan Pub. House, 2004), 197.

[33] Charles C. Ryrie. *Basic Theology: A Popular Systematic Guide to Understanding Biblical Truth* (Chicago, IL: Moody Press, 1999), 46.

[34] Charles C. Ryrie. *Basic Theology: A Popular Systematic Guide to Understanding Biblical Truth* (Chicago, IL: Moody Press, 1999), 47.

[35] Charles C. Ryrie. *Basic Theology: A Popular Systematic Guide to Understanding Biblical Truth.* (Chicago, IL: Moody Press, 1999), 45.

[36] Tony Evans. *Theology You Can Count On.* (Chicago, Illinois: Moody Publishers, 2008), Kindle edition.

[37] http://www.merriam-webster.com/dictionary/mercy (accessed on March 12, 2014).

[38] Wayne A. Grudem. *Systematic Theology: An Introduction to Biblical Doctrine.* (Leicester, England; Grand Rapids, MI: Inter-Varsity Press; Zondervan Pub. House, 2004), 200.

[39] Wayne A. Grudem. *Systematic Theology: An Introduction to Biblical Doctrine* (Leicester, England; Grand Rapids, MI: Inter-Varsity Press; Zondervan Pub. House, 2004), 198.

[40] John F. MacArthur. *Worship: The Ultimate Priority.* (Chicago, IL: Moody Publishers, 2012), Kindle edition.

[41] Evans, Tony. *Theology You Can Count On* (Chicago, IL: Moody Publishers, 2008), Kindle edition

[42] Evans, Tony. *Theology You Can Count On* (Chicago, IL: Moody Publishers, 2008), Kindle edition.

[43] Wayne A. Grudem, *Systematic Theology: An Introduction to Biblical Doctrine* (Leicester, England; Grand Rapids, Michigan: Inter-Varsity Press; Zondervan Pub. House , 2004), 317.

[44] Wayne A. Grudem, *Systematic Theology: An Introduction to Biblical Doctrine* (Leicester, England; Grand Rapids, Michigan: Inter-Varsity Press; Zondervan Pub. House , 2004), 319.

[45] Wayne A. Grudem, *Systematic Theology: An Introduction to Biblical Doctrine* (Leicester, England; Grand Rapids, Michigan: Inter-Varsity Press; Zondervan Pub. House , 2004), 322-23.

[46] Wayne A. Grudem, *Systematic Theology: An Introduction to Biblical Doctrine* (Leicester, England; Grand Rapids, Michigan: Inter-Varsity Press; Zondervan Pub. House , 2004), 338.

[47] Charles C. Ryrie. *Basic Theology: A Popular Systematic Guide to Understanding Biblical Truth* (Chicago, IL: Moody Press, 1999), 51.

[48] Wayne A. Grudem. *Systematic Theology: An Introduction to Biblical Doctrine* (Leicester, England; Grand Rapids, MI: Inter-Varsity Press; Zondervan Pub. House, 2004), 157.

[49] Charles C. Ryrie. *Basic Theology: A Popular Systematic Guide to Understanding Biblical Truth* (Chicago, IL: Moody Press, 1999), 51.

[50] Mark Driscoll; Gerry Breshears. Doctrine: *What Christians Should Believe* (Wheaton, IL, Crossway. 2010), 16.

[51] Shields, M. A., & Hawkins, R. K. (2016). YHWH. In J. D. Barry, D. Bomar, D. R. Brown, R. Klippenstein, D. Mangum, C. Sinclair Wolcott, ... W. Widder (Eds.), *The Lexham Bible Dictionary*. Bellingham, WA: Lexham Press.

[52] Charles C. Ryrie. *Basic Theology: A Popular Systematic Guide to Understanding Biblical Truth* (Chicago, IL: Moody Press, 1999), 51.

[53] Shields, M. A., & Hawkins, R. K. (2016). YHWH. In J. D. Barry, D. Bomar, D. R. Brown, R. Klippenstein, D. Mangum, C. Sinclair Wolcott, ... W. Widder (Eds.), *The Lexham Bible Dictionary*. Bellingham, WA: Lexham Press.

[54] Philip Ryken & Kent Hughes. *Exodus: Saved for God's glory.* (Wheaton, IL: Crossway Books, 2005), pp. 460–461.

[55] Charles C. Ryrie. *Basic Theology: A Popular Systematic Guide to Understanding Biblical Truth.* Chicago, IL: Moody Press, 1999), 51.

[56] Kay Arthur. *Lord, I Want to Know You: A Devotional Study on the Names of God.* (The Doubleday Religious Publishing Group, 2009), 15.

[57] Charles C. Ryrie. *Basic Theology: A Popular Systematic Guide to Understanding Biblical Truth.* (Chicago, IL: Moody Press, 1999), 51.

[58] Charles C. Ryrie. *Basic Theology: A Popular Systematic Guide to Understanding Biblical Truth.* Chicago, IL: Moody Press, 1999), 51.

[59] Charles C. Ryrie. *Basic Theology: A Popular Systematic Guide to Understanding Biblical Truth.* (Chicago, IL: Moody Press, 1999), 51.

[60] Charles C. Ryrie. *Basic Theology: A Popular Systematic Guide to Understanding Biblical Truth.* Chicago, IL: Moody Press, 1999), 57.

[61] Charles C. Ryrie. *Basic Theology: A Popular Systematic Guide to Understanding Biblical Truth.* (Chicago, IL: Moody Press, 1999), 57.

[62] Mark Driscoll; Gerry Breshears. *Doctrine: What Christians Should.* (Wheaton, IL: Crossway. 2010), 12.

[63] Wayne A. Grudem. *Systematic Theology: An Introduction to Biblical Doctrine.* Leicester, England; Grand Rapids, MI: Inter-Varsity Press; Zondervan Pub. House, 2004), 226.

[64] Mark Driscoll; Gerry Breshears. *Doctrine: What Christians Should.* (Wheaton, IL: Crossway. 2010), 12.

65 Mark Driscoll; Gerry Breshears. *Doctrine: What Christians Should.* (Wheaton, IL: Crossway. 2010), 12.

66 Wayne A. Grudem. *Systematic Theology: An Introduction to Biblical Doctrine* . (Leicester, England; Grand Rapids, MI: Inter-Varsity Press; Zondervan Pub. House, 2004), 247-248.

Made in the USA
Middletown, DE
30 September 2020